Resisters

How Ordinary Jews Fought
Persecution in Hitler's Germany

WOLF GRUNER

Yale

UNIVERSITY PRESS

NEW HAVEN AND LONDON

Yale University Press books may be purchased in quantity for educational, business,
or promotional use. For information, please e-mail sales.press@yale.edu (U.S. office)
or sales@yaleup.co.uk (U.K. office).

Set in Electra LH type by IDS Infotech Ltd.
Printed in the United States of America.

ISBN 978-0-300-26719 8 (hardcover : alk. paper)
Library of Congress Control Number: 2022946728
A catalogue record for this book is available from the British Library.

This paper meets the requirements of ANSI/NISO Z39.48-1992
(Permanence of Paper).

10 9 8 7 6 5 4 3 2 1

CONTENTS

CONTENTS

In July 2008, by mere coincidence and only weeks before I moved to Los Angeles, I found the first trace of an individual Jewish resister in an entry of a Berlin police logbook labeled as a "political incident." Police had arrested a Berlin Jew who spoke up against the persecution. I had studied the Nazi persecution of the German Jews intensively for twenty years, but I had never heard of anything like it. This discovery revealed that despite widespread assumptions among Holocaust scholars, Jewish agency and resistance can be unearthed in perpetrator documents, such as police reports and court proceedings. It settled an academic trajectory that started with research on institutions in Nazi Germany, later investigating a diversity of contradictory local and national policies, and then exploring their impact on the Jewish population. Now, I began to focus on the reactions and agency of the German and Austrian Jews toward the persecution.

I always had an interest in understanding the impact of the Nazi persecution on Jewish individuals, and used testimonies and conducted interviews with survivors in Germany, Austria, the United States, and Bolivia for my dissertation. However, the victims were not front and center in my academic work, which concentrated on understanding why and how the persecution policies evolved. During a postdoctoral fellowship at Yad Vashem in Jerusalem in 1998, Yehuda Bauer and I discussed my research in a conversation. He challenged my scholarly approach by asking, "Where are the victims in your narrative?"

It took a dozen years of systematic and intensive research to locate the sources and finally write this book about individual Jewish resistance against the Nazi persecution. As mentioned, it all started in early summer 2008, when I browsed through dozens of dusty police diaries looking for traces of the persecution of the Jews. I discovered police officers' handwritten notes about lost keys, stolen bicycles, drunk people, damaged property, and even apprehended exhibitionists. One day, one entry with the title "political incident" caught my eye. A police officer wrote about the arrest of a Jew who had protested anti-Jewish Nazi policies. Although the note was brief, offering little more than name, birthdate, and address of the arrestee, plus a brief description of place, time, and general content of the protest, it struck me. At the time, most historians would have denied the possibility that Jewish individuals ever protested in public. However, I soon encountered dozens of similar cases, all labeled by the police officers as "political incidents" or "political offenses."

Those unexpected discoveries fundamentally shattered my established scholarly beliefs after decades of Holocaust research. Historians, including myself, had painted a picture of passivity of the persecuted. As discrimination in Nazi Germany gradually increased, the Jews slowly adapted, so went the argument. More generally, the assumption still exists today; Nikolaus Wachsmann, for example, in his book *KL: A History of the Nazi Concentration Camps* (2015), said that "defiance is rare in totalitarian regimes."

The opposite seems true. Since I grew up behind the Iron Curtain in East Germany, the evidence resonated deeply with me on a personal level. My experience of living in a dictatorship until the age of twenty-nine provided me with a distinct acuity. Having been part of the cultural underground in East Berlin, my intimate knowledge of the varieties of dissident behavior, which often resulted in grave repercussions for the individual and his or her family and friends, made me intensely aware how the Communist regime perceived and punished even mild expressions of individual defiance as resistance. Since the persecution in Nazi Germany was so much more brutal, how much more serious must the regime have judged and punished any acts of opposition coming from their racial enemy number one, the Jews? Knowing many people who opposed the Communist government in different ways, I realized it was improbable that German Jewish men and women would not have reacted with defiance and protest to Nazi discrimination policies.

Next, I dug through two thousand court cases in the Berlin archive. Although I did not find any names from the police files in the Special Court (*Sondergericht*) records, a number of new files on Jewish protest and defiance surfaced. They were again rather brief, often solely containing either an indictment or a judgment, three to five typescript pages long. Yet, they would tell us a bit more about the act of resistance and the circumstances as well the profession and biography of the defendants.

Berlin was home to the largest Jewish community in Nazi Germany and often praised as a refuge for Jews because of its size and the potential for anonymity. Both of these factors could have enabled more resistance in the capital. Hence, I expanded my search to see if I could find similar evidence of individual Jewish protest in other places of the former German Reich. During the next years, while teaching at the University of Southern California, I spent my summer breaks in the cities of Hamburg, Frankfurt, Munich, Leipzig, and Vienna, conducting research in local archives. Unexpectedly, they offered similar rich findings about individual Jews and their protest or defiance. I combed through thousands of perpetrator documents, including police reports, Gestapo files, and prison records as well as indictments, proceedings, and judgments from half a dozen Special Courts. Those sources show that Jewish Germans frequently disobeyed Nazi regulations and protested in public against the persecution, despite the imminent danger of denunciations by non-Jewish Germans and subsequent harsh punishments. It was never a lack of sources, but our wrong assumptions, that prevented us from detecting traces of individual Jewish resistance.

Evidence of how Jews actively responded in many other ways to Nazi measures also surfaced; some of them were prosecuted by regular local and regional courts for their acts. I visited the Yad Vashem Archive in Jerusalem and the United States Holocaust Memorial Museum archives, which house copies of files from many German cities and towns. To complement and balance the documentation based on perpetrator files, I added a thorough examination of survivor testimonies. In these more than 170 video interviews from the Shoah Foundation Visual History Archive at the University of Southern California, some of the interviewees confirmed what I discovered in the archives and some provided astounding stories of other types of undocumented individual resistance.

A sabbatical granted by the University of Southern California in 2017–2018 gave me the time to start writing the first chapters. Ironically, the global pandemic, which changed the course of so many lives for the worse, prevented any travel in 2020, giving me the opportunity to finish the manuscript.

This book aims to change the prevailing perspective of passive German Jews during the Holocaust by emphasizing their agency and illuminating the great variety of resistance acts revealed in archival documents and survivor testimonies.

ACKNOWLEDGMENTS

The ambitious and wide-ranging research on the forgotten resistance of German and Austrian Jews would not have been possible without the help of many people. First, I have to thank some students, who assisted in my search. Florian Dannecke, my former research assistant at the German source edition project, helped me with research in Berlin when I was already in Los Angeles. At the University of Southern California, my honors student Jasneet Aulakh transcribed various interviews from the Visual History Archive.

Over the decades, many archivists graciously gave invaluable help to this research, including Bianca Welzing-Bräutigam (Landesarchiv Berlin), Volker Eichler (HStA Wiesbaden), Barbara Welker (Centrum Judiacum Archive Berlin), Monika Nakath (BLHA Potsdam), Franz-Josef Herlt (Regierungspräsidium Darmstadt, Dezernat II 25, Leitung Entschädigung), Dr. Simone Walther (Bundesarchiv Residenzenliste), Nancy Hartman (U.S. Holocaust Memorial Museum Photoarchive).

Many of the archival trips were enabled by research funds accessible to me as the holder of the Shapell-Guerin Chair in Jewish Studies at the University of Southern California. The university fostered an interdisciplinary research environment with brilliant colleagues, inspiring students, supportive staff, helpful librarians, and fast growing resources in the field of Holocaust and genocide studies.

Crispin Brooks, curator of the USC Shoah Foundation Visual History Archive, helped me locate more than 170 relevant video testimonies of survivors at the VHA, which I analyzed with the help of a USC Shoah Foundation Senior Scholarship during a sabbatical semester in 2011. In June–July 2015, a fellowship provided by the German Academic Exchange Service at the Center for Jewish Studies in Berlin enabled me to study the archives of the Jewish community of Berlin and German and Jewish newspapers to explore why there was no discussion of individual or even Jewish resistance in general after the liberation in 1945.

I received important information from various families of Jewish survivors about daily resistance as well as documents, photographs, and memoirs. Sometimes they approached me after presentations, like Monica Simpson in San Diego and Judith Samuel in Los Angeles; sometimes they found my research on the internet. Special thanks goes to Bruce Neuburger in San Francisco, who emailed me when he discovered that I mentioned his grandfather in one of my articles. He generously provided me with dozens of scanned letters and photographs from his grandparents, Benno and Anna Neuburger in Munich, as well as with trial materials from German archives. Without those invaluable materials, chapter 4 would not exist.

I also received materials and information from scholars, such as Linde Apel (Hamburg), Isabel Richter (Berkeley), Christoph Kreutzmüller (Berlin), Benno Nietzel (Bielefeld), Betsy Anthony (USHMM), and Maximilian Strnad (Munich). Others are mentioned in the notes. A whole cohort of people tried to help me solve the mystery of David Bornstein, who vanished from the archives after his successful escape to Palestine. Since the ITS Arolsen archives contained hints of possible immigration to South Africa and Canada, Tali Nates (Johannesburg Holocaust and Genocide Center), Shirley Beagle (South African Jewish Board of Deputies), David Weber (West Park Jewish Cemetery, Johannesburg), Saul Issroff (president, Jewish Genealogical Society Great Britain), Megan Lewis (USHMM), Karen Franklin (Leo Baeck Institute New York), Cara MacDonald (Canadian Museum of Immigration at Pier 21), all worked to solve the puzzle, but unfortunately in vain.

I am thankful for invaluable feedback on articles and the first three chapters I drafted to Martha Stroud (Los Angeles), Marion Kaplan (New York), Peg Levine (Melbourne), Laurie Latham (New York), Naomi and Akin Gruner

Domić, Badema Pitic, Shefali Deshpande, Isabella Lloyd-Damnjanovic, Sayantani Jana (all in Los Angeles), Rob Gould (Florida), Kirril Shields (Brisbane), Peter Hayes (Chicago), Jean-Marc Dreyfus (Manchester/Paris), and Maximilian Strnad (Munich).

Martha Stroud and Badema Pitic provided detailed edits on early drafts of the entire manuscript. I received encouragement and important comments on later drafts from Steve Ross, Paul Lerner (both in Los Angeles), Steve Zipperstein (Palo Alto), Warren Rosenblum (St. Louis), Wendy Lower, and Jonathan Petropolous (both in Claremont). Generously, Jonathan introduced me to his editor at Yale University Press, Jaya Chatterjee. I thank her for taking on this manuscript and the organization of a thorough publication process. I am grateful to the two Yale peer reviewers for their encouragement and suggestions. Finally, Karen Olson helped with a thorough editing of this manuscript and Phillip King provided a fine final copy-editing.

As always, thanks goes to my family, who not only had to endure the mental absence of the author over long stretches, but also had to read parts of my manuscript. This book is dedicated to my ninety-one-year-old father, who, as a former publisher, is still deeply invested in books, including this one of his son.

RESISTERS

Introduction

In early spring 1941, Hertha Reis, a thirty-six-year-old forced laborer in the Nazi capital, was evicted by a judge along with her son and her mother from the two sublet rooms in which they lived. Outside of the Berlin courthouse, she exclaimed in front of passers-by, "We lost everything. Because of this cursed government, we finally lost our home too. This thug Hitler, this damned government, these damned people! Just because we are Jews, we are discriminated against."[1]

Speaking out against the persecution of the Jews in broad daylight in the capital of the Third Reich after eight years of Nazi rule hitherto seemed unimaginable, especially for an ostracized Jewish woman. But the story of Hertha Reis and many other astonishing tales of individual defiance and courage contradict the common perception of an overwhelmingly passive or even fatalistic reaction among the Jewish population oppressed by Nazi Germany.[2]

This book offers a compendium of forgotten stories that changes our view of the past by illuminating unbelievable yet true accounts of individual resistance, hidden in archives since the war ended. The protagonists of this book are ordinary Jewish men and women in Nazi Germany. Because they resisted persecution, the Nazis called them "impudent Jews." These ordinary Jewish men and women found the courage to rebel despite a continuous barrage of discriminating and dehumanizing measures. Their brave acts challenge us to revise our image of victims of mass violence and to unearth the buried history of individual human resistance in times of growing authoritarianism and genocide.

Although many survivors interviewed after the war revealed defiant individual behavior, none of them perceived their actions as resistance, since they were not armed and not members of organized groups. Neither did Max Mannheimer, a twenty-year-old forced laborer at a road construction site in Bohemia in 1940, when he wrote in his diary:

"My home is in a wooden hut behind the tool shed. From there I go to the public park, despite the 8 p.m. curfew and despite the ban on visiting the park. On my way, I count the signs with the slogan 'Forbidden for Jews.' In total, there are six. Later, at eleven p.m., I rip the signs out of the ground and throw some of them in the bushes, some in the creek. However, all my courage proved futile. The next evening, all the signs had reemerged. For a second time, I do not have the courage. I am just not a hero."[3]

Even though he downplays his actions, he broke Nazi laws again during his second visit, twice, by violating the curfew for Jews and the prohibition on visiting the park. Although it was important enough for him to write about it in his diary, Mannheimer did not find this resistance worth mentioning in his interview for the University of Southern California Shoah Foundation in 1996.[4]

With the notable exception of a few scholars—for example, Konrad Kwiet, Helmut Eschwege, Marion Kaplan, and David Engel—most historians seem to dismiss or are unaware of verbal criticism and protests by individual German Jews in public as well as other open acts of defiance, such as sabotage in the workplace or challenging the Nazis with written protest.[5] I have amended Yehuda Bauer's widely cited definition of Jewish resistance to read: "any *individual or* group action in opposition to known laws, actions, or intentions of the Nazis and their collaborators." Expanding the definition to include individuals, not just groups, fundamentally changes our perception, and honors a wide range of Jewish acts of contestation, whether successful or unsuccessful, including protesting in public and breaking anti-Jewish rules.[6] The definition provides us with both a broader perspective and a sharper lens, enabling us to uncover how Jews frequently responded during the Holocaust.

With a Changed Lens: Photographs and Resistance

This new lens changes our view of familiar images and even enables the (re)-discovery of photographs taken by Jews as acts of resistance. When the victims took pictures to document the persecution and their effects, they broke the Nazis' authority over the imagery of the Third Reich and produced evidence of the crimes. If one starts to search, more and more pictures surface, taken by Jews as acts of contestation. During the nationwide Nazi boycott of Jewish stores as well as law and medical practices on April 1, 1933, Jews documented anti-Jewish propaganda harming their businesses. In Stuttgart, twenty-two-year-old Lisa Einstein photographed the entrance of her family's apartment building where members of the Sturmabteilung (SA) had defaced her father's business plaque by posting leaflets with the word "Jew" over it.[7]

One well-known image shows the respected Jewish lawyer Michael Siegel in Munich in March 1933. The Nazis had humiliated him by cutting off his pants legs and forcing him to parade barefoot through the city center. The picture appears in many books on Nazi Germany and usually serves to illustrate the first terror wave after Hitler came to power. However, a closer look reveals that Siegel did not experience random Storm Trooper violence. The SA had forced him to carry a sign that read, "I won't complain to the police anymore."[8] Siegel had protested at the Munich police headquarters against the unlawful arrest of his client, the Jewish owner of the department store Uhlander, and for this reason became a victim of Nazis running amok.[9] He was not the only courageous Jewish lawyer.

Nazi authorities tried to prevent Jews from documenting the persecution. The police president in Riesa, Saxony, prohibited the local representative of the Central Association of German Citizens of Jewish Faith to take pictures of anti-Jewish signs in various Saxonian towns. Yet, in June 1934, Adolf Vogel photographed his father's store in Sandersleben, Anhalt, plastered with boycott signs. Dora Francken defiantly posed next to two signs that read "Dogs are not allowed" and "For Jews no access" at the entrance of the public pool in the small town of Blaubeuren in southwestern Germany. And in the small town of Gross-Gerau, Hesse, Martin Marx documented his family standing next to an anti-Semitic slogan defacing his father's property in 1935, just before he left Germany for the United States.[10]

Storm troopers march Michael Siegel through Munich on March 10, 1933. Photographer, Heinrich Sanden. (Federal Archive Germany Image 146-1971-006-02)

A picture of Lizi Rosenfeld, a Jewish girl, on a Vienna park bench marked "Only for Aryans" documents three offenses at once: sitting on a forbidden bench, allowing someone to take a picture of this rebellious act, and smuggling the negative out of Germany. The Spitzer family later donated the photograph to the United States Holocaust Memorial Museum.[11]

During the violent pogrom of November 9–10, 1938, commonly known as *Kristallnacht*, Jewish individuals responded in a variety of ways to violence and vandalism. Some saved religious objects or private goods; others documented the wreckage in pictures. In Berlin, police arrested Andreas Kirschbaum for photographing damaged Jewish stores.[12] Thousands of private Jewish homes were vandalized, and when Heinz Bauer came home from work to his apartment in Mannheim, he could not believe

Dora Francken poses at the entrance of the local pool in Blaubeuren, circa mid-1930s. (Leo Baeck Institute New York, National Socialism Collection AR 119 F 13387)

Martin Marx's sister, his father Emil Marx, and their longtime Christian maid pose defiantly in front of the anti-Semitic slogan "Jude verrecke" (Perish Jew) painted on the family's home in Gross-Gerau, 1935. Photographer, Martin Marx. (Courtesy of the Ewing Family)

Lizi Rosenfeld sitting on a park bench designated "Only for Aryans," Vienna, August 30, 1938. (United States Holocaust Memorial Museum, Photograph 33983, courtesy of Leo Spitzer)

The destroyed family home of Hans Sachs in Nuremberg after the pogrom of
November 10, 1938. Photographer, Hans Sachs. (Bavarian Main State Archive Munich,
Landesentschädigungsamt 31509)

the extent of the destruction. He took several pictures and smuggled them
out of Germany when he emigrated to the United States. Hans Sachs documented his demolished family apartment in Nuremberg. After the war, he
attached the photographs to his claim for recompense to the Bavarian authorities.[13]

Many German and Austrian Jews documenting crimes and expressing
criticism were denounced, subsequently arrested, and later tried and punished. In the midst of the Sudeten crisis in September 1938, Willi Rothschild said to witnesses in public, "Today, you are laughing, who knows,
who will laugh soon." He was first incarcerated in the Buchenwald concentration camp until May 1939; later the Special Court in Bamberg sentenced
him to four months in prison for this "offense." In his verdict, the judge
characterized his public statement as "impudent."[14]

The "Impudent Jew": Trope or Reality?

The "impudent Jew" (*Der freche Jude*) is an anti-Semitic trope, which Holocaust historians are very familiar with. Hitler and Goebbels frequently used it.[15] There is no precise English translation for the German word *frech*, particularly as it was employed in the Nazi period and the preceding eras. Traditionally in Germany, to be *frech* meant to be assertive and argumentative to the point of rudeness. It had legal implications since such speech was perceived as an insult to the honor of the person on the receiving end, as many defamation prosecutions in Imperial and Weimar Germany demonstrate. I have chosen the somewhat musty and imperfect English word "impudent" because it captures this sense of an act of self-assertion perceived as a violation of another person's status.

We find the term "impudent Jew" in slogans smeared onto store windows as well as in police and court records. In administrative reports at the time, the SS (Schutzstaffel), Gestapo, and mayors often complained about "impudent Jews"; for example, in March 1935, the Gestapo in Aachen reported that "the number of Jews who had sent letters and protested in person has become quite numerous and in their tone often impudent." The county commissioner (Landrat) in Schlüchtern wrote in his March and April report that Jews had started to act impudent again; in a similar manner the president for the Prussian state Hesse complained in his May–June report. In July 1935, the Gestapo in Arnsberg reported frequent denunciations that the Jews would get impudent again, as did the police in Steinach on the Saale River during the same month.[16]

Historians have held that the frequent complaints about the "impudent Jews" allowed the Nazis to justify harsher measures against the Jewish population in Germany. However, most of those complaints referred to actual acts of Jewish resistance. In its July 1935 report for Berlin, the Gestapo emphasized that Jews were born with disrespect for state authority. In the same month, during which weeklong anti-Jewish riots disturbed the capital, the police arrested more than one hundred Jews, mostly for offenses against the German state and the Nazi party. Among them was Rosalie Mielzynski, who had publicly criticized the anti-Jewish riots in Berlin by saying, "Since the German state can't succeed, the Jews are blamed and attacked."

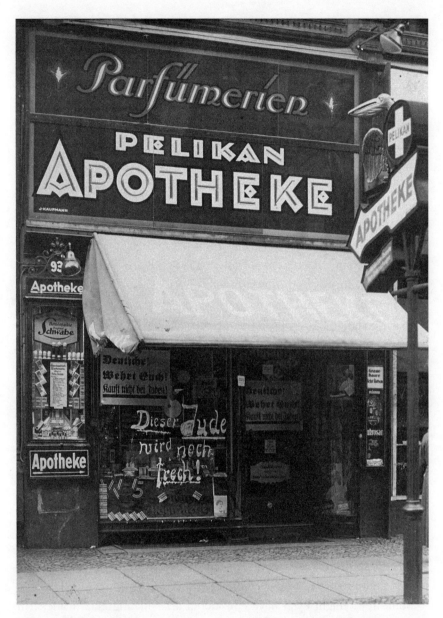

The storefront window of the Pelikan Pharmacy owned by Isaac Bry, in Leipziger Strasse, Berlin, defaced with the slogan, "This Jew still acts impudent," April 1, 1933. (United States Holocaust Memorial Museum, Photograph 07424, courtesy of Raphael Aronson)

However, it did not take riots to provoke individual protest against the persecution. In October 1935, the Berlin police arrested 42 Jews; in November, 57 Jews; and in December, 36 Jews. The number jumped to 73 in January 1936. Among those 208 arrests, 141 cases resulted from "hostility to the state," and 61 involved "race defilement" (*Rassenschande*), the Nazi term for sexual relationships and marriage between Jewish and non-Jewish Germans, illegal since the Nuremberg Laws of 1935.[17]

Ironically, the Nazis also accused Jews of betraying their country, even though the Nazis did not perceive them as Germans. Prosecutors called treason any criticism that in their eyes amounted to a potential preparation for overthrowing the government. Until 1936, no fewer than 46 Jewish Germans, among them 11 women, had been prosecuted or tried for treason in Nazi Germany. Born between 1887 and 1917, these Jews from Breslau, Frankfurt, Cologne, Berlin, and other cities received sentences between three months in jail and fifteen years in a penitentiary (*Zuchthaus*).[18]

In various Bavarian towns, police detained 25 Jews for alleged subversive (*staatsfeindliche*) attitudes and actions between January and October 1936. In its report for 1937, the Security Service of the SS mentioned the incarceration of several "impudent" Jews in Stettin. In September 1938, when Germany found itself at the brink of a war with Czechoslovakia over the Sudeten territories, the Gestapo detained various Jews in cities such as Berlin and Vienna, as well as smaller villages like Buttenhausen, Bigge, and Hüsten, for criticizing Hitler's war mongering and new racist laws.[19] Instead of being simply thrown into a concentration camp, as is often wrongly assumed, such "impudent Jews" were usually prosecuted and put on trial at Special Courts for "treacherous attacks on the Nazi state." They received sentences from several months to years in prison for their alleged crimes. When released from jail before Kristallnacht in 1938, many immediately fled Germany, which often saved their lives.

Some Jews might even have considered assassinating Nazi leaders. In November 1937, the Gestapo in Treuchtlingen, Bavaria, informed the prosecutor in Munich that Bernhard Bermann, a sixty-four-year-old Jewish cattle dealer, had allegedly offered 10,000 Reichsmarks to an acquaintance to kill two local Nazi party leaders. In June 1938, a Gestapo report claimed that

Dr. Bruno Glaserfeld, the head of the National Association of German Jews (*Landesverband Deutscher Juden*) in Berlin, had criticized earlier Jewish illegal activities because they failed to overthrow Hitler. In a gathering with like-minded companions, Glaserfeld propagated the idea of simultaneous bombings of Nazi leadership meetings, such as during Reichstag sessions and the annual party convention in Nuremberg. The Gestapo also reported that sales representative Günther Salter talked about assassination attempts as the only effective political means against the Third Reich. Salter suggested monitoring streets frequently used by Hitler during public events such as his birthday celebration. The Gestapo report underlined that both Jews declared that these plans illustrated the desperation in the Jewish communities.[20]

Aware of such potential danger, Nazi authorities required Jews to surrender any weapons they had. Although the possession of guns had been prohibited in Germany since the 1918 revolution and a 1928 law provided a few exemptions for permit holders, some Jews had kept weapons from their service in the World War, and others owned guns for hunting. In a few cities such as Breslau, Jews were ordered in 1933 to surrender their arms immediately, but in Berlin, the police began to disarm Jews during the fall of 1938. Jews were summoned to the nearest police precinct to hand over their guns and swords, even if they had a permit. In a "special action" (*Sonderaktion*), police raided Jewish homes to search for legally registered weapons and arrested arms-bearing Jews for being hostile to the German state. Alois Adler was arrested on October 3, 1938, after he gave his hunting rifle to a friend to avoid it being found at his home. Immediately after Kristallnacht, police raided Jewish homes in many towns to search for weapons. On November 11, 1938, the Nazi government ultimately prohibited German Jews from owning firearms and any "cutting or stabbing weapons."[21]

Despite or because of the impact of the violent pogrom, the authorities continued to complain about "impudent" Jews. The Nazi party even used the trope in propaganda posters to justify the mass imprisonment of 30,000 Jews in concentration camps after the pogrom.[22]

When the war against Poland began on September 1, 1939, the Jews displayed a more provocative attitude, according to a circular sent to local

Nazi poster calling for mass demonstrations, Munich, November 10, 1938. The lines at the top read: "The synagogue is burned down! The Jewish stores are closed! The impudent-acting Jews are arrested!" (City Archive Munich DE-1992-FS-NS-00195)

Gestapo branches in Berlin on September 6. In Düsseldorf, the local Gestapo issued a decree blaming Jews for neglecting orders and not acting with the necessary restraint in public. A month later, the Gestapo mandated the county commissioners to arrest "in an uncompromising way" all Jews breaking rules or displaying a detrimental attitude toward the Nazi state. In an April 1940 report, the Reich Main Security office emphasized that it had received information about the impudent attitude of Jews from various corners of the Reich. Later that year, Jews were arrested for "impudent behavior" in Munich and for visiting forbidden premises in Vienna.[23] Archival records and survivor video testimonies from the USC Shoah Foundation Visual History Archive confirm that many Jews ignored prohibitions to visit public libraries, parks, swimming pools, and movie theaters everywhere in the Reich.[24]

After the invasion of the Soviet Union, "impudent behavior" of Jews multiplied further in Bohemia and Moravia, according to a report circulating in the Reich Protector office at the beginning of July 1941. In Germany proper, the Security Service of the SS also complained about the "provocative demeanor" of Jews.[25] In response, German and Czech organizations demanded to mark the Jewish population with an armband displaying a Star of David like in Poland. Karl Hermann Frank, the Reich Protector's deputy, wrote to the head of the Reich chancellery, Heinrich Lammers, that the introduction of armbands for Jews would be appropriate because of the "challenging attitude" of the Jews. He pushed to bring this to Hitler's attention.

Subsequently, the notorious "yellow star" identifying and stigmatizing Jews was introduced in Greater Germany, including the Protectorate of Bohemia and Moravia. The decree, which also forbade Jews from leaving their hometowns without permission, was put into effect on September 19, 1941. From this point on, all Jews older than six years had to display the star on their clothes in public, even during forced labor.[26]

This mandate did not help, though, in changing the attitude of Jewish men and women. In Vienna, the daily Gestapo reports reveal that on almost every other day in October 1941, the police arrested a Jewish man or woman, whether for verbal attacks against the Nazi state, unruly behavior, or ignoring local anti-Jewish measures. In Berlin and Vienna, dozens of Jewish forced laborers allegedly committed sabotage and refused to work. Alfred Schirenc, a forced laborer, resisted wearing the notorious "yellow star" and visited restaurants prohibited for Jews.[27] Although some survivors talk casually about not wearing the "yellow star," making it sound more like an adventure facilitating access to forbidden places, such as a movie theater, in reality, not wearing the humiliating badge resulted in serious consequences.[28] In the fall of 1942, after a year of mass deportations, when only 55,000 to 60,000 Jews remained in Germany proper, a substantial number of 1,200 of them served sentences for political or criminal offenses in prisons and penitentiaries across the German Reich.[29]

Individual protests against wearing the "yellow star" confirm that only a radical change in perspective allows us to grasp the full range of individual Jewish behavior during the Holocaust. The forgotten stories demonstrate that the Nazi authorities perceived individual Jewish protest, contestation of Nazi laws and propaganda, and defense against violent attacks as resistance — and they punished such actions harshly. These acts, therefore, need to be integrated into our standard narrative of the Holocaust.

Toward a Broader Perspective of Resistance During the Holocaust

Although many know some details about the Jewish fight against anti-Semitism in Germany before 1933, Jewish resistance and the persecution of Jewish resisters after 1933 have sunk into oblivion despite the existence of some scholarly work on organized efforts at defiance, such as the Herbert-Baum group in Berlin, which attacked a Nazi propaganda exhibition in May 1942, provoking mass reprisals against the Jewish population.[30] The public and even many historians and psychologists still subscribe to the idea of the Nazis having led the Jews like "sheep to the slaughter."[31] Associating Jewish Holocaust resistance exclusively with organized and armed groups such as the Warsaw Ghetto fighters and the Bielski partisans underscores their rare occurrence and, thus, reinforces the notion of Jewish passivity.[32]

It is not that historians have not discussed the topic. Historical commissions established by Jewish survivors all over Europe collected evidence and documented the impact of the Nazi crimes, which in itself was an act of post-factum resistance. *The Black Book: The Nazi Crime Against the Jewish People*, published in 1946, contained a fifty-page chapter titled "Resistance" countering the notion of passivity by presenting examples of Jewish revolts in ghettos and death camps. But it neglected to mention Germany proper and dealt with resistance mostly in terms of organized group activities. Marie Syrkin's 1947 book on Jewish resistance in Europe offered a strikingly similar account, focusing on parachutists, partisans, and ghetto fighters in eastern and southeastern Europe. However, she briefly explores art, education, and historical document as the "struggle of the spirit" by Jews in the Warsaw ghetto as well as Jewish rescue efforts in the Netherlands.[33]

In *The Destruction of the European Jews* (1961), Raul Hilberg said there was an "almost complete lack of resistance" among European Jews. Israeli scholars immediately challenged such assessments by emphasizing moral and spiritual resistance in the ghettos in Poland. Nevertheless, academic discussion soon settled on armed resistance in the eastern occupied territories. In *Perpetrators, Victims, Bystanders* (1990), Hilberg did discuss how some Jews refused to adjust to the growing persecution by hiding, escaping, resisting, or committing suicide. However, he emphasized the rarity of these occurrences, somehow still clinging to a traditional view of group resistance.[34]

Consequently, a thorough evaluation of individual Jewish resistance is missing in almost all prominent Holocaust accounts, surprisingly even in those focusing on the integration of Jewish voices, such as the widely acclaimed books by Saul Friedländer.[35] Friedländer even asserted that the execution of German plans in Europe depended on "the willingness of the victims to follow orders."[36] As if their alleged passivity had enabled persecution and murder.

To evaluate Jewish behavior, most scholars have relied on serial political reports that originated in Nazi institutions, on written testimonies of survivors, and, more recently, on Jewish diaries. Yet, reports produced by the SS, the Gestapo, civil servants, and Nazi party officials for their superiors rarely mentioned resistance of Jews, because in their worldview it conflicted with the dominant anti-Semitic stereotype of "the weak Jew" and the Nazi quest for total control. Out of fear of Nazi censorship, criticism and defiance were almost entirely absent from Jewish diaries and contemporary letters. In postwar testimonies, survivors and witnesses left out such acts because the authors themselves defined resistance in a traditional way: as organized and armed acts.

German authorities, however, harshly punished Jews for the smallest individual actions. In December 1934, a Special Court in Saxony sentenced Walter Meyer to a year in prison for saying in public that Hitler would behave like a hysterical lady.[37] In a stark difference from how they viewed other political enemies of the Third Reich, such as Communists and Social Democrats, many prosecutors and judges saw Jews only as "guests in Germany" who needed to behave with particular restraint. After the Reichstag in Berlin—the home of the German Parliament—was destroyed by a fire, the Nazi-controlled Parliament passed the Enabling Act on March 23, 1933, handing Hitler unprecedented powers to govern. Two days before that, President Paul von Hindenburg had issued a decree prohibiting "treacherous attacks" against the "Government of the National Awakening," to criminalize any type of political opposition. Special Courts were established across Germany. In December 1934, the Nazi government enacted the "Law against Treacherous Attacks on the State and the Party, and for the Protection of Party Uniforms."[38] The Special Courts, with the exception of the People's Court and the main regional courts (*Oberlandesgerichte*), received jurisdiction under the new law providing them with sweeping powers to prosecute protests against the regime now deemed as "political offenses."[39]

Historians have overlooked the fact that Special Courts not only prosecuted political enemies, but also widely employed the "Treacherous Attacks Law" to punish any type of criticism expressed by Jews against the Nazi state and its persecution. Since the separation between private and public spheres, as well as the protection of private homes, soon ceased to exist in the Third Reich, courts sent Jews to jail even for critical comments they made in the privacy of their own apartments. Although only a handful of Jews still lived in the Sudeten district after its annexation to the Third Reich, the Special Court in Eger tried Jews in 17 percent of its cases in 1940. The same Special Court also punished Jews more harshly than other defendants, although the Special Courts in Troppau and Leitmeritz (both Sudeten) did not treat them differently than other opponents of the Reich. In some cases, Special Courts as in Freiberg, Saxony, did not allow Jewish lawyers to represent their clients because of the "political nature" of the offenses. Hence, the treatment of the Jews expressing criticism depended on the prosecutors and judges in each individual courtroom.

Moreover, not only Special Courts, but almost every local and regional court in Nazi Germany tried Jews for "criminal acts." Historians have yet to appreciate how these court proceedings can reveal patterns of defiant behavior during the Third Reich.[40] Jews not only opposed a wide range of anti-Jewish decrees and measures, but because of the circumstances also broke both general German and specific Nazi laws. However, the traditional assumption of a steady Nazification of the judicial system and law enforcement from 1933 on is too simplistic. The reality was more complicated. Some accounts reveal surprising acts of solidarity with Jews: police officers offered help, witnesses testified favorably, and judges acquitted Jews, even late into the war. Every denunciation of Jewish acts of defiance or protest needed proof in court. Despite the common myth, most of the time (with some exceptions), the Nazis could neither jail a Jewish man or woman nor incarcerate them in a concentration camp without proper legal procedures. If accusations could not be corroborated, judges either dismissed them or acquitted the defendant.

Interestingly, the new broader perspective emerging from the diverse set of new sources revitalizes older ideas about resistance. Shortly after the end of World War II, the survivor Philip Friedman outlined future scholarship on the persecution of the Jews and listed multiple forms of resistance, including "spiritual, moral, individual, collective, spontaneous, and organized."[41] Similarly, survivor Meir Dworzecki reflected early on multiple categories of resistance: economic, medical, cultural, and moral. He promoted the concept of *Amidah* (stand), which he described as encompassing "all expressions of Jewish 'non-conformism' and . . . all the forms of resistance and all acts by Jews aimed at thwarting the evil design of the Nazis."[42] While lamenting the limited possibilities of armed resistance, the Israeli historian Yehuda Bauer took up Dworzecki's *Amidah* concept, focusing on semi-organized activities, education, hiding, and religious acts.[43]

At the core of the current *Amidah* understanding is the preservation of Jewish religion, culture, and education against Nazi prohibitions, which was very important in the ghettos in occupied Poland. Yet this was a non-issue in Germany proper, where the Nazis forced the Jews to maintain their culture and education in segregated associations and schools until 1942.[44] Similar to the Israeli scholars, in the 1980s the Australian historian Konrad Kwiet and East German survivor Helmut Eschwege widened the definition of Jewish resistance by including individual activities for Nazi Germany.[45]

Comparable small deeds of resistance have been discussed in other contexts. In the 1980s, during a debate about anti-Nazi resistance, historians looked at a wide range of activities, including non-conformism and protest. At the same time, the microhistorical approach of everyday life history (*Alltagsgeschichte*) emerged in Germany, emphasizing *Eigensinn* (obstinacy) of the powerless as well as their asymmetrical responses.[46] Another important train of thought originates from the sociological and anthropological studies on daily resistance of oppressed people in authoritarian and repressive environments. James Scott, for example, proposed to define resistance simply as any action that rejects subordination; subordination defined as any ideas, practices, and systems that devalue one group and place it under the domination of another.[47] Similarities to individual Jewish resistance can be explored in the day-to-day resistance of African Americans under slavery, which included flight and work sabotage.[48] Relevant here are also general studies on non-violent social and political resistance.[49]

Recent studies on Jewish resistance during the Holocaust emphasizing Jewish agency and responses still describe organized armed activities as the "real" resistance.[50] Only a very few of the individual resistance acts emerged in the vast literature on the persecution of the Jews.[51] Frank Bajohr and Christoph Kreutzmüller have shown how Jewish merchants and businessmen developed their own defense strategies.[52] Jürgen Matthäus called one tactic "evasion by compliance," when Jews tried to exploit Nazi racial laws. In petitions, for example, women declared their children offspring from an extramarital relationship with an "Aryan."[53]

However, such petitions formed part of a large and complex body of written opposition to the Nazi persecution of the Jews. Jews authored countless petitions addressing local and regional administrations, the Nazi government, and its chancellor Hitler. Most historians have neglected them as written in vain, since Nazi authorities rejected the requests in many cases.[54] Not many scholars would think of these petitions as acts of resistance. However, new research establishes that in such entreaties, Jews did not only ask to be exempted from certain laws and restrictions, thus contesting their classification by the regime, but often protested persecution in general. Jews used their petitions to reclaim their rights as taxpayers, citizens, and Germans, directly challenging the prerogative of Nazi persecution.[55]

If a Jewish person in Germany decided not to wear the "yellow star," he or she disobeyed a Nazi decree and, if caught, was punished with time in prison. Actively choosing to do nothing could be prosecuted as resistance. In occupied Europe, evading persecution by fleeing one's country was not a rare occurrence, and was also a type of resistance. Legal emigration and illegal border crossing dominated the period from 1933 to 1939. Emigration never meant just leaving your home and your country, but included smuggling money or belongings and served to escape imprisonment or trials. Fleeing from labor camps, disobeying prohibitions to leave hometowns, escaping deportations by concealing identities in hiding, and illegally crossing borders dominated the years from 1939 to 1945.[56]

In 1937 and 1938, the Gestapo issued dozens of arrest warrants for Jews, either because they had already escaped the country or because they had protested Nazi persecution or broken Nazi laws. Twenty-five-year-old Werner Cohn, who was wanted for "race defilement" and other alleged crimes, fled to the Netherlands. In 1938, the Gestapo had warrants for "atrocity propaganda" on six Austrian Jews, who tried to escape via Germany to western Europe. After the beginning of mass deportations in the fall of 1941, many Jews decided to flee. In February 1942, the Gestapo in Munich searched for fifty-year-old Heinrich Skapowker, who had escaped from one of the camps, the *Arbeitserziehungslager* in Berlin-Wuhlheide, established for people who sabotaged forced labor. In January 1942, the Gestapo arrested two twenty-year-old Jews who attempted to cross the border to Hungary after a successful escape from the Litzmannstadt ghetto. Dozens of Jewish women and men from Vienna fled, either from occupied Poland after the Gestapo forcibly relocated them, or before they were deported. They went into hiding, or they tried to cross the border into Hungary or Yugoslavia.[57] The Joint Distribution Committee, a Jewish aid organization, reported that as of January 1942, six thousand Jews had found shelter in Hungary, mostly from Greater Germany and Poland.[58]

Calling it "flight resistance" (*Fluchtwiderstand*), Tanja Fransesky has shown that Jews jumped from deportation trains in France, Belgium, and the Netherlands by the hundreds.[59] In Germany, the head of the Order Police issued a nationwide decree calling for the police and train personnel to search for, detect, and fix floor planks in the train wagons, which Jews often loosened to escape. In Berlin, Jacob Levin avoided his deportation and lived in hiding off the black market until the criminal police caught him in May 1943. In November 1943, a teenager told police that her mother, the non-Jewish Anna Glatzig whose husband fought at the front, sheltered a former neighbor, Max Marcus, who had escaped deportation.[60] Thus, escape and hiding were often intertwined.[61]

Although escape is still an understudied phenomenon, hiding has become more prominent over the past few decades, first indirectly with research on rescuers, and more recently with local studies on hiding in Warsaw, Munich, and Berlin.[62] The number of hidden Jews in Germany is estimated to have been between 10,000 and 12,000. In Berlin alone, 5,000 to 7,000 Jews (out of nearly 73,000 total) went into hiding after the transports began in 1941. That is almost one out of every ten Jews.[63] Twenty Jewish functionaries disappeared after receiving the deportation order in October 1942. In their angry response, Nazis shot several representatives of the Berlin Jewish community and the Reich Association of Jews.[64]

Some Jewish men and women died in hiding, and others perished after being captured and deported to the occupied East. One German Jew, who had successfully hid until the end of the war, was hanged in Düsseldorf shortly before the liberation. Still, in Berlin, 1,700 Jews survived submerged.[65] And even while hiding, individual Jews frequently disobeyed anti-Jewish rules and regulations and resisted in many unexpected ways, as we can learn from the diary of Victor Klemperer and autobiographical accounts by Marie Simon, Cioma Schönhaus, and Zenon Neumark.[66]

Others tried to escape Nazi persecution by committing suicide, "the ultimate refuge," as Konrad Kwiet called it. However, opinions among scholars vary on whether suicide can be counted as resistance. It is seen as either a common Jewish response in times of intensified persecution, a mere act of despair, an attempt to maintain some dignity, an act of disobedience, or a form of protest and resistance.[67] Categorizing the act as protest rings true in a number of cases. In January 1942, the fifty-eight-year-old former merchant Leopold Schneider, who had received his deportation order, shot himself in front of his parents' grave at the Jewish cemetery in Berlin-Weissensee. He used a handgun that he had not surrendered after Jews were ordered to relinquish their arms in 1938. A few days before the tragic incident, he told his brother that he would not obey the deportation order.[68] Other Jews left suicide notes condemning the Nazi persecution. Hedwig Jastrow took her own life after Kristallnacht and declared in a letter that this was neither an act of despair nor an accident. Contesting the Nazis, she declared that she did not want to live without a fatherland, ostracized and reviled.[69]

Are acts such as sitting on a forbidden park bench, photographing an anti-Jewish sign, disparaging Hitler, not wearing a "yellow star," flight, and suicide *really* resistance? It might be considered too expansive to interpret these acts as resistance, yet the reality in a dictatorship is that the authorities perceive every expression of a differing opinion, every diversion from the prescribed mainstream behavior, and every defiance of an ideological, political, social, or economic rule much differently than would be the case in an open society. An authoritarian government does see all such acts as threats to its power, and therefore will persecute those responsible. This is even truer in the case of the German Jews, whom the Nazi state punished as both political and racial enemies.

The book tells five stories of courageous acts, standing as an example for a certain type of individual resistance. Each main story is embedded in an exploration of the personal life of the resister and the local history of persecution surrounding him or her. Moreover, to avoid the impression that these stories of courage are isolated instances, the second part of each chapter highlights a series of other stories of the same type of resistance. The five categories of individual Jewish resistance that emerged from this research are "Contesting Nazi propaganda," "Oral protest," "Defying anti-Jewish laws and restrictions," "Protest in writing," and "Physical self-defense."

The many forgotten stories of individual resistance challenge the still widespread misconception of Jewish passivity under the Nazis. The evidence unearthed in these accounts restores agency to the persecuted. The stories of Hertha Reis and so many other Jews in Greater Germany demonstrate the myriad possibilities in which, even under the most perilous circumstances, individuals of an oppressed group can and, indeed, do resist discriminatory policies in a dictatorship.

ONE

Contesting Nazi Propaganda

David Bornstein in Hamburg and Others

On August 12, 1936, David Bornstein, thirty-nine, dressed in a gray summer suit, accompanied his wife Margarethe to a bus terminal at the outskirts of Hamburg. Margarethe was going to visit her parents in Bad Segeberg, and her bus was scheduled to leave at 1:30 p.m. Bornstein sat on the bus next to his wife until departure was imminent, and then he got off the bus and chatted with her through the window from outside. According to court documents, Max Schümann, the driver of another bus, said that while waiting for his departure he spotted Bornstein scratching the swastika over the *Deutsche Reichspost's* white logo on the bus with his walking stick. He claimed Bornstein then took a step back, looked at the swastika, and scratched it again. The driver approached Bornstein and asked, "What are you doing there? That's outrageous." Bornstein turned around, surprised. "Are you talking to me?" Schümann said, "Yes, you," and, pointing at the swastika, he added, "You just did this." According to Margarethe, her husband responded, "I did not. Why would you allege something like this?" Schümann approached the driver of Margarethe's bus, Richard Kalkreuter, who was busy collecting fares from passengers, and pointed out the scratches that were approximately ten centimeters long on the swastika. Both Reichspost employees confronted David Bornstein.[1]

Bornstein vehemently denied being responsible for the damage. He exclaimed that he would confirm this under oath and even lifted his hand as if he would start to swear to it. He stepped into the bus to ask passengers if they had witnessed him doing anything wrong and took down the names of those who said no. Schümann then showed Bornstein how he had damaged the bus by scratching the emblem with his cane. He added that he had seen Bornstein look down to see if the stick had been on target. Eventually, Bornstein admitted to it, but claimed it was an unconscious act. Pointing out the layout of the scratches, Kalkreuter did not believe that Bornstein had damaged the Nazi logo by accident. He asked for his name and address, and Bornstein furnished a Hamburg light-rail pass with a photo. Kalkreuter took down the information but had no time to find a second witness, since it was time to leave for Bad Segeberg.[2]

After the Reichspost coach's arrival at its destination, Kalkreuter reported the damage and the name of the suspected culprit to an official at the post office. The next day, he went back to give a formal statement. Consequently, the official called the post office in Ulzburg, where Schümann was stationed. Schümann filed an official complaint with the police precinct near the Hamburg bus terminal where the incident had unfolded. In his description of the incident, he expressed his suspicion that, because Bornstein was a Jew, he had deliberately tried to destroy the Nazi symbol.[3]

David Bornstein, blond and blue-eyed, was born in the Polish town of Żyrardów, forty miles west of Warsaw, on January 18, 1897. For more than a decade, he resided in the German city of Hamburg, where he earned a living as a sales representative. He established his own business selling picture frames and dining trays, switched to toiletry products, and by July 1928, opened a wholesale store specializing in brushes, make-up brushes, combs, and wash-leather in an impressive seven-floor building called Wallhof. In 1933, the mixed commercial and entertainment complex, located in the city center close to Hamburg's big train station at Glockengiesserwall 2, housed sixty-two businesses, stores, and offices as well as beer pubs and cabarets.[4]

Despite the Nazification of Germany and the steadily intensifying persecution of the Jews, Bornstein was able to grow his business in the entrepreneur-friendly city. Still, his earnings seemed to be modest. In 1936, he lived with his new wife, the raven-haired Margarethe Meier, in a sublet apartment on the ground floor of Haynstrasse 11 in Eppendorf, in the northern part of the city, forty minutes by public transport from his work.[5]

However, long term, he saw no future in Nazi Germany. Even without a law existing against Jewish enterprises, across Germany Nazi boycotts, city restrictions, and violent attacks pressured Jewish business owners into either selling or liquidating their stores and companies. In other cities between half and two-thirds of Jewish businesses had been closed down or "aryanized"; in Hamburg, by contrast, this was true for "only" 20 percent of Jewish businesses in 1937. But this situation could not last forever.[6]

As a sales representative, David Bornstein was not shy. He frequently found himself in arguments. Neighbors felt provoked by his sometimes impudent and pretentious attitude; he had called the caretaker in his apartment building an "idiot." Many disputes resulted from politics, especially after Hitler took power. In the eyes of his neighbors, Bornstein presented himself as overly proud as a Polish Jew. Once, he had confidently claimed that ten German Jews would be expelled before he, as a Polish Jew, could be deported.[7] Bornstein's "impudent" comments and "unpleasant" personality were frequently cited during the investigation and subsequent trial.

After the formal complaint about the scratched swastika was made, police handed the case over to the Gestapo on August 14. A few hours later, a secret police officer questioned both of the bus drivers. Kalkreuter stated that he had not seen anything until Schümann alerted him. However, he claimed that Bornstein was fully aware of what he was doing. He added that he knew Bornstein as a notoriously unpleasant person. Schümann assured the police that he had seen Bornstein deliberately targeting the swastika. After the questioning, the police officer staged a reenactment of the incident: the denunciator Schümann portrayed the suspect, demonstrating how Bornstein supposedly scratched the swastika.[8]

When the Hamburg Gestapo tried to bring David Bornstein in for questioning, they learned he was on a business trip to the Ore Mountains. The manufacturing of brushes and combs was a common family business in the region between Saxony and Thuringia. After a pre-scheduled visit to the famous annual international fair in Leipzig, Bornstein was supposed to return to Hamburg on September 8.[9]

Independently from police and the Gestapo, the Reichspost Directorate in Kiel informed the office of the Hamburg prosecutor about the alleged

Denunciator Max Schümann poses as David Bornstein, and a police officer as Bornstein's wife inside the bus, during a reenactment for the Gestapo investigation, August 1936. (State Archive Hamburg, 213-11/54253, fol. 13)

incident. Contradicting Bornstein's claim of innocence, the official stated that the suspect, a Jew, had done it on purpose because he hated the swastika and wanted to show that there were enemies of the Nazis everywhere. In the name of the Reichspost, the post official demanded a swift prosecution of Bornstein.[10]

It did not take long for the main prosecutor in Hamburg responsible for investigating "political crimes" at the so-called Special Court to act. In a letter to the Gestapo, he requested more details about the incident: Why would the drivers believe that Bornstein deliberately damaged the bus? Did Bornstein chat with his wife in a lively manner? Where was the emblem located on the bus? Where was Bornstein, inside or outside of the coach?

Were there other witnesses? Finally, the prosecutor also requested a photo-graph of the ruined swastika logo.[11]

A week earlier than expected, on September 2, Bornstein showed up at the police office for questioning. In his signed statement, he explained that in or-der to be able to speak through the high window to his wife, who was inside the bus, he had to be up on his toes. To avoid losing balance, he had to lean for support on his walking stick. According to his statement, it had been pure coincidence that the tip of his walking stick touched the emblem on the side of the vehicle. He never intended to scratch the swastika. Boldly, Bornstein claimed that if he ever planned to do something like this, he would never do it in front of a bus full of passengers. Rather, he would seek darkness as a cover. He concluded his statement by emphasizing that he had never been a member of any political party and organization or politically active in any other way.[12] The police proceeded to question the two bus drivers again.[13]

During the next weeks, the Hamburg prosecutor's office prepared Born-stein's indictment. However, the main prosecutor at the Special Court tem-porarily put a hold on the process. Before trying the incident as a political offense, he needed to make sure that Bornstein's defense of having done it by accident would not hold up in court. He asked the Gestapo to thor-oughly investigate the suspect's reputation, including what previous occur-rences had motivated the bus driver Kalkreuter to call him an unpleasant person.[14]

This request slowed down the prosecution considerably. The Gestapo questioned the bus driver again in November, three months after the inci-dent. Kalkreuter explained that Bornstein had frequently bothered him by asking to open a window that had just been shut or pestering the bus drivers with questions during their breaks. Even more unpleasant was Bornstein's affectionate attitude toward his wife. To say goodbye, Bornstein would al-ways occupy the seat next to her, and until departure, they would passion-ately kiss and tightly hug each other. Such intimate behavior in public was not common in northern Germany and made him and the majority of pas-sengers uncomfortable, said the driver.[15]

The Gestapo also requested information from the local Nazi party. The party branch in South-Eppendorf, where Bornstein lived, wrote that his neighbors did not like him at all since he supposedly displayed an impudent and pretentious, sometimes aggressive, yet cowardly attitude.[16]

After looking at all the testimonies, the prosecutor's office did not see enough evidence to charge Bornstein with a political offense, and therefore shelved the idea of trying him at the Special Court. Instead, the office decided to charge him in a regular court for damaging or destroying an emblem of the state. This was a compromise. Although this specific charge would yield a lesser punishment than a political offense, destroying a state symbol could be politically motivated and therefore carry a heftier sentence than ordinary property damage. In January 1937, the prosecutor's office handed the case over to the Hamburg court.[17]

The court opted for a quick procedure at a summary court and charged David Bornstein with maliciously damaging an emblem of the state under paragraph 135 of the Penal Code. Due to the now significantly less severe accusations, the judges requested only Bornstein's appearance in court instead of his arrest. They also summoned several witnesses, namely the two bus drivers as well as tenants of the building where Bornstein lived.[18]

With the trial looming, Bornstein asked a lawyer, Bernhard David, to represent him. In his authorization letter to the court, the lawyer emphasized that Bornstein vehemently denied having done anything to damage the bus while he waited for his wife's departure at the station. The defense lawyer asked the court to call Bornstein's wife and another woman, who was also a passenger that day, as witnesses. He was confident that they would confirm that Bornstein had done nothing more than chatting with his wife through the bus window.[19]

The trial began on January 15, 1937. It was open to the public, and the court director (*Amtsgerichtsdirektor*) Krause functioned as the presiding judge. Bornstein appeared with his lawyer. Prosecutor Dr. Oelbrich read the charges, and the judge called the witnesses. None of the neighbors had come, only the two bus drivers and the two passengers, Margarethe Bornstein and Ella Hähnsen. When the judge asked Bornstein to tell the court what had occurred, he said, "I was just chatting with my wife through the bus window. Suddenly, a bus driver approached me and asked me what I am doing there. Supposedly, I had damaged the emblem. I must deny this claim." Bornstein told the judge that he might have touched the swastika with his cane, again reiterating that it was by accident.[20]

Margarethe Bornstein took the witness stand despite her right to decline testimony as the wife of the accused. She said she did not see her husband damaging the emblem and she could not believe that he would ever do such a thing.

A discussion ensued about the extent of the damage. Before a painter had repaired the emblem, the police had taken photographs of the damage. The first driver claimed that the swastika had not been scratched before the incident. Bornstein countered by saying that the police photo showed more scratches than he remembered from that day. He suggested that someone produced more damage in order to harm him personally.[21]

After a weeklong break, the judge summoned the bus drivers again, as well as Margarethe Bornstein, Ella Hähnsen, and four new male witnesses from Bad Segeberg, among them two Reichspost employees. Bornstein stood by his previous statement, and Schümann and Kalkreuter confirmed their testimonies. The main postmaster (*Oberpostmeister*) in Bad Segeberg testified that immediately after the bus's arrival, Kalkreuter pointed out three long scratches on the swastika. Another Reichspost employee confirmed the number of scratches. The sixty-four-year-old painter Richard Reuter, who had repaired the damage, did not remember exactly how many scratches he had seen, but recalled smaller blemishes next to the bigger ones. By contrast, Ella Hähnsen testified that she had only noticed two scratches. The judge also called the defendant's seventy-two-year-old father-in-law, Levin Meier, but he testified that he had only heard about the incident from his daughter.[22]

The prosecutor, in his concluding remarks, requested a sentence of six weeks in jail for Bornstein. The defense lawyer asked for an acquittal. The defendant repeated that he had not done anything wrong. Ultimately, the judge declared Bornstein guilty of damaging an emblem of the state under paragraph 135 of the German Penal Code. He sentenced him to five weeks in prison and obliged him to pay the cost of the trial proceedings.[23]

At the beginning of the written judgment, the Hamburg court emphasized that David Bornstein was a Jew, stateless, and of Polish origin. The

The Gestapo photograph showing the scratches on the swastika emblem painted on the side of the bus, 1936. (State Archive Hamburg, 213-11/54253, fol. 13)

court pointed out that Bornstein had admitted to having caused the scratches, perhaps unintentionally, yet denied a malicious will. Notwithstanding, the court invoked common sense by quoting Schümann's observation of Bornsteins's actions. Nobody, according to the court, would dare to handle a heavy walking stick so close to delicate car paint; therefore, Bornstein must have scratched the swastika on purpose. The judge took into account that the second bus driver might have testified under the influence of animosity based on Bornstein's alleged behavior in the past. In the end, the court based the judgment on Schümann's statement, who had never had an encounter with Bornstein before. Moreoever, the court was convinced of

Bornstein's malicious intent, particularly because he was a Jew and from Poland. Although Bornstein had never done anything against the Nazi government before and had been cautious regarding criticism of anti-Jewish measures, his origin made him, in the judge's eyes, a natural enemy of Nazi beliefs. Therefore, because of previous personal experience or chagrin, the defendant supposedly had willfully attacked an emblem of the Nazi state. Because of the absence of a criminal record, Bornstein's sentence was reduced from six weeks to five weeks in jail.[24]

The judicial affair cost David Bornstein nerves and money. After the trial ended, he appealed to the prosecutor's office for a postponement of his jail sentence, because the Bornsteins had planned a trip to Palestine to scout business opportunities, and his wife Margarethe wanted to visit her son from her first marriage, who had emigrated to the Mediterranean country the previous summer. Another motive, which he did not reveal, was to prepare for emigration. They were scheduled to depart from Hamburg on March 7, 1937, with their steamship *Gerusalemme* leaving on March 10 from Trieste. Bornstein assured the security police that they would be back on April 20, since the booking of a discounted trip forced them to take a return ship from Haifa on April 10.[25]

The Gestapo, however, did not make it easy. The officers wanted some kind of security that the Bornsteins would return. Interrogated about his savings, Bornstein disclosed that he possessed 10,000 Reichsmarks, most of it tied up in his store, and his most recent annual income was 5,000 Reichsmarks. For the temporary deferment of his sentence, the Gestapo requested a fee of 500 Reichsmarks, which was 10 percent of his annual income and more than many people earned in two months. They ordered Bornstein to bring a receipt from the court cashier's office the next day. As mandated, on February 27, he appeared and submitted the receipt as well as a letter, in which the prosecutor's office administered a sentence postponement until April 27. The Gestapo finally agreed to his trip but called the local tax investigation office to make sure he would not leave without paying outstanding taxes.[26]

During the next days, the couple obtained transit visas for Austria and Italy at the respective consulates in Hamburg. They had already received the visas for Palestine from the British consulate general. The couple arrived in Palestine on March 15 and stayed until April 7, 1937.[27]

Before Bornstein had even tried to get permission for his Palestine trip, his lawyer Bernhard David filed a petition for clemency. Shortly after his client's return, the lawyer received word that the sentence was postponed until April 1940. To avoid serving prison time, he needed to display immaculate conduct and pay another large fine of 1,500 Reichsmarks. After three years, the prison sentence and his criminal record were to be expunged.[28]

Margarethe was pregnant when the couple went to Palestine. Their daughter Ruth was born on September 17, 1937. According to German law, only children of Germans could automatically become German citizens. Ruth not only looked like her father, with her blonde hair and blue eyes; she, like her father, was registered as stateless. By this time, the family had moved into another apartment on the ground floor of Schlüterstrasse 12 in Hamburg. Their new home was in the city center and only twenty-five minutes by foot from Bornstein's store in the Wallhof.[29] In May 1938, David Bornstein's in-laws moved from Bad Segeberg to Hamburg, closer to the couple and their grandchild.[30]

All things seemed to be pointing in the right direction. Yet suddenly, on June 16, 1938, David was arrested and held at the police prison Hamburg-Fuhlsbüttel for a week. From there, authorities transferred him to the concentration camp Sachsenhausen near Berlin.[31]

When Hitler ordered that "asocial and criminal Jews" were to be seized for forced labor deployment, the head of the German police, Reinhard Heydrich, merged the order with the independently planned "action against asocials," which included vagrants, beggars, so-called Gypsies, pimps, and persons with a criminal record. Subsequently, 2,500 male Jews with criminal records, even for minor convictions such as smoking in a forest during wildfire season or crossing a street on a red light, were incarcerated in concentration camps. David Bornstein's postponed sentence for damaging the swastika put him on the radar for this raid. In Sachsenhausen, he was interned with 823 German Jews. In the concentration camps, SS guards treated the incoming "asocial and criminal" Jews harshly, harassing and frequently beating them. One hundred sixty-nine Jews incarcerated as "asocials" died before 1939. If they survived, many spent months in this concentration camp until they could secure emigration papers.[32]

Compared with others, David Bornstein got lucky. One month after his arrival in Sachsenhausen, the SS released him from "protective custody," together with two other Jews interned as so-called asocials in late June. It seems likely that Bornstein provided some emigration paperwork to facilitate his release. The authorities registered his emigration to Palestine on September 8, 1938.[33] This was only two days after Hitler spoke in front of the German Reichstag, proclaiming the establishment of a Greater Germany now including the annexed Austria.[34]

Bornstein's wife and daughter left Germany with him.[35] They escaped just in time to avoid two brutal and violent nationwide anti-Jewish raids. At the end of October, Reich Leader-SS and Chief of the German Police Heinrich Himmler ordered the mass expulsion of Jews of Polish origin. Seventeen thousand people, including many women and children, were corraled by police guards with bayoneted rifles and deported without their belongings by bus and train to the Polish border. Since the Polish border guards refused to let many of them cross into Poland, the Germans dumped thousands of Jews in the no-man's land between the two countries.[36] Two weeks later, the Nazis struck the entire German Jewish community with unprecedented violence during Kristallnacht. After the pogrom, the Nazi leadership decided on new drastic measures, including a total prohibition for Jews to own and manage businesses, the "forced Aryanization" of firms, shops, and assets, segregation in schools and welfare, and forced labor, as well as a special tax levy of one billion Reichsmarks to drive Jews out of Germany in anticipation of a war.[37]

If David Bornstein had stayed in Nazi Germany, he would have lost his business, and possibly also his home and his life. After he left for Palestine, his store still appeared in Hamburg's 1939 address book at Glockengiesserwall 2, since one had to register far in advance for an entry. From 1940 onward, his name and store disappeared, but no one seemed to have rented his spot, even though the other nine offices and organizations that occupied the neighboring spaces on the third floor of the Wallhof reappeared with entries in the newly printed annual directories. Standing empty for years, his shop seems like a visual symbol for the hole that Bornstein's emigration left in German society.[38]

David and his family arrived in Palestine on September 19, 1938. Two and a half years after their immigration, the family applied to obtain citizenship at the Government of Palestine–Department of Migration. Finally leaving persecution behind, the stateless Jewish couple David and Margarethe Bornstein and their daughter became naturalized citizens of Palestine on June 8, 1941.[39]

Other Stories of Jews Contesting Nazi Propaganda

Bornstein's tale demonstrates how German Jews actively battled Nazi propaganda and the regime itself in unexpected ways. Yet this is not an isolated case. Since 1933, the police across Germany had been arresting Jews for destroying Nazi posters or symbols, sullying displays of the anti-Semitic newspaper *Der Stürmer*, and contesting the Hitler salute.[40]

During the nationwide anti-Jewish boycott on April 1, 1933, former frontline Jewish soldiers challenged the Nazi propaganda by wearing their uniforms from the World War in cities and towns across Germany. Jewish shop owners donned their war decorations and medals, contesting, as Michael Geheran has emphasized, "a crucial element of Nationalist Socialist discourse: the claim that Jews had been cowards and unpatriotic shirkers during the war." In Wesel, Westphalia, Erich Leyens printed large quantities of fliers criticizing Nazi treatment of Jewish war veterans, and on the day of the boycott next to the SA guards, he distributed those texts to passers-by while wearing his wartime uniform with the Iron Cross First Class. This provoked sympathy and solidarity; many people reacted "with open dismay" to SA men harassing a former soldier in the war. In Berlin, a former U-boat officer, the Zionist Max Haller, stood before his business with his medals on display. The growing crowd eventually brought traffic on the street to a standstill. In Stettin, Olga Eisenstädt, a soldier's widow, stood in front of her small shop and educated passers-by about her service during the war. By battling Nazi propaganda and anti-Semitic tropes of Jewish physical and moral inferiority, lack of courage, and service during the war, these Jews reclaimed their Germanness.[41]

Displaying German symbols versus Nazi symbols was another way to challenge anti-Jewish propaganda. German Jews proudly displayed traditional

German colors, as the Weimar tricolor (black, red, and gold) flag or the flag of the German empire. Because of this attitude, the Nuremberg Race Laws included a prohibition for Jews to fly the Reich and national flags.[42]

During the first year of Nazi rule, Moritz Natho pulled down a swastika flag in Leipzig, Saxony.[43] German Jews also destroyed Nazi posters. Joachim Boin, a member of Jewish sports clubs who lived in Cottbus in eastern Germany, ripped down Nazi posters several times in different places.[44] In 1933, the thirty-one-year old chemist Dr. Paul Wolff removed anti-Semitic posters, and during the summer of 1934, he tore a page from Hitler's *Mein Kampf* and damaged two other Nazi books in a bookstore. Wolff also sent letters to Hitler and local courts criticizing defamation attacks against the Jews. In January 1935, he insulted German civil servants. In two trials, courts sentenced him to a total of thirteen months in prison.[45]

While serving his sentence, Wolff exclaimed in front of a guard, "Hitler verrecke" (Hitler die a miserable death). Later, he gave a guard a piece of toilet paper on which he had written: "Hitler and Streicher are slanderers of the Jewish religion." These were not the only incidents, but he got away with minor disciplinary punishments. However, during the daily walk in the prison yard on July 10, he shouted loudly: "What Hitler wrote in his 'Kampf' on pages 312 and 313 about the Jewish religion is a great lie." Not only the thirty to forty other prisoners and the guards had heard his critical words, but supposedly also the families of the guards living in apartments nearby. Later, he bothered the guards, criticized the Nazi Sterilization Law of 1933, and complained that people were forced to use the Hitler salute. The next April, the prison warden confiscated a letter Wolff had written to Dr. Wilhelm Stapel, co-editor of the monthly journal *Deutsches Volkstum* (German Peopledom). Wolff challenged Stapel's anti-Semitism, particularly for calling the Jewish soldiers weak. In the letter, he reminded him that 12,000 Jews had given their lives for Germany during the war and cited Hindenburg's words honoring them. Put on trial again in 1936, Wolff defended all of his actions criticizing propaganda against the Jews. Investigated by a doctor for his mental health, Wolff emphasized that he fought out of conscience against the defamation of the Jews. Even before Hitler took power, he attended anti-Semitic meetings and smacked the speaker in his face. Moreover, he told the judge that he could not promise to change. Taking into consideration a history of schizophrenic attacks—he had spent time in a sanatorium in the 1920s—the Special Court in Freiberg (Saxony) acquitted him of some of his offenses under the Treacherous Attacks Law of 1934, but still sentenced him to three more months in jail.[46]

On August 12, 1935, the county leader (*Kreisleiter*) of the Nazi party district Eimsbüttel-Nord reported Jacob Heilbut, the Jewish owner of the house at the corner of Schwenkestrasse and Stellingerweg, to the Hamburg Gestapo for allegedly removing a propaganda poster from the wall next to the entrance of his bread shop. Three witnesses, among them the owner of another bread shop across the street, said they had spotted Heilbut using a bucket of water and a spatula to scrape off a poster that read, "Deutsches Volk horch auf" (German people, listen up). The poster had been issued by the Nazi party to whitewash previous Nazi attacks on churches and to blame Catholics and Communists instead. The text said: "German people, listen up! Unscrupulous agitators are working to push you into a culture war! . . . This sabotages the inner peace of our nation." The poster was printed and distributed by all Nazi *Gau* (district) leaderships, and it went on to warn pedestrians to be aware of dangerous wolves coming disguised in sheep's skin.[47] At the same time, another nationwide anti-Semitic campaign took place. In Göttingen, Storm Troopers put up posters with the slogan "Recognize Satan in the Jew" on shops owned by Jews. The campaign culminated in a speech by Goebbels in Essen on August 4, 1935.[48]

Matthias Espen, a member of the Nazi party, emphasized that this was the second time Heilbut had removed a poster without authorization. In addition to reporting it to the Nazi party, Espen informed the nearby police station, but ironically, the regular police would not interfere, since the law prohibited posting bills on private walls. On August 23, 1935, the Gestapo took Jacob Heilbut into custody, charging him with malignant removal of official posters of the Nazi party. During the interrogation, more details of the story emerged. Members of the local Nazi cell had posted the propaganda poster around midnight on August 7. After discovering it the next morning, Heilbut decided to remove it immediately. Questioned by the Gestapo, he defended his action by saying he had already cleaned parts of the building's exterior and by coincidence was planning to clean the section with the poster that day. The Gestapo did not believe him. They accused Heilbut of subversive actions against the state and the Nazi party. Three days later, the local court charged him with damaging property under section 303 of the German Penal Code. The judge issued an official arrest warrant, suspecting that, as a Jew, he would try to escape. During the short trial on September 10, the prosecutor demanded a sentence of two months in prison. Judge Dr. Bertram ultimately sentenced Heilbut to six weeks in prison, since the destruction of the poster was perceived as a conscious act of sabotage against the measures of the Nazi district leadership.[49]

After the court declined an appeal for clemency in December, Heilbut asked for a delay of his imprisonment, since his wife was not able to run the bread shop alone with two small children during the busy holiday season. The court granted him a postponement until January 6. Heilbut then served his remaining time, counting the pre-trial detention. Because of this criminal record, in June 1938 he became a victim of the raid against "asocial and criminal" Jews and was sent to the Sachsenhausen concentration camp, where he was not released until January 1939. Soon after, he fled to England and later to the United States. In 1952, the German state paid for his travel, and he returned for the first time to Hamburg. There, he demanded a revision of his trial, the abolishment of the sentence, and its deletion from his criminal records, citing the political nature of both the trial and the judgment. His appeal was successful, and the court granted the abolition of his sentence.[50]

Jacob Heilbut was not the only German Jew who ripped down one of the "German people, listen up" placards. On August 12, 1935, the police arrested Isidor F. for the same reason in the small town Walldorf near Meiningen, Thuringia. Attacking Nazi propaganda posters was just one of many expressions of defiance. Jews also fought back against individual actions by anti-Semites, sometimes in sophisticated ways. Henry Schuster's parents rented out the store in their house to a non-Jewish merchant, who—after he opened his business—placed a "Strictly Prohibited for Jews" (Für Juden strengstens verboten) sign at the home's private entrance, which was used by the Schuster family. One night, Henry's mother changed one letter on the poster so that it read "Strictly Prohibited for Everybody" (Für Jeden strengstens verboten).

Die Juden sind unser glück

A defaced display box for the anti-Semitic newspaper *Der Stürmer*, Saint Peter, Baden, 1933. The slogan has been altered to read, "The Jews are our Fortune," instead of "The Jews are our Misfortune." (United States Holocaust Memorial Museum, Photograph 18523, courtesy of Miriamne Fields)

The shop owner denounced the Jewish family to the authorities, which led to an investigation. The town's mayor personally questioned the family's son Henry, who was a young boy at a time. However, no evidence surfaced, and the Schusters were never charged or punished for this offense.[51]

Even after the violent pogrom in November 1938, Jews attacked Nazi insignia and other displays of propaganda for the Nazi party and state. In June 1939, Leipzig police charged a Jewish man for trying to bring down and destroy a Nazi flag.[52] Display cases of the anti-Semitic newspaper *Der Stürmer*, which could be found everywhere in Nazi Germany, also were a target. Jews smeared or spit at the glass protecting the newspaper editions. In February 1941, the Vienna Gestapo detained twenty-three-year-old Georg Lichtenstern for three weeks after he ripped down a note from a *Der Stürmer* display case, which warned: "In case of a spit attack, the next Jew will be made to lick it off." After his release, the Gestapo planned to hand Lichtenstern over to the Central Office for Jewish Emigration under Adolf Eichmann for "relocation" to occupied Poland.[53]

In November 1941, the Gestapo intercepted a letter that had been written by a pensioner, Marie Schmidt, in which she urged her sister in Switzerland to facilitate emigration for her and other family members. Because she had attached a news magazine clipping with a photo of Hitler in which she had punctured his eyes, as well as the tiny Nazi party badge above his heart, the Gestapo arrested Schmidt.[54]

As the stories of David Bornstein and others illustrate, Jews actively contested anti-Jewish propaganda and attacked symbols of the Nazi dictatorship. The forms of this individual resistance varied: Some Jews destroyed Nazi flags, others removed propaganda posters; some defaced anti-Semitic newspaper stands; still others altered signs with anti-Jewish restrictions, pierced Hitler's eyes on a propaganda photo, or damaged a swastika logo on a public bus.

Unlike other defiant actions, such as public protest and neglecting laws, this form of individual Jewish resistance often took only a brief moment to execute and happened without human interaction. Much harder to recognize or detect, such behavior has not left many traces in German archives.

Although one might assume that such actions were more widespread during the early years of the Nazi regime, the unearthed evidence shows that Jews continued to contest Nazi propaganda even during the war. For the German state, these were attacks to the very foundation of the dictatorship. When they were discovered, whether by chance or by eyewitness denunciation, the punishments for these seemingly small acts of defiance were swift and profound, life altering and, in some cases, life-ending.

TWO

Verbal Protest Against the Persecution

Henriette Schäfer in Frankfurt and Others

Henriette Schäfer, née Neu, was the daughter of a Jewish shoemaker in the small town of Odernheim am Glan, Rhineland-Palatinate, near Bad Kreuznach. She perceived herself as a German patriot. During the World War, she worked in an ammunition factory, and in her spare time, she sewed knapsacks for the German army. She married a very conservative non-Jewish German man, but she had never been politically active, especially not since 1933.

After Reich President Hindenburg handed over power in Germany to Hitler, Henriette Schäfer began to have a hard time coping with the daily news, which included the nationwide anti-Jewish business boycott, soon followed by the first anti-Jewish laws, and a steady stream of humiliations. Newspaper headlines printed in black or red screamed that Jews were murderers and traitors. "Traitors" must have been particularly hard for Henriette to swallow, since she felt so patriotic. Every year, the situation worsened for Jews in Frankfurt. In 1938, drawings showing Jews hanging from gallows covered windows of Jewish store owners. Ultimately, the violent attacks against German Jews during Kristallnacht put an end to her patience.

Henriette Schäfer was born on August 20, 1882. She had a slim face with brown eyes and a straight nose. In 1909, she married the merchant Wilhelm Schäfer and moved to Frankfurt am Main in the German state of Hesse, where they

A drawing of a Jew hanging from a gallows and the words "It's about time," on the window of A. M. Joseph's shoe store in Frankfurt am Main, May 1, 1938. Photographer, Hannah Reeck. (Institute for City History Frankfurt, S7Z Nr. 1938-30)

rented part of an apartment at Schlossstrasse 63 in Frankfurt-Bockenheim. The couple did not have children.[1]

Once Hitler became Reich chancellor in 1933, the conditions for Jews deteriorated everywhere in Germany, but particularly in Frankfurt. According to the first Nazi-organized census in 1933, 26,158, or 4.71 percent, of the city's 555,000 inhabitants reported that they were Jewish, the largest percentage in any big city in Germany. The new lord mayor, Friedrich Krebs, a lawyer and local Nazi party functionary since 1922, became one of the most fanatic city officials. Immediately after assuming his post, just days before the nationwide anti-Jewish boycott in April 1933, he abolished all city contracts with Jewish businesses and prohibited municipal employees from shopping in stores owned by Jews. In addition, he fired all Jewish employees and put all Jewish municipal officials on mandatory leave. During the following years, the Frankfurt city government and the regional Nazi party leadership harassed Jews in many ways.[2]

In November 1938, Hitler used the assassination of a German diplomat in Paris by a young Polish Jew as a pretext for an attempt to drive the remaining Jews out of the Third Reich. On the evening of November 9, Joseph Goebbels instructed the Nazi party leadership to launch a nationwide pogrom against the Jews; in Hitler's words, to unleash "the people's rage." Armed with axes, sledgehammers, gasoline, and guns, Storm Troopers, SS, and other Nazi gangs systematically demolished and looted Jewish private properties as well as their community institutions, including schools, and orphanages. They forced their way into Jewish homes and apartments, vandalized Jewish-owned stores, and set the majority of synagogues in Germany ablaze, while beating, sexually abusing, raping, and murdering innocent German Jewish men and women. This pogrom left several hundred Jewish men and women dead, and thousands more injured, including women and children. The Gestapo sent 30,000 men to concentration camps, where hundreds more would perish because of abuse, hunger, and frost.[3]

Henriette Schäfer certainly must have been outraged and frightened by the events. The following morning, she entered the grocery story on the ground floor of her apartment building, where she approached the elderly shopkeeper Agnes Orschel, her landlord and neighbor, and asked, "What are you saying about the fact that everything is being destroyed and the synagogues are being set on fire?" The shopkeeper responded along official lines, justifying what had happened by saying that it was not right for a Jew to kill a harmless person, and the people had been outraged. Schäfer snapped, "This is not the people, but the government. They are all blackguards, scamps, and criminals. Hitler is the biggest bandit. If I could, I would poison them all." She added, "Our people, the Jews, will eventually take revenge." The shopkeeper told her to keep quiet and that she should be pleased that all the neighbors let her live in peace as a Jew. There were no other clients in the store during the exchange. Henriette stopped talking and abruptly left when another customer entered the store.[4]

The burning Börneplatz synagogue in Frankfurt am Main, November 10, 1938. (Courtesy of Yad Vashem, Photoarchive)

A few months passed, but on March 30, 1939, the Nazi party block leader responsible for monitoring activities in Henriette Schäfer's building informed his local branch about the exchange between the Jewish woman and the store owner. He also reported that when Schäfer heard that someone had requested a donation from her family for *Kinderlandverschickung,* the organized recreational evacuation of children from the cities managed by the head of the Hitler Youth, she became upset and exclaimed in front of a neighbor, "It does not cross my mind to feed his bastards," meaning Hitler. Moreover, she allegedly added, "I would like best, if I could poison this rascal and scoundrel." The report also mentioned an argument with her sister-in-law, Anna Köninger, who lived with the Schäfers, which resulted in her eviction from the couple's apartment only the day before the denunciation. According to the Nazi party report, Henriette had threatened to commit suicide. The block leader requested a quick intervention not only because she had threatened to kill herself, but because she might potentially try to flee the country. The owner of the building, Adam Hieronymus, had also reported to the Gestapo that she had called Hitler a "bandit." Gestapo officers had already spoken with him and prepared witness interviews for the coming days.[5]

Henriette's husband, Wilhelm Schäfer, wrote to the Gestapo immediately in order to deflect the accusations. He explained that during his wife's travel his sister Anna Köninger had badmouthed the couple in front of neighbors. The sister had been staying at his home temporarily after her release from the concentration camp Lichtenburg, where she had been incarcerated as a Jehovah's Witness. After Henriette's return, arguments escalated, and he threw his sister out of the apartment. Later, Hieronymus had advised him to stay away from his wife, and Schäfer emphasized that was exactly what his sister wanted to accomplish: to separate him from Henriette. He said Anna was a fanatic in her faith and that she acted crazy sometimes. He also noted that he was a member of various Nazi organizations, including the supporting circle for the SS, and ended his letter with "Heil Hitler."[6]

The Gestapo questioned three female witnesses named by Adam Hieronymus who all lived in the same building.[7] Shop owner Agnes Orschel, who was Hieronymus's mother-in-law, described her earlier exchange with Schäfer in November 1938, but emphasized that Schäfer had not made hostile comments to her about the Nazi state at any other time. However, Orschel mentioned that the neighbors knew Schäfer as a rabid person and were scared of her, adding that her tenant Erna Breitbach had told her about a similar outburst.[8] After the windows of the Jewish shops were smashed, Breitbach said she met Schäfer on the stairs, who told her that this was not right. Breitbach responded that one could not change anything. When the Gestapo pressed further, she said that they usually did not talk about politics when they ran into each other on the stairs. Breitbach, who had lived in the building only since August 1938, said she and Schäfer were not friends, just neighbors, and at first she did not even realize Schäfer was Jewish. Breitbach assured the Gestapo that she would not pursue conversations with Jews anymore.[9]

The third witness was Anna Sailer, who had lived in the apartment next door to Schäfer since 1935. Although she characterized Henriette Schäfer as a brazen and impertinent person, she also assured the Gestapo that Schäfer never talked negatively about the German state, because she knew Sailer was a Nazi party sympathizer. When Agnes Orschel told Sailer that Schäfer had insulted Hitler, Sailer confronted Schäfer: "You damned Jewess; you insulted our Führer, for which you belong in a penitentiary." Schäfer allegedly responded that she would soon leave for America anyway. However, she denied the Hitler insult and asked who would have told her something like this. Sailer brought up a second incident from February–March 1939. When Schäfer came back from a trip and heard about the request for children camp donations, she supposedly got upset in front of her: "They can kiss my ass. They should raise their bastards alone." According to Sailer, Schäfer's husband warned her to keep her mouth shut if she wanted to avoid going to a concentration camp like Dachau. Anna Sailer concluded that she was very anxious and had memory issues, but she stood by her recollections of these incidents.[10]

Wilhelm Schäfer sensed that his wife was in grave danger. In a second letter to the Gestapo, he emphasized that after he and his wife had moved into the new flat, an electrician warned him about Adam Hieronymus, who would often solve disputes with his tenants in court. No tenant would stay long. This could be easily verifiable by looking at the court files, and Wilhelm Schäfer was sure that after hearing from former neighbors, the Gestapo would be hesitant to believe Hieronymus and Orschel's accusations. Schäfer wrote that Hieronymus, who was a Nazi party member, had told him about his relationships with Gauleiter Sprenger and the Prince of Hesse. Yet, contradicting himself, he later called the prince a dirty pig. When the Nazi party expelled Hieronymus, he assured Schäfer they were all bandits. Schäfer added that Agnes Orschel had told him she was happy that her son-in-law was not with the party anymore since they saved the membership fees. He also claimed that Hieronymus and Orschel had patronized Jewish businesses until recently, saying they preferred Jews over Christians because their own "blood relatives" had betrayed them. He accused Orschel of selling meat products from a wholesale butcher shop, which were cheaper, and in every desired quantity, and her son illegally bred Easter bunnies in his coal cellar. Next-door neighbor Anna Sailer could not be trusted either,

Schäfer added, saying she was full of envy and vindictiveness. In the neighborhood, people called her the "Bockenheim gazette," as she was talking about everything to everybody. Schäfer insisted that he and his wife had never said anything against the Hitler government or its measures, particularly since they were in favor of them long before 1933, verifiable by their voting records. Schäfer urged the Gestapo to reprimand those who publicly shame innocent people and signed with "Heil Hitler."[11]

Henriette Schäfer was interrogated on April 17 by a Gestapo officer named Bleser. She declared that she had a good relationship with Adam Hieronymus and, until recently, she did all her grocery shopping at Agnes Orschel's store. After her sister-in-law's arrival from the concentration camp on Christmas Eve 1938, Orschel and Sailer turned more hostile toward her; arguments and altercations also unfolded in her own household, which ultimately resulted in her sister-in-law's departure. Schäfer denied that she had criticized the government and called Hitler a bandit. Only the story about the camp donation was true. However, it was taken out of context. She insisted that she argued with her sister-in-law because Köninger had told the donation collector that Henriette was Jewish. Henriette denied having said anything like "kiss my ass" or "raise your bastards alone" to her neighbor, which her sister-in-law could have overheard. She also vehemently disputed all her other allegations, including Henriette's husband telling her to shut up to avoid going to a concentration camp, a plan to move abroad, or using derogatory terms when talking politics. All the accusations by her sister-in-law were born out of revenge.[12]

When questioned, Wilhelm Schäfer characterized his wife Henriette as very reserved. He stated that she never said, "They should raise their own bastards." However, he confirmed that his sister had told everyone that his wife was Jewish, including the donation collector, and denied that he told her she would end up in Dachau.[13]

The Gestapo did not believe either Henriette or Wilhelm. They called Wilhelm's letter an act of vengeance, trying to turn the tables on their neighbors. The main prosecutor asked Anna Sailer to confirm if Wilhelm had been present during their argument.[14] She repeated that the sister and husband must have heard everything, although they were in the kitchen, while she and Henriette argued outside.[15] Henriette's sister-in-law Anna Köninger had moved to her birth town of Gaggenau near Rastatt in Baden, so she could not be interviewed by the Frankfurt Gestapo, but in June 1939, local police questioned her about the episode. She told them that someone from the National Socialist Welfare organization (NSV) had dropped by while Henriette was away and asked if the family could take in a child. Köninger declined, saying her sister-in-law was Jewish. After Henriette returned, she learned that Köninger had disclosed the truth about her mixed marriage not only to the visitor, but also to her neighbors. Köninger reiterated that Henriette had said that they could kiss her ass and should raise their bastards alone; supposedly, she was still very upset because of the "Jew action." Köninger added that her brother suffered in this marriage and he was increasingly in favor of how the government handled the "Jewish question."[16]

The main prosecutor recommended prosecuting Henriette Schäfer under the Treacherous Attacks Law of 1934 for insulting Hitler.[17] He described Henriette Schäfer as a Jew, impertinent and impudent, living with a German-blooded husband. He laid out the accusations regarding November 1938, and even though Schäfer denied everything and called the reports an act of vengeance, he considered her guilty in this case as well as in the second incident from 1939. Since Schäfer had not signed her interrogation statement with the forced middle name "Sara," now required to identify all female Jews, he started a separate criminal proceeding. The main prosecutor expected a clear verdict by the Special Court. A month later, the Reich Ministry of Justice gave the green light for a trial.[18]

On July 31, 1939, the main prosecutor for the Special Court at the State Court Frankfurt indicted Henriette Schäfer for slanderous comments about leading figures of the German state on two occasions. On August 11, the public proceedings against her began. The court provided her with a defense counselor for the trial.[19] Anna Köninger declined to testify, but Henriette's husband did. In the ruling, the court concluded that although Henriette Schäfer had denied all the accusations, the judges believed the witnesses, even Anna Sailer, who was open about her differences with the defendant. The court found Henriette Schäfer's comments to be a testament to her hateful attitude, undermining the trust of the German people in their political leadership; she should have known that her hostile comments could reach the public. The Special Court sentenced her to six months in prison on two counts under the Treacherous Attacks Law and ordered her to bear the costs of the proceedings. However, the court took into consideration that she was very upset about the violence on November 9, and supposedly spared her an even tougher sentence.[20]

Three days after the verdict, Henriette Schäfer appealed. By this time, the couple had rented a new apartment at Fichardstrasse and moved out of Schlossstrasse. Obviously, the situation with their neighbors had turned sour. Henriette emphasized that she could not remember the things she was accused of and emphasized that she had no prior criminal record. Because her husband was absorbed by his business and needed her to take care of their home, she asked the court to put her on parole and change her jail sentence to a fine. Her request was not granted; the prison sentence would start within a week. For the court proceedings and the upcoming months in prison, she also owed the Third Reich over 360 Reichsmarks.[21]

On September 13, 1939, at 9:10 a.m., Henriette Schäfer reported to the women's prison in Frankfurt-Höchst. The prison warden noted her appearance, including that she had graying hair and sketchy teeth, with a weight of 155 pounds; the warden judged her healthy and capable of work. Because of the conditions in the jail, however, Henriette began to lose weight, which her husband must have noticed when he visited her on October 15 and November 16. After she had served half of her sentence, Wilhelm Schäfer asked the court to release her on parole, arguing that her statements had been merely indiscretions. Echoing his wife's earlier appeal, he repeated that she had no criminal record and her imprisonment put a heavy burden on him, since he worked eleven hours a day and still had to purchase food for himself after work.[22]

The court denied probation on December 23, 1939. The prison director had not been in favor of parole because of the nature of the crime; the head of the Special Court also rejected the idea. Henriette Schäfer served her full sentence and was released from prison on March 13, 1940. She had to report to the police on a regular basis, beginning the day after her release.[23]

Her ordeal was far from over. Even though she was living in a "privileged mixed marriage" with an Aryan husband, Schäfer was forced to wear the "yellow star" beginning in September 1941. In Frankfurt, the Gestapo began to organize mass deportations to the occupied territories in eastern Europe. Jews in "mixed marriages" were to be spared; however, after most German Jews had been deported, some local authorities included Jews from mixed marriages. In 1943, in spite of her "privileged mixed marriage," as it was called, Henriette Schäfer had to move into a segregated dormitory managed by the remnants of the Jewish community.[24]

In June 1943, only 639 Jews remained in Frankfurt, 344 of them in mixed marriages. Forced labor and segregation now beset their everyday lives. At the beginning of 1944, the Gestapo everywhere in Germany deported Jewish partners from dissolved mixed marriages, where partners had died or divorced, to the ghetto in Theresienstadt (Terezin) in the Protectorate of Bohemia and Moravia; in Frankfurt am Main, this affected 56 Jews, mostly women. Only months before the end of the war, as the final act, the SS leadership decided to move all German Jews living in mixed marriages to Theresienstadt.[25]

On February 14, 1945, the Gestapo deported Henriette Schäfer and 190 other Jews from Frankfurt; including people from other towns, 615 Jews arrived four days later in the old garrison town of Theresienstadt. First established as a ghetto to confine Czech Jews, it became a dumping ground for elderly and "privileged" German and Austrian Jews. Most of the Czech Jews, and later many German and Austrian Jews, were deported from there to the East and murdered. Henriette survived the ghetto until the liberation in May 1945.[26]

Before 1933, Frankfurt had been home to the second largest Jewish population in Germany, with more than 26,000, but by the end of the war a mere 160 Jews still lived in the city. Despite the massive destruction in the city during the war, when Henriette Schäfer returned, the municipality assigned her to a new home in August 1945. Reunited with her husband, they moved into an apartment at Höhenstrasse 19.[27]

Some years later, Henriette Schäfer appeared at the prosecutor's office in Frankfurt. She declared that the Frankfurt Special Court had tried her in 1939 and that she had served her entire sentence in prison. Since the end of the war, she had been recognized as a racial and political victim of the Nazi regime, which was not easy for Jews in mixed marriages, who were mis-judged as "privileged" survivors.[28] Although she had received some support to buy furniture or pay medical bills, Henriette Schäfer now sought com-pensation from the German state. For her application to get the Nazi verdict reversed under the law for the Restoration of Nazi Injustices (Wiedergutma-chung nationalsozialistischen Unrechts in der Strafrechtspflege) of May 29, 1946, she needed proof of having served her prison sentence. The Frankfurt prosecutor's office tried to locate the people involved, but Adam Hierony-mus, Agnes Orschel, and Anna Sailer had not survived the war.[29]

Only three weeks after Henriette's formal appeal, on Christmas Eve 1949, the verdict was reversed and the sentence expunged from her criminal record. Justice was served. Many German Jews did not survive to experience the same. After she formally filed for a recompensation claim, Henriette Schäfer died in June 1951. For years, her husband fought to receive the com-pensation she would have deserved.[30]

Other Stories About Verbal Protest Against the Persecution

Henriette Schäfer was not an exception. Hundreds of Jews had spoken up in public and in private against national and local discrimination since 1933. As revealed by police and court records, Special Courts punished most of them: first by employing the Decree of the Reich President of March 21, 1933, prohibiting treacherous attacks against the national government, and later the Treacherous Attacks Law of December 1934.

As early as spring 1933, a Special Court in Frankfurt am Main put at least seven Jews on trial for publicly criticizing the beatings and murders of fel-low Jews by SA gangs as well as the torture of Jews in concentration camps by SS guards. The prosecutor at the State Court in Frankfurt indicted the young merchant Erich Löwenstein for "spreading rumors." First in a shop and later on the street, Löwenstein interrogated two acquaintances, both members of the Nazi party, about the party's goals regarding the Jews, asking specifically whether the Nazis wanted to drive the Jews out of Germany or harm them in any way. He said that Nazis recently had killed Jews, and openly criticized such actions. Referring to (probably foreign) newspaper reports, he claimed a Jew had been hanged in Worms and a Jewish lawyer had been shot in Kiel. It became a heated conversation that attracted a large gathering of fifteen to twenty people. On April 1, 1933, the day of the notorious nationwide anti-Jewish boycott, a Special Court handed down a sentence for Löwenstein of one year in prison for telling *"Greuelmärchen"* (atrocity tales)—that is, disseminating supposedly wrong information.[31]

Jews made similar critical comments in the next weeks and months in Frankfurt and elsewhere.[32] In Maxsain, Rhineland-Palatinate, the Jewish livestock trader Hans Oster told a local innkeeper, Johann Oberreuter, that twenty uniformed SA members had dragged another Jewish livestock trader out of his bed in a neighboring village and blackmailed him at gunpoint to sign over 1,000 Reichsmarks. For telling this story, Oster received six months in jail. Subsequently, the authorities declined his application for a trade license, ending his whole livelihood.[33]

Jews criticized Nazi leaders, their policies, and certain events, such as the so-called Röhm putsch, the violent purge of Hitler's perceived opponents in 1934.[34] Even after being taken into custody, some Jews did not stop. While riding on the police truck on his way to jail after his arrest for currency offenses in June 1933, the almost fifty-year-old Bertram Stern told other prisoners that in his view, Hitler and the new government were state criminals and belonged in a penitentiary. He said the government would "deny the ill-treatment of the Jews, despite that the facts were well known and documented abroad." The Gestapo interrogated Stern, but he denied making the comments. During the three months in so-called "protective custody" before his trial, he attempted suicide. Only because the prisoner who reported the comments was deemed not trustworthy, the Special Court acquitted Stern. In 1934, Sruel-Chaskiel Kawelblum, a twenty-five-year-old concentration camp inmate on transfer, told his fellow cell mates in a Munich prison how the SS abused and mistreated inmates, especially Jews, in Dachau. Beatings during arrival were followed by extreme work until total exhaustion in a quarry. For sharing these facts, he received seven months in prison.[35]

The lines between public and private conversations quickly became blurred under the Nazis. Special Courts prosecuted comments made in private under the notion that they could potentially reach the wider public. In January 1936, a court sent Max Sternberg, who owned a wholesale business, to prison after he told an old business partner in a private conversation that forty-five Jewish children had recently been expelled from a local orphanage in Diez.[36] In 1935, during a discussion with several tenants and property owners at an apartment in Wiesbaden, Raimond Ullmann claimed that the real arsonist who had set the Reichstag fire in 1933 was Hermann Göring, the second man in Hitler's government; the Nazis had blamed the Communists. Ullmann bragged about getting information from foreign newspapers and radio broadcasts. He had already had an encounter with the Gestapo, after smuggling material disparaging the Nazi persecution to Luxembourg. The texts were wrapped underneath a bandage on his prosthetic leg, and included a photo of a Jew who had been beaten and dragged around the streets in Worms. For his accusation about Göring, a Special Court sentenced him to fifteen months in jail under the Treacherous Attacks Law of 1934.[37]

Jews fought back by filing their own complaints with the police. In Hamburg in 1934, Isaak Gottheimer protested being called "*Mistjude*" (dirty Jew or dung Jew). The police recorded similar cases in Berlin.[38] In synagogues, rabbis like Dr. Joachim Prinz and Dr. Max Nussbaum in Berlin and Dr. Joseph Carlebach in Hamburg used sermons and prayers to subtly criticize Nazi politics, all under increasing Gestapo surveillance in their synagogues. Prinz, for example, spoke in public about the increasing segregation, or the "neighbourless ghetto," that Jews were forced to live in.[39] Some German Jews tried to win the public over. Georg Cohn, his wife, and their daughter were arrested after standing on the sidewalk and trying to persuade patrons to boycott the "Wachsmuth" bakery, because the Nazi owner had instigated arrests of Jews during the weeks of anti-Jewish riots in Berlin in the summer of 1935.[40]

Jews openly criticized the Nuremberg race laws. In Munich, sixty-four-year-old Wolf Monheit commented on the prohibition of sexual relationships between Jews and non-Jews: "The Aryans are crazy. When the Führer sees a Jewess, he will rape her." The Special Court acquitted him in October 1935, since the judge did not trust his accuser, a fourteen-year-old boy who had mentioned that he expected a reward for every Jew caught. When the thirty-eight-year-old physician Fritz Lehmann moved out of his Berlin rental apartment in the spring of 1936, he sarcastically told the new tenant that he should thank Hitler for the lack of cleanliness, because the Nuremberg Laws had taken away his outstanding help. The Berlin General prosecutor indicted Lehmann for insulting the Führer.[41]

Paula Klopfer, during a conversation at the Café Imperator in Berlin in 1936 with Max Zintl, Paul Leciejewski, and Police-Major Hans Bauer, commented that the newspapers could not be trusted, since they printed a lot of exaggerations and lies, for example, that Communism was a Jewish invention. She also challenged Hitler's claim that Communist Russia's leadership consisted of 98 percent Jews. When one of the men mentioned that he could not picture the ugly Kurt Eisner, the Jewish leader of the Munich Revolution, as the head of Germany, Klopfer replied that Goebbels would not look much better. She added that he also should not father children because of his clubfoot, since the Nazi state purged hereditary illnesses by law. The Reich Ministry of Justice mandated her indictment. The fifty-eight-year-old Fritz Philippi, a bank clerk in Berlin, was denounced and later indicted for his "poisonous remarks" about leading Nazis, especially those criticizing Hitler's annual Nuremberg speeches in which as he said "the Führer" always blamed everything on the Jews.[42]

During the next year, Jewish men and women in Berlin, Frankfurt, and Munich received prison sentences between two and six months for either insulting Hitler and other Nazi leaders or telling jokes about them.[43] One summer evening in 1937 at a beer pub in front of witnesses, Kurt Ascher, a fifty-five-year-old advertisement specialist, called Der Stürmer a "smear press" (Hetzblatt) and said the German newspapers were writing on orders from Goebbels. He was arrested. The Gestapo called him a "typical impudent Jew," who continued his criticisms in jail. In a rather unusual move, the Gestapo interned him until his trial in a concentration camp, where he died two weeks later.[44]

In February 1938, police arrested a Romanian citizen, Rubin Oling, in Dresden because a former neighbor reported that he had stated that Hitler and his measures were short lived. Oling had claimed that although the persecution of the Jews might last, there would be a day of change and then others would judge those measures. Interestingly, the Special Court found that the neighbor was not credible and dropped the case. A month later, Gestapo officials questioned the owner of the Leiser-Langer furniture store in Dresden. His wife, Reisel Langer, snapped and shouted: "Go with them, Leiser, we are fair game. Let them shoot you." Surprisingly, the Special Court in Freiberg did not pursue charges against her under the Treacherous Attacks Law. In this case, the prosecutor argued that even though this was an attack on the state, it could not undermine the trust of the German people in their government, since it came from a Jew. The anti-Semitism leading to the arrest apparently saved the victim from punishment.[45]

In many cities, welfare departments forced poor Jews to perform compulsory work (*Pflichtarbeit*) in segregated gangs in order to secure welfare benefits, while sparing non-Jewish welfare recipients. Since March 1938, Salomon Kuniansky, fifty-four, had worked for the city of Plauen (Saxony) at a construction site in such a gang. During a break, the workers were telling each other jokes, and Kuniansky proposed "Radio," an acronym for "Raus aus Deutschland Ihr Ostjuden" (Out of Germany you Eastern Jews). Spelled backward, "Radio" meant "Ohne Juden Deutschland auch ruiniert" (Without Jews Germany also ruined). After a denunciation, co-workers defended him by stating that he did not want to ridicule the government, so the Special Court in Freiberg dropped the case.[46]

In June and July 1938, Berlin saw more than four weeks of new violent attacks against Jews instigated by the Nazi party, which Hitler himself later stopped after they drew too much international attention. Kurt Adler, thirty-two, openly and repeatedly criticized the omnipresent Nazi and SA processions in the city. After a neighbor turned him in, the police handed Adler over to the Gestapo for alleged disparagement of the Nazi party.[47]

At the same time, the political tension had been worsening between Germany and Czechoslovakia because of increasing Nazi agitation by the Sudeten Germans. Jews and non-Jews responded anxiously. During the height of the Sudeten crisis in September 1938, the head of a police station in Berlin-Wedding ordered a thirty-five-year-old shop owner, Kurt Rosenberg, to remove from the sidewalk two large ceramic vases placed at both sides of his store entrance as an advertisement. Rosenberg asked a neighbor if the police officer saw himself as a little Hitler who ruled his district as a dictator and could harass people only because they were Jews. Rosenberg also criticized the recent introduction of special license plate numbers for cars owned by Jews and predicted that soon Jews would receive food only with yellow ration cards. He exclaimed that the German state would not stop inventing things in order to victimize the Jewish people. Referring to a possible war, he said the German state deserved to get its ass kicked. The neighbor denounced him to the police, who handed Rosenberg over to the Gestapo.[48] In Munich, the retired merchant Franz Landauer exclaimed that in case of a war, one must shoot Hitler first, since he was responsible for the fighting. Landauer got lucky. The criminal and other police branches did not communicate, and his passport application went through, which enabled him to leave Germany a week before his trial.[49]

In reaction to the pogrom violence in November, more Jews like Henriette Schäfer spoke up. In Augsburg, sixty-four-year-old Josefine Fleischmann received one month in prison for telling several women in a nursery store that the SA had also beaten Jews to death during the annexation of Austria. Back then, Jews had to lick the blood off Storm Trooper boots, she said. In Krumbach, a small Bavarian town, Minna Klopfer, thirty-seven, told the owner of the dairy store in front of half a dozen locals that once things calmed down, the Catholics would be next.[50]

Heinrich Mugdan, a so-called Jewish *Mischling* (mixed blood), confronted fellow train passengers in Berlin ten days after the pogrom, calling it and its results "barbaric." Other Jews did the same during the next weeks and months. In reaction to an eviction notice after the pogrom, which forced her father to leave their apartment within forty-eight hours, the twenty-three-year-old stateless mischling Else Cohn, sterilized by the Nazi state in 1935 because of an alleged "mental deficiency," exclaimed during a discussion in a staff lounge of the Löwenbräukeller, a well-known Munich restaurant and brewery: "I could spit the Fuhrer in his cunt for bringing up the law that the Jews have to go." The Special Court sentenced her to four months in prison. The war-decorated tanner Ernst Nachmann, forty, told his wife and a neighbor after his release from the Buchenwald concentration camp about the frequent beatings by the SS, their abuses of rabbis, and the fact that twenty to thirty men died every day. He called Hitler "a dog, mean fellow, and tramp" (*Kelef, gemeiner Kerl, Stromer*). The Frankfurt Special Court sentenced him to three months in jail.[51]

Even years after the pogrom, Jews continued to criticize the violence. At the end of January 1940, the divorced former upholsterer Moritz Hirsch snapped at a neighbor after she made a comment about the snowfall in front of his house, saying that the snow should pile up high as a mountain as a punishment for the burning of the Jewish places of worship. Every day, he said, he must walk by the ruins. Hirsch, who was a forced laborer for the city, said that the whole government was keen to murder and soon there would come the time that those who murdered would be executed. When the Special Court in Frankfurt am Main tried Hirsch under the Treacherous Attacks Law, he defended himself by arguing that he had been drunk and could not remember what he had said. He also used his time spent in a mental institution as a defense, and for that reason the court acquitted him.[52]

The anxiety about a looming war with Poland led to even more criticism. The city of Vienna had started to concentrate Jews in so-called "Jews' houses," established under a Nazi law abolishing protections for Jewish tenants in April 1939. Jews were mandated by city governments to sublet their properties, which led to several Jewish families cohabitating in one living space. On August 21, 1939, the sixty-two-year-old married lawyer Dr. Arthur Singer loudly protested at the Vienna housing office, publicly calling Hitler a scoundrel (*Hundsfott*) who would take money from the Jews but would not let them live. He said Jews should not be forced to sublet to other people and urged the other dozen or so Jews waiting with him to join his protest against the city order, storm the offices, and beat up the city officials. Some Jews did go into offices, yelled at officials, threw their summons at the official's feet, and declared they would not sign the mandatory sublet orders. When a tumultuous situation ensued, a city official called the Gestapo. After months of detention, the Vienna State Court, functioning as a Special Court, sentenced Singer, who denied all accusations, in June 1940 to one year in prison under the Treacherous Attacks Law. However, the court acquitted him of the charge of inciting public unrest, since the other Jews present at the time refused to confirm those allegations.[53]

A few days before the German invasion of Poland, homemaker Felizi Weill, née Hamburger, while doing her laundry at a laundromat, commented publicly, "Now war comes again. . . . Hopefully we will still live to see the big shots die a wretched death; they have more compassion with a dog on the street than with us Jews." She added that if she were forced to leave her home, she would move into the Isar, which was Munich's main river. All her silver and her money had been taken from her, she said, and they would probably take her laundry, too. After she was arrested, the prosecutor alleged that she was driven by hate against the German state and its measures. By contrast, the defense emphasized the insignificance of the occurrence and brought up her possible emigration. In January 1940, the Special Court stopped the proceedings under an amnesty newly issued by Hitler for minor offenses committed during the war. Felizi Weill and her husband left Germany for the United States in March 1940. Some other outspoken Jews, for example Arthur Schlesinger in Dresden and Margarete Hirsch in Baden near Vienna, also benefited from Hitler's amnesty during the next months. Other critics did not, like Alfred Lauffer in Dresden and Hugo Heinrich in Berlin. In December 1939, police had arrested Heinrich, a sixty-two-year-old former ironer, in Berlin. In a pub, he pretended to be from Sweden, communicating in broken German. When the owner asked him why he criticized Germany so much, Heinrich stated that he was a friend of the Jews and they lived in a very bad situation in Germany. Heinrich was indicted under the Treacherous Attacks Law. Two years earlier, he had been punished with eight months in prison for criticizing Hitler's politics.[54]

The war, new restrictions, and the evening curfew for Jews aggravated everything even more. The failed attempt to assassinate Hitler in November 1939 provoked some reactions among Jews. In Munich, Franz Kohn expressed his view that the "assassin" was actually a rank-and-file Nazi, and they would find and kill Hitler anyway. He paid for these words with five months in prison in 1940. This was not his first punishment. For defying the decree about the forced Jewish middle names in March 1939, he was sentenced to pay 15 Reichsmarks or serve three days in jail. In September 1940, the widow Julie Wagner called Hitler a bloodhound and expressed regret that the assassination attempt in the Munich Bürgerbräukeller of the previous year had failed. For her frequent critical comments about Hitler, the Special Court in Munich punished Wagner with the extraordinary sentence of five years in prison. When she wrote letters from jail, she never signed them with the discriminatory middle name "Sara," and consequently received a sentence of ten additional days in prison. In June 1942, the judiciary handed her over to the Gestapo, who deported Wagner to Theresienstadt, where she died a few months later.[55]

Police and court files reveal plenty of evidence how German Jews continued to criticize Nazi persecution both in private and in public. Welfare recipient Max Lehr, seventy, approached shoppers in the restaurant of the Karstadt department store in Berlin. At a crowded table, he stated loudly, "They have expelled almost all Jews to Palestine and took away all our money. That is the biggest wrong done to us."[56] Former sales clerk Louis Herbert Korn gave subversive speeches at a private library in Zwickau, Saxony. After the Gestapo detained him, the Special Court in Leipzig sentenced him to six months in prison in November 1940 for criticizing the Nazi government's policies. The next day, newspaper reports mocked him as a Jew, writing that the court had punished him because "as a guest in Germany" he had launched treacherous attacks against Hitler and the Nazi state. The attitude of the newspaper must have hurt especially, since Korn had lost one foot fighting for Germany in the World War and walked with a prosthesis.[57]

Both former shop assistant Sara Lassore and Artur Goldschmidt, at the time a forced laborer, received one-year jail sentences for treacherous attacks against the Nazi state. Both had repeatedly criticized the Nazi government in the privacy of their apartment. Goldschmidt predicted the fall of Hitler and read aloud the text of his own honorary cross award for war veterans, which, in his words, would henceforth serve only to "wipe his ass." He added while the Germans were complaining about the alleged atrocities of Polish Jews, they themselves were guilty of torturing their own Jews. Lassore confirmed that, as she had talked to many former camp prisoners of Sachsenhausen, where the Nazi gangs severely mistreated the Jews. She said that soon a day of reckoning would come. They were denounced by a couple subletting a room in Lassore's apartment, which led to their arrest in April 1940.[58]

Living in Vienna since 1903, David Gutwurzel was well known in a barbershop as one of the patrons who always talked about politics. One day, he called the Nazi government a "bandit and murder regime" and added, "The current Reich government is a government of criminals, since they stole everything from the Jews." Denounced by the barber, he received eight months in prison under the Treacherous Attacks Law in June 1940. Josef Sonnenfeld, twenty-three, was arrested for taking pictures of a military compound. During a search of his Vienna home, Sonnenfeld told a bystander that if the Gestapo kept bothering him, he would kill one of their officials, even if he had to pay for it with his own death. In a rather unusual move, he was interned at a concentration camp. In May 1940, Mirl Rachel Wiener, who had grown up in Galicia, never gone to school, and was living on welfare, approached a group of "Aryan" women on the street in Vienna who were on their way back from grocery shopping. She called Hitler names, which quickly drew a large crowd. Among the approximately one hundred onlookers were also some Jewish women, who sided with Wiener when she exclaimed that the "Aryans" would take everything from the Jews. One "Aryan" woman, who denounced her later, tried to stop her. Wiener smacked her in the face. When police arrived, she yelled, "Your Führer should die a miserable death," and then laid herself down on the pavement and refused to move. The police had a hard time bringing her to the precinct. Although she denied the accusations, the court sentenced her to one year in prison under the Treacherous Attacks Law.[59]

After the Nazi leadership started mass deportations of German Jews, verbal protests continued. Representatives of the Reich Association of the Jews in Germany (*Reichsvereinigung*) protested the transports from Baden and the Palatinate to France in the fall of 1940. In response, the Gestapo arrested Julius Seligsohn and Otto Hirsch, two close colleagues of the association board member Leo Baeck, and interned them in concentration camps, where they perished.[60]

In Hamburg, the fifty-one-year-old Melanie Krohn entered a police station on December 21, 1940, and shouted, "Down with Hitler!" She was an actress who had moved from Vienna to Hamburg in 1920. Until 1933, she performed in countless plays at the Thalia Theater and the Schauspielhaus. After the

Nazis ended her career, her husband divorced her since she was Jewish. At the police precinct, she cried and exclaimed that she had no will to live anymore. She was immediately arrested, and afterward the lawyer for the Jewish community in Hamburg, Dr. Max Plaut, defended her. He tried to establish a family history of mental issues by explaining that Krohn's mother had been mentally ill, her sister had committed suicide, her brother had vanished for some time, and Krohn herself had suffered from depression and repeatedly expressed the will to die. Plaut suggested transferring the Jewish woman to a mental institution. Krohn, who was a forced laborer at the time, nevertheless had to stand trial. However, the Hamburg Special Court sentenced her to only two weeks in prison. Presiding Judge Dr. Bertram believed that she was acting out of despair and in a state of depression. He only punished her for general mischief, whereas courts across the country had given Jews six months or more prison time for similar comments under the Treacherous Attacks Law. Soon after the mass deportations started in November 1941, Melanie Krohn was deported along with more than four hundred Hamburg Jews to the Minsk ghetto in the occupied Soviet Union. Only two days before their arrival, the SS had murdered thousands of Soviet Jews who were incapable of working, to free up space for German Jews. The German Jews performed forced labor for the German army, the SS, and the German railway. Many Jews from Hamburg, if they did not die from exhaustion or diseases, were shot or killed in gas vans in the early or late summer of 1943.[61]

In 1941, the Vienna Gestapo arrested several Jewish women and men for making comments against Hitler, the persecution of the Jews, and the treatment of the mentally ill. Some of them received harsh punishments of up to two years in prison. Similar arrests occurred in Berlin. Some of the delinquents had already received sentences for other "crimes," such as for not brandishing their marked ID cards.[62]

Hertha Reis, a forced laborer, left a Berlin courthouse on March 17, 1941. As mentioned in the introduction, a judge had just evicted her, her mother Franziska Reis, née Kaufmann, and her ten-year-old son Rudolf Alexander from the two small rooms at Neue Königstrasse 42 that she had sublet from one Dr. Epelstein. He had canceled her contract and sued for eviction. Hertha Reis felt she had nowhere to go; she crossed the street of Hallesches Ufer and tried to commit suicide by throwing herself into the river. Stopped by a passerby, she exclaimed desperately, "I got baptized, nevertheless I am an outcast. The Jewish community won't accept me anymore and I am mistreated everywhere. We lost everything. Because of this cursed government, we finally lost our home too. This thug Hitler, this damned government, these damned people! Just because we are Jews, we are discriminated against." After a pedestrian criticized her for these words, she responded, "I am as much a German as you are!" Since three witnesses, two women and an SS man, all confirmed that she had cursed Hitler, police took her into custody. It was not the first time she had been investigated for politically charged comments. In 1937, teenagers had called her and her son, then six years old, "Jew, Jew!" and sang a Nazi song behind their backs as they walked along the street. She snapped and responded, "You Hitler Youth and SA are the real criminals in Germany. God will punish you for this." Fortunately, she got away with a warning back then. Although the archival sources do not reveal anything about her trial at the Special Court, we know that the Gestapo deported Hertha's mother to Piaski in Nazi-occupied Poland in March 1942. The shock of this probably led Hertha to commit suicide a month later. Her son, Rudolf, having lost his mother and grandmother, ended up in a Jewish orphanage. In October 1942, the Gestapo deported all of the children in the orphanage to Riga, where they were murdered on arrival.[63]

In February 1942, the Special Court in Vienna indicted Karoline Rist. Two months earlier, customs officers had searched her hotel room for hidden jewelry. In front of hotel staff and the customs agents, she exclaimed, "This is Hitler's business! The party stole my apartment, and they robbed me of everything. Hitler should be hanged." The court never proceeded with a trial; instead, she was handed over later to the Gestapo. During the same month, Gabriele Reich (born in Vienna in 1885) was indicted for a laundry list of offenses: so-called "radio crimes" (listening to foreign broadcasts), insulting Hitler, and criticizing anti-Jewish measures. According to the indictment, the previous summer, Reich had exclaimed that the Nazis were all criminals, Hitler was a bandit, and the SA would raid Jewish homes and steal everything. The Special Court sentenced her to ten months in prison.[64]

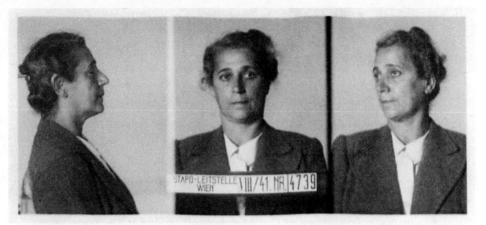

Gabriele Reich in Gestapo custody, Vienna, August 1941. (Vienna City and State Archive, Sondergericht, SHv Strafakten, A1: 6131/47)

Serving prison time did not stop some Jews from openly expressing their scathing opinions about the Nazi persecution even during the war. The former merchant Otto Karpowitz spent five months in the Berlin-Plötzensee prison for so-called economic crimes (*Wirtschaftsvergehen/Devisenvergehen*). During the summer of 1942, he told his fellow Jewish cell mate Alexander Löwenstein: "The shit head Goebbels incites pogroms with his speeches; however, after this time there will come another time, and for every Jew who had suffered, there will be coming 1,000 others and more." His remarks were overheard, and the Special Court in Berlin sentenced him to two additional years in January 1943, arguing that he should have known his comments could reach the public, even when expressed in a chat inside a prison cell. Long before the end of his prison sentence, the judiciary authorities handed him over to the Gestapo, who deported him to Auschwitz in September 1943. Alexander Löwenstein, Karpowitz's cell comrade, had already died in the penitentiary in Luckau.[65]

The stories of Henriette Schäfer and so many others in this chapter provide ample evidence that verbal protest was not a rare occurrence. Jewish men and women spoke up against persecution in government offices, at restaurants, on the streets, in their workplaces, and in their apartment buildings.

They courageously criticized Hitler, the Nazi government, and the anti-Jewish legislation in general, as well as local violence, the theft of property, and local restrictions on Jews' everyday life.

When Jews fell victim to a denunciation, the local Gestapo investigated and Special Courts prosecuted them for treacherous attacks against the Nazi state. With time, the lines between public and private increasingly became blurred. The courts punished utterances that were overheard in private settings, with the argument that even such private comments could reach the public. In most cases, Jews who were found guilty of protesting or criticizing the authorities were sent to prison, with sentences ranging from a few weeks to several years. The punishments tended to be more severe during the war.

Speaking out against injustice and discrimination is always a conscious and deliberate act—all the more so in a dictatorship. Since Hitler's taking power, Jewish men and women were aware that criticizing the Nazi government or its policies of persecution—whether in public or in private—could result in prosecution and punishment, endangering their own lives and also those of their family and friends. Such "impudent Jews" as Henriette Schäfer, however, and so many others, nevertheless decided to take the risk. Even in Hitler's Germany, they spoke out against terror and injustice.

THREE

Defying Anti-Jewish Laws

Hans Oppenheimer in Frankfurt and Others

Hans Oppenheimer left his four-story apartment house and carefully let the heavy wooden door swing back slowly to avoid any noise. Not a single light illuminated the street in front of him. The city of Frankfurt had ordered a brownout as protection from Allied air raids. After Hans finally arrived at his destination a few blocks away, he hid in a doorway. As the city anxiously waited for the Allied bombs to fall, Hans waited too.

For weeks, he had been leaving his home every night, breaking the curfew established for Jews since the beginning of the war. Hans was a mere seventeen years old, but he had already toiled as a forced laborer for a year and a half, most recently unloading stones and bags of cement from river barges for ten hours a day. He earned only pennies and felt constantly harassed. He had never been to a movie or a play, because these were prohibited for Jews.

As a Jewish adolescent, he saw no future in Nazi Germany. Since the war prevented him from leaving, he had decided to do something. Every night, he waited, excited, for the bombing raids. All he longed to do was to break the thin protective glass so he could get to the small handle of the fire alarm.

Hans Oppenheimer had blue-gray eyes, a snubby nose, and reddish hair. He was the first-born son of the merchant Siegmund and his wife Martha. His father sold linings and other sewing accessories to tailors in Frankfurt. Soon after Martha gave birth to Hans on January 3, 1923, she died, and his father quickly remarried. His new wife, Anna Fischer, was twenty years younger than he was. The family lived in an apartment building at Wittelsbacher Allee, an imposing boulevard in the city's northern district of Ostend, where many Jewish families lived.[1]

Hans attended the Linné elementary school, named after Carl von Linné, a Swedish botanist and natural scientist, around the corner from his home. Around 1932 or 1933, the family moved to another apartment on the ground floor of Scheidswaldstrasse 72, just one block from their previous home. Because of local Nazi measures and the nationwide boycott against Jewish businesses of April 1, 1933, many Jewish entrepreneurs and merchants lost customers, suppliers, and trade partners, and soon their entire livelihoods. That was the last year Siegmund Oppenheimer's shop appeared in the business section of the city's address book, where it had been an annual fixture since 1921. It was also the year that Hans's parents enrolled him in the Philanthropin, one of the most famous Jewish schools in Germany. Founded in 1804 by the Rothschild family, the Jewish elementary and secondary school was housed in an impressive building featuring a tall tower at the corner and three large gables on the roof, close to the city center in Frankfurt-Nordend. It took the ten-year-old Hans thirty minutes to walk to school. Despite the increasing persecution that affected every family, the Philanthropin was able to shield its roughly one thousand Jewish students from danger, at least during the 1930s.[2]

After Hans graduated from middle school in 1937 with good grades, he wanted to learn a manual profession, for two reasons: to support his family, and to gain a long-term skill that would enable him to leave Germany. Anti-Jewish laws and local policies made life miserable for the second largest Jewish population in Germany. In the fall of 1936, Frankfurt reduced welfare benefits for the Jewish poor and separated them from other welfare recipients during office hours. Frankfurt's regulations were soon cited by the German Council of Municipalities as an example to instruct other city governments on how to prevent Jews from visiting parks, public pools, markets, libraries, and sports fields. Later, Frankfurt pressed for banning Jews from municipal zoos, museums, and theaters; the city also initiated "Aryanization" of real estate, private foundations, and art collections.[3]

Metalworking shop at the Jüdische Anlernwerkstatt, Frankfurt am Main, after 1933.
(Courtesy of Jewish Museum Frankfurt am Main, F005-682)

To prepare for a future abroad, Hans started a locksmith apprenticeship at a Jewish vocational school, the Jüdische Anlernwerkstatt. Established in an abandoned factory in 1936, the school trained male teenagers to become carpenters, locksmiths, or gardeners. All of these vocations improved the students' chances of emigration to Palestine, the United States, and other countries. By offering training to 130 teenagers and adults, the Anlernwerkstatt provided a striking example of a Jewish community response to the worsening conditions in Nazi Germany.[4]

For eighteen months, Hans learned every locksmith skill, including autogenous welding, a then-modern technique in which strongly focused heat melted the surfaces of two metals together without using any filler material. The downside of attending this Jewish metalworking shop was that the training was not certified by the German state as a regular apprenticeship. Hans also did not gain much practical experience, since businesses were now refusing to take Jewish interns. In the spring of 1939, Hans graduated from the vocational school and registered as unemployed at the Frankfurt labor office in order to find work.[5]

In the beginning of 1939, the Nazi state obliged all German Jews to adopt discriminatory Jewish middle names and file for a special identity card that was marked with a "J." Hans's official name became Hans Israel Oppenheimer. He was also required to become a member of the Reich Association of the Jews in Germany, an institution officially founded in July 1939 and tightly controlled by the Gestapo.[6] Soon after his registration, the Frankfurt labor office deployed him as a forced laborer, part of the recently introduced German labor administration's program to exploit all unemployed registered Jews who sought work or received unemployment benefits. During the summer of 1939, more than 20,000 Jewish men toiled in segregated work gangs at road constructions, street cleanings, and hydraulic works everywhere in Greater Germany. From 1940, all Jews had to perform forced labor, but by then mostly in industries. At the peak of the forced labor program, more than 60,000 German and Austrian Jewish men and women worked for hundreds of German companies, receiving only minimum wages and no benefits. Many had to leave their homes for months, even years, to live in forced-labor camps run by private enterprises and public builders.[7]

The labor office sent the sixteen-year-old Hans Oppenheimer to a labor camp for Jews in Stein Neukirch, almost seventy miles away from his hometown. He worked for the Firm Häbel (Marienberg/Westerwald). After hours and on Sundays, the mayor made Hans perform extra labor, preparing haystacks or cutting wood for the villagers. After he was dismissed from the camp in the fall of 1939, Hans was a forced laborer for the city of Frankfurt, and then in March 1940, the labor office put him on a train to another forced-labor camp for Jews in Kelkheim, in the Taunus Mountains.[8]

In 1939, Wilhelm Graf, the mayor of Kelkheim, wanted to build a road from Kelkheim to Frankfurt, and the state labor office in Frankfurt granted him twenty Jewish men to work on its construction. The mayor deliberately did not choose a contractor who wanted to pay regular wages to the Jews, but instead went with a construction firm offering minimal payments. When the Jewish men arrived in April, Graf ordered immediate beatings.

The Jews had to perform sixty hours per week of heavy manual work. To separate the Jews from the town's residents, Graf restricted their movement within the city limits. A camp was established in the local inn "Taunus-blick" (Taunus View), where the men slept in bunk beds rented from a local company. A police officer guarded the camp. Every week, Kelkheim councillors inspected the conditions; one of them intervened in order to keep the Jews from using the guest toilets of the Taunusblick inn. From time to time, the mayor ordered more beatings, to "speed up" their work. Most of the forced laborers had no experience in manual work, yet they were made to break stones in a nearby quarry. Soon many became exhausted and fell ill. Seven men were sent home. One man, Julius Becker, could not cope with the humiliation on a daily basis, and he committed suicide. When the road was finished, the labor camp closed, in October 1939.[9]

The mayor's appetite for cheap workers, however, had been whetted. So the Frankfurt labor office sent Jews again, including Hans Oppenheimer. He spent almost eight months in Kelkheim. Even though the small town of Kelkheim was only ten miles from his hometown, Hans did not see his family for many months. Jewish forced laborers were not allowed vacation time, a result of new anti-Jewish labor regulations. Frustrated by his treatment as a forced laborer, Hans supposedly rebelled and smashed windows in town.[10]

Hans finally returned to Frankfurt in November 1940. The labor office sent him to Geldmacher, a building supply business, where he earned the weekly minimum wage of 25 Reichsmarks. He lived with his parents, even though he did not get along with his stepmother. His younger brother Rudolf had learned gardening. His father, Siegmund, had lost his business, so the family had been depending on public welfare. But after the November pogrom, the Nazi government issued a decree to expunge all Jewish poor people from the public welfare rolls, and Frankfurt stopped paying benefits to Jews in the summer of 1939. After that, the Jewish community had to step in.[11]

Hans Oppenheimer was arrested on December 10, 1940, just as he was about to smash the glass on the fire alarm box on Habsburger Street. A fire-fighter had set up a trap. The moonlight illuminated the street that night, so

Hans was easily spotted by Heinrich Dielmann, district staff sergeant of the fire protection police.

It wasn't the first time Hans had set off a fire alarm: he had done so in three different locations during the previous weeks. Because of the curfew for Jews, he had to be careful of the frequent night patrols so he could reach all of the locations within ten or twelve minutes on foot: the corners of Sandweg-Thomasiusstrasse, Wittelsbacher Allee-Thüringer Strasse, and the corner of Friedberger Anlage-Sandweg.[12]

When the Gestapo interrogated Hans, he confessed to setting off nine false fire alarms using pay phones and fire alarm posts. He also admitted that he usually waited around until the fire brigade arrived. Sometimes he would pull the handle again to set off another alarm after the firefighters had left. Hans claimed he was merely pulling pranks, influenced by bad company, and did not think about the consequences. The authorities were convinced, however, that he acted alone and on purpose to divert the fire trucks from actual bombing sites and in more cases than he had admitted, since dozens of false fire alarms had been set off in his neighborhood in previous weeks.[13]

After more than a week, the police transferred Hans from the police station to a pre-trial detention jail. Waiting for weeks in his cell no. 221, he asked for permission to subscribe to a newspaper, the *Neueste Frankfurter Zeitung*, and a magazine, the *Hamburger Illustrierte*. In March, he added another newspaper. He also was granted access to a "legal adviser," the former lawyer Dr. Popper. In 1938, most Jewish lawyers had lost their licenses. The state permitted only a limited number to represent Jewish clients as so-called "legal advisers" (*Rechtskonsulenten*). The title was degrading, since in Germany, nonprofessionals without law degrees serving poor clients were traditionally called legal advisers.[14]

Hans waited four months in prison. On April 12, 1941, the main prosecutor at the State Court in Frankfurt am Main, who was acting as the head of the Special Court, indicted him on four counts of damaging public property and charged him with several felonies according to the criminal code and for offenses under the decree against "Public Vermins" (*Volksschädlinge*). The decree, enacted after the war started, allowed Nazi Germany to use capital punishment for minor offenses to "protect" the home front.[15]

Since 1939, using the war as a cover, the Reich Ministry of Justice had pressured the state and local judiciary to prosecute crimes more harshly.

The indictment declared that Hans Oppenheimer was a "full Jew." The prosecutor cited the Gestapo investigation and the claim by a Gestapo officer named Wetzel that Hans was an unstable, lazy, and dishonest human being who was always willing to destroy things. The prosecutor expressed his suspicion that Hans was responsible for far more crimes; forty-four false alarms had been reported during recent weeks, and the series allegedly ended with Hans's arrest. The prosecutor blamed Hans for supporting the enemy's bombing campaign by consciously setting off false alarms with the purpose of diverting fire trucks from the actual bombing sites. However, the German People's Court was not able to prove a military treason charge, which would have resulted in the death penalty, and the German Army High Command had not found sufficient evidence for crimes punishable under the decree for the protection against impairment of national defense. Therefore, the main prosecutor charged Hans with less serious crimes: Breaking the protective glass at fire alarm boxes in three cases counted as destruction of public property under Paragraph 304 of the German penal code, and doing it under cover of the state-mandated air-raid protection brownout counted as sabotage under the "Public Vermin" act. Although Hans had broken the curfew for Jews multiple times, ironically there was no provision punishing him for this in the respective anti-Jewish police order.[16]

The prosecutor for the case wrote two letters. With the first, he informed the Reich Ministry of Justice in Berlin about the matter and proposed a sentence of six years in a penitentiary. He argued that the punishment should be particularly harsh for a Jew who had acted as an enemy during the war of the German people. Imprisonment in a German penitentiary usually meant stricter prison conditions as well as hard manual labor, for example in quarries, on a daily basis. In a second letter, to the Frankfurt general prosecutor, he demanded to try Hans as an adult, although the teenager had been seventeen years old when he set off the alarms. He insisted that Hans appeared morally and intellectually more mature than his age, so to protect the German people, it would be necessary to treat him as an adult, considering his reprehensible actions. Nevertheless, he had to backtrack. Hans had admitted to having set off nine false fire alarms, but the prosecutor could not charge him for the five times when the teenager used public pay phones. He could have done the same without consequences during peacetime. Therefore, the prosecutor suggested lowering the potential sentence to three or four years in penitentiary. Only days before the trial, the general prosecutor in Frankfurt recommended including the pay phone cases and pursuing a punishment of five or six years in penitentiary based on the dangerous acts of the defendant and his alleged "Jewish character."[17]

Hans's trial before the Frankfurt Special Court started on May 2, 1941, at 9 a.m. in room 125 on the third floor of the "old building," a Neo-Renaissance structure erected in the 1880s. There was neither a defense lawyer nor a "legal adviser" present. Hans, now eighteen years old, defended himself. The court charged him with nine cases of malicious acts of setting off false fire alarms during the months of November and December 1940. Hans did not deny responsibility, but he again suggested that he had set off the alarms solely as pranks. *Landesgerichtsdirektor* Kalb, as the judge, did not buy this argument, and sentenced Hans to three years in prison for being a "Public Vermin" sabotaging the war effort. Fortunately, the judge did not grant the prosecution's request to put Hans in a penitentiary or to convict him as an adult; a medical expert witness had recommended trying him as the adolescent that he was. The judge also took into account that Hans did not have a criminal record. However, in his verdict the judge emphasized that, as a Jew, Hans should have paid special attention to the law, since he was only tolerated as a guest in Germany.[18]

Hans Oppenheimer's case in Frankfurt triggered legal discussions in Berlin. Officials in the Reich Ministry of Justice complained about the lack of adequate legal means to punish the abuse of pay phones or alarm boxes to set off false fire alarms. At first, the officials thought of including a corrective paragraph in a newly prepared decree about "state crimes"; however, Hitler scrapped the proposed draft. Later, they debated and enacted an addendum to the Air Defense Law, making the abuse of fire alarms during air raids a punishable offense.[19]

On June 7, 1941, Hans Oppenheimer was transferred from Frankfurt to a prison in the small town of Diez (Diez an der Lahn), approximately fifty miles from his hometown, where he was incarcerated for the next two years. This correction facility, holding more than six hundred prisoners, was built in the form of a cross as a Panopticon, a design intended to allow a single security guard to observe many prisoners. It was also one of the first German prisons to be equipped with electric lights. During the Third Reich, many Germans convicted of treason were incarcerated there, and because they were considered political enemies, the Gestapo often transferred them to concentration camps after they had served their sentences. Diez also served as a place to execute the death penalty. It still exists today as one of the largest prisons in the German state of Rhineland-Palatinate.[20]

When Hans arrived at the prison, he had to write a résumé. He used this opportunity to lay down his wishes for the future, writing that he hoped his relatives would arrange the necessary papers for an emigration on his release from prison in 1943. He wanted to work, perhaps in his profession as a locksmith, and to learn how to drive in order to establish a good living abroad. He was not worried about finding a job, since he knew all of his former employers were satisfied with his work. He also declared himself healthy on paper, even though he had previously been hospitalized.[21]

The prison director put Hans in solitary confinement, most likely for being Jewish. To prevent any contact with other inmates, he did not get permission to work outside his cell. Isolated for months, folding bags and envelopes day in and day out, the conditions took a rapid toll on Hans. His only lifeline was his practice of writing monthly letters to his family. He begged his parents to visit and bring him medication. He did not know that some of his messages ended up shelved in his prison file, censored by the warden for being too outspoken about his miserable prison situation and the lack of help for his quickly deteriorating health.[22]

Yet despite his growing aches and ongoing isolation, which exhausted him both physically and mentally, he did not back down. Several times, he petitioned the prison director, protesting maltreatment by his guards and overly hard labor assignments. Sometimes, the guards caught him sitting in his cell and not working. Even after sharp rebukes by his work supervisor, he did less than half of the daily prison workload. To the prison doctor and the main work inspector, Hans complained about his deteriorating health and unmanageable work tasks. "You need to complain even if you are a Jew," he told his work supervisor, who described the inmate's general behavior as "impudent and defiant." During a cell inspection, Hans informed the warden that the guards had delayed his requests to see a doctor for weeks. As a result, he was given a warning, since the prison personnel thought he was just pretending and being lazy.[23]

In August 1941, the prison administration confiscated a letter to his parents, who, just a month earlier, had been evicted from their apartment in Scheidswaldstrasse, where they had lived for eight years. City authorities forced them to sublet a room at Hegel Street 21 in Frankfurt-Ostend, one of the "Jews' houses" (*Judenhäuser*) in Frankfurt Nordend-Ost. Under a law from April 1939, cities evicted Jewish tenants and relocated them to these "Jews' houses," often as sublets of existing tenants. Dresden and Leipzig had started to segregate Jews in 1939; Frankfurt waited until 1941. In these "Jews' houses," several families lived in one flat, sharing kitchen and bathroom, if one existed.[24]

In the intercepted letter, which is still in his prison file, Hans referred to an earlier message to his parents, in which he had said that three years in prison would ruin his future. He understood that there was no possibility to appeal a Special Court sentence. He assured his parents that he would not make mistakes again and the prison labor inspector had told him that if his conduct improved, he could soon receive regular treatment like other prisoners. Still, he frequently got into trouble because the doctor did not believe his health issues. Hans asked his parents to solicit documentation from the hospital about his stay during the previous year. As a short-term remedy, Hans asked for a painkiller, such as *Pyramidon*, and some vermicide, because he thought he was suffering from worms; he had lost almost three kilograms in weight since his arrival in Diez. Because he had performed exhausting forced labor before his imprisonment, he had no body fat to spare. Hans did not dare to make a request for extra food, as some inmates did, because he wanted to avoid the impression that a Jew was getting more food than other prisoners.[25]

Hans's solitary confinement had gone on for eight months by this time. When his parents asked him to change his behavior, Hans responded that this was not his fault alone. In one of his confiscated letters, he wrote at the end that thinking about his life would make him go crazy. "You know best," he told his parents, "that I never visited a cinema, theater or a cabaret." The city of Frankfurt had banned these entertainments for Jews since he became a teenager.[26]

Hans suffered from increasing health problems. A hernia, probably originating from his heavy manual work, seemed to get worse. His father asked for permission to provide his son with a hernia suspensory, almond meal as a balm for his heavily irritated face, a book to learn English, and his locksmith certificate. Although the prison doctor had recommended the suspensory and the almond meal, the warden denied the request with the argument that packages were prohibited in principle. Without a chance to communicate with other prisoners and battling several health problems, including being malnourished, Hans lost more than twelve pounds within a few months, and at five feet six inches tall, was now down to only 115 pounds. In addition to the hernia and his inflamed skin, his teeth were hurting.[27]

Isolated and depressed, Hans saw no light at the end of the tunnel, and on October 10, 1941, he strangled himself with a neckerchief. A guard found him in his cell and revived him. Afterward, he was transferred to a "pacification" or cooling-off cell (*Beruhigungszelle*). Since he threatened to try to kill himself again, the guards tied him up and kept him longer than usual in the special compartment. Eleven days later, Hans was allowed back to his cell, but on December 17, he attempted to take his own life again, this time trying to jump over the railing on the fourth floor of the prison. Prison guards prevented him from falling. The warden ordered guards to tie Hans up in the pacification room again and keep him on the ground floor at all times. On New Year's Eve, the guards released his shackles and transferred Hans to a cell at Station I.[28]

The depression and enormous pain only got worse for Hans during the next year. The prison officials did not respond to his complaints, and they did not dare to inform his parents about the problems. His concerned father requested information from the prison, since they had not received a letter since November; they did not even know about their son's second suicide attempt.[29] The prison had withheld two letters with the argument that Hans would only tell lies. In the confiscated messages, Hans complained that the intense pain from his chronic skin disease and decaying teeth was keeping him awake all night. He wrote that his only hope for salvation was death. He begged his parents to get permission from the prison for him to take his own life.[30]

Hans again reported sick on March 6, 1942, this time because of swollen feet. The prison doctor injected him with Salyrgan, a common practice at the time to achieve a diuretic effect. Responding to a letter, his father assured Hans that this would be curable and there was no reason to give up on life. Soon, his father wrote, he would visit Hans in Diez, but he was waiting to get permission to leave town, which he needed because of the "yellow star" decree. The prison director confiscated the letter, arguing that this was the second letter in one month and the content was not important. Hans never got the chance to read his parents' comforting words.[31]

Since he lived in fear of the station warden, Hans directly petitioned the prison director on April 16, 1942, regarding his illness and his previous behavior. He wrote that the doctor at the pre-trial detention in Frankfurt had confirmed the severity of his health issues. After some weeks in Diez had passed, he wrote, he started to suffer from severe aches in his head and heart, for which the doctor prescribed him tranquilizers. Yet, during the next months, the unbearable pain triggered a number of "rebellious acts." The documents reveal nothing about the nature of these acts, but the warden punished Hans with extra harsh conditions. Only after realizing that he had edema and it was treatable with injections did Hans understand what he had done wrong as a result of the severe pain; he asked the warden to forgive him and to erase his extra sentences. He also requested permission to write to his parents once a week, for a toothbrush and toothpaste, as well as access to the *Leuchtturm* (Lighthouse), the official magazine for prison inmates in the Third Reich. Hans assured the warden that he had not tried to commit suicide again after attempting to jump over the railing, and the following four months of solitary confinement without work and recreation had "cured" him. Surprisingly, the director granted work—folding more envelopes—and access to the magazine. He even allowed him to write to his parents on a weekly basis and to ask them for a toothbrush. Two days after receiving permission, his father could finally visit Hans, after almost a year of being incarcerated at Diez. This was only the second time that Hans was able to see someone from his family. A few weeks later, his father's third and final visit took place, on July 20, 1942.[32]

The daunting prospect of deportation hung over all German Jews, so Hans's father sent a package containing a winter coat, a three-piece suit, and two shirts for him. He assumed there was a good chance he would not see his son again; nevertheless, he wanted Hans to be prepared when he was released from prison.[33] Toward the end of August, his father mailed another twenty-three pieces of clothing, including two suits (one three-piece, striped, and one two-piece in light green), a brown sweater, shirts, socks, underwear, and a pair of black shoes. With permission, he also sent a two-volume Jewish prayer book containing an emotional note urging Hans to use the book and to think of his parents and brother in case they were deported. But Hans never received these things. The warden threw the prayer book in a locker with the rest of his belongings and attached the letter to the inmate file.[34]

In a letter dated August 27, 1942, which the prison staff also withheld, Hans's parents wrote that they expected their "evacuation" at the end of September to the ghetto Theresienstadt near Prague, the destination for all German Jews older than sixty-five. They knew Hans could not accompany them on this fateful journey. They expressed their growing concerns about not knowing the whereabouts of his younger brother Rudolf, and two aunts, Fanny and Pauline. Hans had inquired in his last letter about the kind of rules his parents had to follow on a daily basis, and they confidently responded that when they obeyed all laws, nothing would happen to them. His father promised a last visit before their deportation, and his stepmother wrote that she would trust in God and recommended Hans to do the same. His father, who had mentioned sending the prayer book earlier, noted the dates of the upcoming Jewish high holidays. The letter was handwritten with a fountain pen. On the left margin of the front page, the father added with a pencil: "Just received the request to be prepared for the 09/2. Hence, fare thee well!"[35]

On September 1, 1942, the Gestapo deported the sixty-nine-year-old Siegmund Oppenheimer and his wife Anna to the Theresienstadt ghetto in the Protectorate of Bohemia and Moravia. Unknown to his parents, Hans's stepbrother, Rudolf, had been deported earlier to the East. Only two days before his parents were deported, on August 30, he had died in the Majdanek hybrid concentration and extermination camp, near Lublin in eastern Poland.[36]

Hans's stepmother had some hopes for their relocation to Theresienstadt. Since she was born in Bohemia, it meant a return home, though an involuntary one. However, neither would see anything more than the ghetto walls. Hans's father died two months after their arrival. On January 23, 1943, the Gestapo deported his stepmother to Auschwitz-Birkenau. She arrived at Auschwitz with 2,028 other ghetto inmates. Most were killed in the gas chamber. The SS spared only the young and strong for their labor. It seems unlikely that Anna Oppenheimer, then over fifty years old, survived the selection.[37]

In mid-September 1942, the newly appointed Reich minister of justice, Otto Thierack, had agreed to hand over all "asocial elements," including all Jews, before the completion of their sentences from the judicial correction system to the SS for "extermination through work." Normally, this would have meant the transfer of these prisoners to a concentration camp. Yet the head of the SS, Himmler, gave the order to clear all concentration camps in Germany proper of Jews by relocating them to Auschwitz or Majdanek. On November 3, the Frankfurt general prosecutor requested the transfer of the Jewish prisoners in Diez to Auschwitz. The mayor, acting as the head of the local police, sent the three Jews to Frankfurt, where they arrived on the 18th.[38]

While waiting in the prison Frankfurt-Preungesheim for his deportation, Hans rebelled one last time. During an Allied air raid, he did not brown out the small window of his cell. He might have wanted the enemy planes to spot his light from the sky and put him out of his misery. The prison staff punished him with two days of strict arrest, which meant losing his bedding, work, and the daily hour for an outside walk, with food rations reduced to water and 700 grams of bread.[39]

One day before New Year's Eve 1942, the Frankfurt prison handed over the Jews from Diez to the police for transport to Auschwitz. Hans did not survive there for long, due to his weakened state. He probably never knew that a transport carrying his stepmother had arrived a few days earlier from Theresienstadt. Hans Oppenheimer's death was recorded on January 30, 1943, just after he had turned twenty years old.[40]

Other Stories of Disobeying Anti-Jewish Laws and Decrees

Even though Hans Oppenheimer's story is indeed extraordinary, his personal acts of individual defiance resemble countless others recorded in archival documents and survivor testimonies. Jewish women and men violated a long list of national anti-Jewish regulations.

Courts penalized Jews, including Manfred Feldmann in Hamburg, for not obeying the Nazi order to turn in their handguns in November 1938 under the new anti-Jewish gun decree.[41] Jews ignored or acted only partly on the decrees to hand over all precious metals and jewels in February 1939, to deposit all liquid assets and money in frozen bank accounts, and to leave all valuables behind in Germany upon emigration.[42] Often, they defied a combination of these rules. For such alleged crimes, Jews were punished by either Special Courts or local courts.[43]

Wilhelm Sander, a former merchant, was sentenced by the Special Court in Frankfurt in 1940 to seven months in jail for hiding cash at home and smuggling money into Switzerland before his emigration to Palestine. When Gustav Beiersdorf, a former sales representative and war veteran who lived in a hotel in Frankfurt, was arrested for not registering with the police for more than a year, police discovered that he possessed 5,000 Reichsmarks in cash and ten gold coins. Although the Gestapo pushed for his incarceration in a concentration camp, a Special Court arraigned him, put him on trial, and sentenced him to four months in prison. His younger brother Arthur, a former tailor and war veteran, was sentenced in January 1941 for similar reasons to five months under the war economy act and the hard currencies decree.[44]

Because of the increasing number of anti-Jewish regulations, multiple offenses became almost the norm during the war. In February 1942, Hamburg police arrested Martha Frank because she openly criticized officials who declined to provide her with food ration cards at a special office for Jews (*Sonderdienststelle für Juden*). She was not wearing the "yellow star" and had not registered with the police after she moved from Berlin to Hamburg in 1941. The investigating Gestapo discovered that she was hiding jewelry in her underwear as well as precious metals and foreign currency at home. She had not registered her assets in 1938 as required for all Jews. Furthermore, she had already received two sentences for not displaying the special identification card required for Jews. For this litany of violations, a Hamburg court sentenced her to six months in prison. According to prison records, even in jail she continued to behave "impudently." After serving her sentence, the Gestapo arrested Frank again in February 1943 and deported her to Auschwitz.[45]

Breaking the evening curfew that Nazi Germany had imposed on Jews after the beginning of the war in September 1939 was common. In most instances, it was not only leaving one's home at night for a walk, but rather to visit parks, restaurants, bars, cinemas, or theaters, deliberately patronizing prohibited establishments and not identifying themselves as Jews. Some publicly criticized the Nazi state and the persecution in public and at these establishments.[46]

In February 1941 in Vienna, the widow Laura Rechnitz committed offenses against three Nazi regulations at once, by going out after 8 p.m., visiting the Esterhazi bar, which was forbidden for Jews, and telling political jokes, such as how a German doctor bragged that he had removed the brains from 82 million Germans and they would still move around. The Vienna police officer who filed the charges after a denunciation alleged that Rechnitz was really talking about Hitler. He also noted that she had defended Jews during her bar conversation. She received a six-month jail sentence for insulting the German Reich.[47]

When Jews defied the order to hand over their radios in the fall of 1939 and listened to forbidden foreign broadcasts during the war, courts in Frankfurt, Hamburg, and Vienna punished them with harsh sentences of up to two years in penitentiary under the general ordinance against "radio crimes."[48] Some Jews, however, were never caught for tuning in to foreign radio stations. Ruth Epstein remembers listening to such broadcasts on her father's short-wave radio after the Nazis had prohibited Jews to own one; even family friends would come to get international news.[49]

After Kristallnacht in 1938, when the Nazi state prohibited Jews from running businesses in Germany, some of them refused to close their shops. The former merchant Max Grossmann defied various anti-Jewish restrictions in November 1939 by selling rubber bands, entering a cafe in Hamburg against restrictions, and not introducing himself as a Jew in sales negotiations with a café owner and Nazi party member named Kleist. For this trio of offenses, he received a sentence of one year in prison. Frankfurt and Vienna authorities discovered Jewish business activities as late as 1940 and 1941.[50]

Soon after the war started, the Nazi state prohibited Jews from acquiring new clothing and shoes and granted Jews only limited food rations. Over time, such restrictions created a dire situation, driving many to purchase goods from the black market or to perform illicit trade activities themselves. For their defiance, many Jews were incarcerated in Greater Germany. In the small village of Schwanstein, a woman kept dozens of boots after the "aryanization" of her shoe store. In Vienna, Hugo Abeles, Friedrich Blum, and Leo Blum traded with toasted coffee. They were prosecuted for "economic crimes during a war." In Prague, a German newspaper announced arrests of Czech Jews for similar offenses on a daily basis.[51] In Berlin, Siegfried and Gülda Zadek and their sixteen-year-old twin daughters were denounced for disobeying the restricted shopping hours for Jews that had been introduced there in July 1940.[52] At the end of September 1942, the police arrested Robert Prochnik, an employee of the Jewish Community Vienna, and two other members of his family for illegally buying meat and butter, which they were not allowed to receive through their limited rations for Jews.[53]

After the introduction of the nationwide forced labor program, many Jews tried to evade the recruitment by the labor offices, others resisted wearing discriminating armbands during their work, and many refused their work orders. Logbooks of 1940 and 1941 show that in Berlin police arrested a number of Jewish men and women for refusing or sabotaging their forced labor assignments by private companies. A Berlin court sentenced the twenty-eight-year-old Hildegard Lewithan to three months in jail for repeatedly refusing her work orders in October 1941. She resisted even though her husband, Alfred Lewithan, had been in jail since the fall of 1939 for "impudent" behavior. Soon after her release from prison, police arrested Hildegard again for stealing. In June 1942, the Gestapo deported her directly from prison via Minsk to the extermination site Maly Trostinec.[54]

As opposed to most other Jewish "crimes," some of the defiant laborers were not tried and were sent directly to Gestapo-run re-education labor camps (*Arbeitserziehungslager*), or even concentration camps. A group of Jewish forced laborers who protested against their minimal wages toiled for months in the re-education labor camp in Berlin-Wuhlheide.[55] For more than a year, the forty-nine-year-old Henny Stern worked for a Düsseldorf metal firm, whose management denounced her several times to the labor office and later to the Gestapo for her insolent attitude, her defiance of her forced labor duties, and her attempt to influence other Jewish forced laborers. In December 1941, the Gestapo took her into "protective custody" for her subversive behavior and sent her to Ravensbrück, the women's concentration camp, where she died six months later.[56]

Three years before the Nazi state introduced the notorious "yellow star," in summer 1938, it ordered all Jews to carry marked identification cards and adopt the discriminatory middle names "Israel" and "Sara." Starting in January 1939, Jews had to present themselves everywhere in public by using the marked ID and those names. These two decrees were meant to identify and humiliate Jews in public. Interestingly, the Nazis could not simply force the Jews to adopt these discriminatory names, because German law required citizens to put in a formal application for any legal name change. Equally, they had to file an application to acquire an identification card and do so under the discriminatory regulations. The local archives in Hamburg, Vienna, Berlin, Leipzig, Frankfurt, and Munich offer ample evidence that many Jewish men and women refused to file the necessary paperwork. The sixty-eight-year-old painter Max Antlers, for example, declined the Berlin police's repeated requests to complete the application form for the marked identification card. Even after the police summoned him, Antlers refused and was arrested in February 1939.[57] When seventy-six-year-old Hedwig Jastrow took her own life after the November pogrom, in her suicide letter she declared that she wanted to be buried with the untainted name her parents had given her.[58]

Elderly Jews in particular rejected these Nazi orders. Some, many of them women, were able to hide their identities successfully for years. Ida Schneider, seventy-three, never applied for the special identification card or adopted the compulsory middle name "Sara." She did not introduce herself as Jewish in public, either. For her "crimes," Schneider received seven months in prison in 1941. Johanna Quaas, sixty-five, and Frieda Schütze, fifty-three, hid their Jewish origin until 1942, when they were discovered. The Leipzig court sentenced Quaas to six months and Schütze to seven weeks in prison. The Gestapo sent several women for hiding their Jewish identities, among them Herta Prenzlau from Berlin, to the Ravensbrück concentration camp.[59]

Even some Jews who complied with the obliged name changes refused to use them in public. In October 1940, Dr. Edgar Fels, a former lawyer downgraded to "legal adviser," and his female companion, Paula Breslauer, took a taxi together even though it was forbidden in order to make it on time to a private event in Hamburg where they were supposed to play violin and piano. When police stopped the car, they did not identify themselves as Jews, fearing retaliation. For multiple infractions, a court punished them each with sentences of ten days in jail. As Luise Solmitz wrote in her diary, her Christian husband, Friedrich Wilhelm, registered his dog at a Hamburg police precinct and did not reveal his Nazi categorization as a racial Jew, for which the police charged him with an offense. Dreisa Kaste did not introduce herself as "Sara" when she was brought to a police station in 1941 after an officer caught her during curfew with a lit flashlight on the street. This had been forbidden since the beginning of the war by the law on air defense. A Hamburg court sentenced her to four days in jail or a payment of 20 Reichsmarks. In Leipzig, Frieda Stelzer received eighteen days in jail for not introducing herself with the name "Sara" in 1942. In Vienna, numerous Jews refused to employ the new "names" in public.[60]

These German Jews knew that non-compliance with Nazi laws and decrees would have serious consequences. Failing to reveal their Jewish identities may seem at the lower end on a spectrum of resistance, but it still produced potential prison time. Even in letter exchanges with authorities and private recipients, Jews had to identify themselves by using the discriminatory names and mentioning their identification card numbers. In Würzburg, the Gestapo filed charges against Johanna Samuel for not using "Sara" in an intercepted private correspondence and a postcard. In June 1941, Adolf

Katzenstein, who toiled as a forced laborer in construction, sent a petition to the Hamburg state governor and party district leader (*Reichstatthalter* and *Gauleiter*) Kaufmann, in which he criticized losing his beloved work as a chef because of his "race." Katzenstein did not sign with "Israel" or put down his special identification number, even though a court had already punished him for not applying for the Jewish identification card a year before. In Leipzig, Frankfurt, and Hamburg the police recorded dozens of similar cases.[61]

Although courts often sentenced them to pay minor fees for the infractions, most Jews had no income other than minimal forced labor wages. The penalties could be the equivalent of a week's wages, which many could not afford to pay, which meant they would have to go to prison. Even if they had savings, they now had a criminal record, which made them particularly vulnerable.

Jews had to inform municipal and other offices about the "name changes," and in some cases, the consequences for defying these Nazi orders even just on paper could be grave. Living in Leipzig, Margarete Engel did not tell the civil registries of Berlin and Bremen, where she was born and got married, so those offices could issue updated birth and marriage certificates. Arrested in January 1942, she defended herself by saying she did not know about the details of the decree. The local court sentenced her to two weeks in jail with an order to hand her over to the Gestapo after her sentence. In March 1942, she was sent to Ravensbrück concentration camp. Two months later, she was transferred to a mental institution in Bernburg, on the Saale River. Engel was murdered there under the "14f13 program," in which inmates incapable of work were separated from the others and euthanized.[62]

Concealing one's Jewish identity and "passing" as a non-Jew still became a common way to defy anti-Jewish persecution. A story with the headline "Again a Jewish 'Aryan' " in the Nazi newspaper *Völkischer Beobachter* on January 18, 1940, in Vienna revealed that Adolf Friedman, forty-three, had been arrested for "race defilement" while working for an "Aryan" store and pretending to be an "Aryan." Friedman had been in a fifteen-year relationship with a non-Jewish woman, whose former husband seized the opportunity to denounce the Jew. In another case, Robert Zwicker secured from a church a birth certificate of a person with the same name. With this, he received a permission to marry his non-Jewish girlfriend in 1939. He also forged ration cards and invented the murder of a cousin to manage his old business under his new identity. Once discovered, he was sentenced to death. In April 1942, the Special Court in Vienna sentenced the hairdresser Edith Weiss, twenty, to one year and three months in a penitentiary for visiting film theaters, swimming pools, and cafes forbidden for Jews; for establishing relationships with non-Jewish Germans; occasionally wearing a Nazi party badge; and having sexual relations with an "Aryan" soldier. She used a forged name and did not wear the "yellow star."[63]

Many people perceived the yellow badge as a stark humiliation and refused to be marked and treated as outlaws. In October 1941, the Gestapo had pressured the Jewish Community Berlin to have its representatives warn the local Jews about concealing the "yellow star" with collars, pocketbooks, or portfolios. Similarly, the Gestapo in Olomouc (Protectorate) warned the local Jewish community that refusing Jews would face harsh punishments. The Gestapo frequently intervened since even after this stark warning Jews did not sew the stars properly and tightly on their clothes. The Prague newspaper *Der Neue Tag* reported as a warning that the local court in Plauen (Vogtland) sentenced sixty-nine-year-old Israel Bentler with a fine of 40 Reichsmarks after he covered the star with his arm in public. Siegfried Weininger used his briefcase to cover the yellow badge when entering a tobacco store in Vienna. After an interrogation, the Gestapo included him in the first transport of the mass deportations to the occupied East.[64]

Margot Liu, née Holzmann, a Jewish lesbian living in Nazi Berlin, found a different way to challenge the humiliating obligation to wear the "yellow star." Despite being in a relationship, she met a Chinese waiter named Chi Lang Liu, who had lived in Germany for a decade. On October 11, 1941, while celebrating his birthday, they became engaged. By marrying him a month later, she secured Chinese citizenship, so "wearing the Star of David" was no longer required for her, and she was not subject to deportation, as the criminal police noted. On their wedding night, however, Margot abandoned Chi and went to sleep in her girlfriend Martha's bed.[65]

Munich courts tried various Jews for disobeying the "yellow star" rules during the next year. Some resisters had to pay fines; others received jail sentences of several weeks. Berthold L. received a sentence of six weeks in jail for not wearing the "badge" at the end of 1942. Temporarily spared because of his forced labor, he went into hiding before being summoned to jail. In Leipzig, Fanny Zimmermann went to jail for three weeks for not wearing the star in February 1942. In Essen, Moses Bader was denounced for the same reason in April 1942. Some Jews refused to wear the discriminatory badge even after they had already been punished for the same "crime" once. In Austria, the Gestapo arrested a Jewish farmer, Franz Bier, who still did not wear the "yellow star" in spite of previous sanctions by the county commissioner.[66]

Not wearing the "yellow star" was a mass phenomenon, albeit a costly one. Opposition was common among Jews everywhere and often resulted in large numbers of arrests in a single city or town. In his monthly report of November 1941, the district commissioner (*Oberlandrat*) in Moravian Ostrava commented that the "yellow star" encountered a lot of resistance. Several Jews had been arrested for not wearing the notorious badge. In December, this district commissioner said that seven Jews had been arrested for not wearing the star and twelve for covering up the yellow badge. In the month of January 1942 in Vienna, the Gestapo arrested twenty-nine Jews, fifteen women and fourteen men, for the same offense. They received prison sentences from four to six weeks, and after their releases, they were deported to Nazi-occupied Poland.[67]

After the mass deportations went into full swing, Jews took off the star and went into hiding to protect themselves. Sometimes they were caught on the street, as was Max Zickel in Berlin in September 1943. Zickel could not produce a marked identification card, and after he admitted to not wearing the "yellow star" for a year, the Gestapo transferred him to a collection camp for deportation. Some Jews in hiding were caught when they went to their former homes in order to retrieve their belongings. The residences had been sealed by the police after their flight, so they had to break in. Sometimes police found Jews in hiding during raids of the homes of non-Jews, such as that of Karl and Helen Merchel. In May 1943, Merchel's neighbor Ernst Braese denounced him for bringing fat home from his work and selling it illegally. Police discovered not only large amounts of raw and processed grease, eigh-

teen bottles of wine, liquor, meat, perfume, shoes, and three cans with pep-
per, but also four Jews in hiding: Gerhard Beigel, Rudolf Goldbach, Jakob
Lewin, and Sara Schmidt. All had resisted boarding the trains to Auschwitz.
They were among the several thousand Jewish men and women who took
off the "yellow star" and hid in the capital of the Third Reich.[68]

Clearly, very many Jewish men and women disobeyed anti-Jewish restrictions and Nazi laws. Seemingly minor acts of defiance, like Hans Oppenheimer pulling a fire alarm, triggered swift and harsh punishments. Jewish
men and women kept stores open, after the Nazi state prohibited it, refused
to hand over precious metals when it was ordered, and hid hard currency.

Equally, when Jews concealed their identity by refusing to adopt "Jewish" names, display the "yellow star," or carry marked identification cards,
German courts perceived such minor acts as a threat to the Nazi state and
its policies. Even harsher punishments for Jews resulted from so-called radio
and economic crimes during the war. These forms of defiance were often
desperate responses to the increasing lack of access to resources, such as information and food.

These Jewish resisters and countless others whose individual defiance
did not leave traces in an archive, were not complacent and passive at all.
They resisted anti-Jewish policies with boldness, audacity, persistence, and
sometimes despair in an environment where it was life threatening to do so.

FOUR

Protest in Writing Against Nazi Persecution

Benno Neuburger in Munich and Others

B enno Neuburger had never been a member of any political organization or association. He had voted for a liberal party, which many
German Jews supported, and joined the local Jewish community. Living in
Munich, however, home to the Nazi party headquarters, Benno had been
exposed directly to Hitler's anti-Semitic rhetoric since the 1920s. He began
to despise the party's leader, especially after his rise to power in 1933 and the
enactment of anti-Jewish policies across the country.

Under the new mayor of Munich, Dr. Karl Fiehler, a long-standing and
high-ranking member of the Nazi party, the city stopped doing any business
with Jews in March 1933. Earlier than other cities, Munich prohibited Jews
from participating in public auctions and visiting municipal swimming
pools. Without the existence of a corresponding Nazi law, the Munich welfare department was among the first to reduce benefits for the Jewish poor.

Benno's rancor against Hitler grew with the radicalizing policies against
the Jews. The persecution dispersed his family. As a result of the pogrom in
November 1938, he suffered several weeks as an inmate in a concentration
camp, solely for being Jewish. After returning home, he had to make room
for relatives, and later, on city orders, for strangers. All of this he might have
endured without rebelling. But his abhorrence for the Nazi leader was drastically exacerbated by the frequent proclamations Hitler made beginning in
1939 that he would exterminate the Jews in Europe. When the Nazis forced
German Jews to wear the "yellow star," the humiliation of being visibly

ostracized from German society appears to have been the last straw for the seventy-year-old Benno Neuburger.

Benno was born in Munich, the capital of the German state of Bavaria, on March 4, 1871, as the fifth child of the real estate broker couple Max and Jette Neuburger. After vocational school and an apprenticeship, Benno worked as a sales clerk at the Elias Cohn Königsberger fabric store for fifteen years. In 1902, he joined his father's real estate company. After his parents passed away, Benno took over the family enterprise in 1915, but hardships after the war and the Treaty of Versailles culminated in the political and economic crisis of 1923. In November of that year, the politically ambitious Adolf Hitler and his small Nazi party entourage set out to exploit the fragile political and economic situation and topple the Bavarian government in Munich. Their coup attempt was modeled after Mussolini's march to Rome, and it was supposed to be the first step on the way to taking over Berlin. The German army, however, quelled the amateurish "Beer Hall Putsch," and Hitler went to prison. But because of the hyperinflation that resulted from the destabilized economic conditions, Benno lost most of his savings of more than 160,000 Reichsmarks; the once substantial family fortune had turned into worthless paper.[1]

Benno could not afford to buy new real estate. To make a living for his family, he started selling the remaining real estate stock of his company piece by piece. In 1907, he had married Anna, née Einstein, who was almost six years younger and came from a cattle trader family in Laupheim, in Württemberg. First, they lived together in his parents' house in Munich. The couple soon had children: Fritz, born in 1908, and Johanna a year later. In April 1936, the family moved to Trogerstrasse, which was close to the city center and near Prinzregentenstrasse, where Hitler lived.[2]

Daughter Johanna, Hani as the parents called her, started to get increasingly desperate about the expanding anti-Jewish restrictions and longed to escape Nazi persecution. She came close to a nervous breakdown. Finally, in September 1937, she was able to leave Germany and emigrated to the United States. In New York, she got married in August 1938, a week after her thirty-year-old brother Fritz joined her in the city. In a letter, their mother

Fritz and Johanna Neuburger (the two at right) in their late teens, with their cousins behind them, somewhere in Germany, no date. (Courtesy of the Neuburger-Stoll Family)

Benno, Anna, and daughter Johanna Neuburger (first, second, and fourth from left) with others in a beer garden, probably in Munich, no date. (Courtesy of the Neuburger-Stoll Family)

wrote: "I can't believe that [I'm] without children here, but [I'm] happy that it worked out for Fritz and he is gone as well; even though the farewell has not been easy. I will rest a[nd] take care of myself so that [I'll] be able to join you some day."[3]

In Munich, the situation became more difficult every month. In June 1938, the main synagogue in the city center had been demolished on Hitler's order. The Neuburgers wanted to join their children sooner rather than later. They tried to get the necessary papers at the U.S. consulate. With visa fees and passage tickets, however, emigration was costly. Although Benno and Anna found a buyer for their remaining apartment shares, the money did not come through. As they witnessed the steady departure of acquaintances and friends, the Neuburgers could not afford to emigrate.[4]

During Kristallnacht in Munich, the attackers demolished homes, schools, shops, and department stores and set ablaze the two remaining

Anna Neuburger, no date.
(Courtesy of the Neuburger-
Stoll Family)

main synagogues. Many Jews were blackmailed, and beaten; at least one man was murdered in the city. Thirty-three Jews committed suicide. Police and the Gestapo detained more than a thousand men and brought them to the nearby concentration camp Dachau. Two days after the pogrom, Anna Neuburger wrote to her daughter in the United States: "Dear Hani, We have received your letter from November 4. We are happy that you children are doing so well. With myself, everything is the same. I'm alone but dad will be getting home soon."[5]

The last sentence was a hidden reference to the fact that police had taken Benno Neuburger to the Dachau concentration camp. However, he would not be coming home soon. In Dachau, the SS guards beat the Jews upon arrival, especially older men. It was already winter, and the inmates were provided with only very thin clothing and they had to endure endless roll calls. Food was scarce; brutal treatment was common. By November 25, the day Benno Neuburger was released, the SS in Dachau had already registered the deaths of nine Jews; by December 16, the number rose to twenty-four. Those who survived came home exhausted and sick. Ironically, Benno Neuburger had suffered near the very same location in Dachau where, as a German soldier, he had guarded a munitions factory during the last year of the first World War.[6]

During the pogrom, the attackers had invaded and destroyed Jewish homes everywhere in Germany. Countless Jews became homeless and sought shelter. Anna Neuburger's relatives, the Holzers, were driven from their home in Traunstein after SA and civilians attacked and partly destroyed their house. The Holzer family left the small town, which claimed to be "Jew free" soon afterward, and moved into the Neuburgers' Munich apartment. Two days after the pogrom, the Holzers added a postscript to Anna's letter to her children, "My loved ones, as you can see we are still with your mom. Don't worry, she's doing well considering the circumstances. We'll remain here until we can return home. Of course the best thing would be to go to America right away."[7]

Since private homes, the last refuge, had been violated, many Jews tried to get out of Germany. Separated from her incarcerated husband, Anna became desperate. Two weeks later, she wrote to her children again: "Dear Fritz and Hani, We received your letters from 11 and 15 November. We just wish we could already be with you. Dad is still out doing things. Hopefully, you can get your citizenship quickly. I'm sure things will get easier then. Every day we are waiting for mail from the authorities but nothing so far. There's so much to take care of. But meanwhile all we can do is wait. . . . I'm just so happy that all of you children got away. We just have to wait to be reunited with you again. Every day I'm praying to the Almighty that we stay healthy until we get to you."[8]

On the day she posted this letter, Benno, at sixty-seven years old, returned from the concentration camp. Life became even more complicated. A month later, the Holzers still occupied the smaller rooms of the apartment, while Benno and Anna were forced to camp out in the living room. It was not only that the apartment was crowded, but the younger relatives were noisy. They yelled at their children and had bad manners. The Neuburgers were depending solely on their savings. They waited for the outstanding

Benno Neuburger, no date.
(Courtesy of the Neuburger-Stoll
Family)

money from the sold apartment shares. Benno wrote to his children: "You really have no idea how things are. Just be happy that you got away."[9]

Weeks and months passed while the Neuburgers desperately waited for news from the U.S. consulate in Stuttgart. In January 1939, they sent packages of gingerbread to their children and letters spiced with ever more despair. By the end of March, temperatures rose in Munich, yet the hopes of the elderly couple sank even lower. However, they refused new emigration ideas proposed by their children, such as going to Cuba. Benno was still waiting to collect the outstanding 8,000 Reichsmarks from the apartment shares, which was a small fortune, and he needed time to sell the remaining real estate pieces, as he wrote in May.[10]

With the beginning of the war in September 1939, borders closed and emigration stalled. The Neuburgers felt trapped. Local restrictions also increased. In Munich, Breslau, and Frankfurt am Main, the city governments forced the Jews to shop in a few assigned stores; in Berlin and Dresden they introduced limited shopping hours. Under the law of April 1939, the Neuburgers were forced to sublet a room to another woman and an aunt had moved in, creating even more crowded conditions.[11]

In 1939, only half of the original Jewish population of 1933 still lived in Munich. Despite their desperation, the Neuburgers would not entertain the idea of leaving for Cuba. They wanted to live close to their children. Benno wrote to them in November 1939: "We are just too old for this kind of adventure. . . . We probably would be completely without income over there—not knowing the language, the culture and the people. I think I would feel immensely lost and helpless."[12]

The separation from their children became more and more heartbreaking. The parents missed Johanna's wedding and were only able to learn through letters about her pregnancy and the birth of their first grandchild. For every tiny shred of information, Benno and Anna had to wait weeks and months: the good news, the name of the newborn and, finally, the first picture of their granddaughter Karolina. Later, they also missed the engagement and the wedding of their son. Finally, in September 1940, they received the necessary U.S. sponsorships for their immigration. However, Benno discovered spelling errors in their names and a wrong birth year for his wife in the paperwork. Why were the children not more careful? This could spoil their chances to get out of Nazi Germany.

But there seemed to be hope on the horizon in December 1940, as Benno wrote to his children: "We are happy to report that Stuttgart has contacted Chicago and it looks like we'll be able to leave earlier than expected." On February 20, 1941, Benno reached out with even more hopeful news: "There's a rumor going around that up to 50,000 people will be allowed to emigrate within the next few months. Well I should say the ones who are in possession of a passage. . . . Who knows, we might soon be reunited. That would be wonderful." Four days later, he asked the children to pay for the ship passages. He needed "to name the ship, the cabin number and to have a receipt for the payment of the passage. If those requirements are not fulfilled the visa will not be issued."[13]

The United States did not make it easy for Jewish refugees because of widespread anti-Semitic sentiments in the State Department and other parts of the government. In addition, the Neuburgers had "to pay a capital tax" to Nazi Germany. Since they had not received the money for the property they had sold three years earlier, their son sent five hundred dollars. He also paid for their ship passages, which his parents finally received at the end of March 1941. However, it had taken far too long to secure the rare ship passages. Despite having their U.S. immigration quota number, they could not get out, because their sponsorships had to be renewed. The couple started to lose hope again. Friends and relatives experienced similar dramas when passages were canceled because they could not get an appointment at the consulate on time, and vice versa, in a vicious cycle.[14]

More desperate than ever, Neuburgers began to envy the people leaving for Cuba. In April 1941, Anna wrote, "Life is tough these days. A lot of people suffer in pain. We'll just have to do our best to stay healthy. Me and dad we certainly would love to leave to be with you." Yet their chances became slimmer every week. In June, the Nazi government ordered all U.S. consulates to close, in retaliation for President Roosevelt's order to shut down German consulates in the United States. In September 1941, Benno sent this message: "We are so ready to leave here. Let's just hope it'll happen soon. The only problem is that so many want to do the same thing."[15]

He wrote these desperate words the very day after all Jews older than six years were forced to wear the notorious "yellow star." The only accessible newspaper for Jews, the *Jüdische Nachrichtenblatt*, had published the text of the humiliating decree. A few days later, he had to pick up the pieces of bright fabric for Anna and himself at the offices of the Munich Jewish community. On September 19, 1941, he had to leave his home for the first time wearing the "yellow star" above his heart. In spite of Hitler's attacks on the Jews before and especially after 1933, Benno had still perceived himself as a proud German from Munich. Now, he must have felt othered, humiliated, branded like an animal.

However, he did not want to give in to the Nazis. Between September 20, 1941, and February 28, 1942, Benno Neuburger applied Hitler stamps to dozens of postcards and wrote abusive comments on them. The first read: "The eternal mass murderer Hitler. Disgusting!" On October 1, he wrote: "Son of a bitch Hitler," "Murderer." Benno prepared all the postcards secretly, without his wife knowing. He put them in mailboxes in his neighborhood, most of them in a single mailbox on Troger Street, only a few houses away from his apartment. He mailed three such postcards in September and October anonymously and with no addresses on them. Strangely, according to the Gestapo records, he didn't mail any others until the end of the year.[16]

It seems unlikely that Benno stopped mailing postcards in November and December, especially since Hitler gave his annual speech in Munich on the evening of November 8 to commemorate the Nazi "martyrs" of the failed 1923 putsch. In Breslau, the German-Jewish historian and high school teacher Willy Cohn noted in his diary that this year Hitler had called "the international Jewry" the world's prime arsonist and blamed them for the war. The speech was supposed to justify the beginning of the mass deportation of German Jews.[17]

In the pouring rain on November 20, the Gestapo took the Holzer family to the train station at 4 a.m. and put them on the first deportation train from Munich bound for Nazi-occupied Lithuania. Benno and Anna would never hear from them again. Five days later, these Jews from Munich as well as more from Berlin and Frankfurt were all shot in Kowno's Fort IX. They were the first Jews from Germany who were murdered.[18]

The situation in Munich was desperate. Suicides spread like wildfire among the remaining Jews.[19] The first weeks of 1942 saw Benno sending out his protest postcards more frequently. His comments drastically sharpened in tone. The first card on January 11 contained a whole poem. The post stamp bore the words "Heil" and "Murderer," and the text read: "The Almighty is in Heaven. The 4rer [German: *Vierer*; sounds like 'Führer'] is an atrocity person. God decides for all people everything and doesn't tolerate other gods—Hail he is himself a God indeed." Over the next five days, he sent several postcards. On the 16th, a card bore the sole word "Tyrant."

Around January 22, Benno sent two more postcards. On one of them he had written on Hitler's face "Hail," "Terror government," and the "The new God," while on the back of the card one could read the prophetic "Murderer of 5,000,000." One card sent on February 23 bore the lines "Beast, murderer, thug" and "die a wretched death" across Hitler's face. The last card secured at the post office showed a sketched cross on Hitler's etched face; the symbol stands for the deceased in Germany.[20]

Benno became more and more bold and furious. His anger was most likely refueled by a new speech in January 1942, in which Hitler doubled down on his rhetoric about the extermination of the Jews from three years before. In that notorious speech on January 30, 1939, Hitler had proclaimed, "In the course of my life I have very often been a prophet, and have usually been ridiculed for it. . . . Today I will once more be a prophet: If the international Jewish financiers in and outside Europe should succeed in plunging the nations once more into a world war, then the result will not be the Bolshevization of the earth, and thus the victory of Jewry, but the annihilation of the Jewish race in Europe!" Now, on January 30, 1942, he reiterated his notorious "prophecy." Moreover, Hitler exclaimed, "For the first time, there will be applied the old-Jewish law: an eye for an eye and a tooth for a tooth!"[21]

On March 16, a new local anti-Jewish measure affected Benno and Anna: The city of Munich forced them to give up their home and "resettle" in a barrack camp in Milbertshofen on the outskirts of the city, one of two residential camps recently established for Jews. Until the invasion of the Soviet Union, the Nazi leadership hesitated to establish ghettos for Jews in Germany proper. Nonetheless in summer 1941, the Gestapo, in collaboration with city governments or district administrators, started to concentrate segments of the Jewish population in so-called "residential communities" (*Wohngemeinschaften*) in preparation for upcoming mass deportations. Authorities established such camps in closed mines, confiscated and vacated monasteries, abandoned institutional buildings, and run-down castles. Soon over 3,200 Jews lived in more than forty such "labor and residential camps" throughout Germany, from Cologne to Breslau. Inadequate food supply, poor sanitary conditions, lack of privacy, heavy manual labor, and psyches

Jews from Munich arriving at the camp in Milbertshofen, November 1941. (City Archive Munich DE-1992-FS-NS-00022)

damaged from years of persecution resulted in a high mortality rate among older Jews in these mini-ghettos.[22]

In Munich, the Nazi party had discussed plans to segregate the Jews in 1940. Despite the initial hesitation of the Reich Main Security Office in Berlin, Munich's Mayor Fiehler was given the green light in March 1941 to force Jewish men, including the elderly, to build barracks in Milbertshofen. In October, 400 male and 38 female Jews lived in Milbertshofen. Every inmate had to pay 0.50 Reichsmarks per day as rent to cover the camp's construction costs.[23]

In spring 1942, the number of inmates at the camp Munich-Milbertshofen rose to more than 1,200 in anticipation of mass deportations. When the elderly Neuburgers arrived at the *Judensiedlung I* (Jew colony), one can only imagine their shock. Stripped of most of their belongings, they were lacking

Interior of one residential barrack at the camp for Jews in Milbertshofen, 1941/1942. (City Archive Munich DE-1992-FS-NS-00030)

any shred of privacy in the overcrowded camp barracks. Both slept in bunk beds without any separation.[24]

A week after the couple's forced relocation, the Gestapo took Benno Neuburger into custody on March 24. Since he had mailed the anonymous postcards without any postal addresses on them, the post office employees in his district filtered them out and passed them on to the Gestapo. Unfortunately, Neuburger had overlooked that one of the recent postcards displayed a stamped seal of the family's real estate company. The Gestapo officers interrogated the seventy-one-year-old man and tried to force him into a confession. After initially refuting their allegations regarding the postcards, Benno gave in, probably because he was beaten and tortured. His mug shots reveal bruises and swellings on one side of his face.[25]

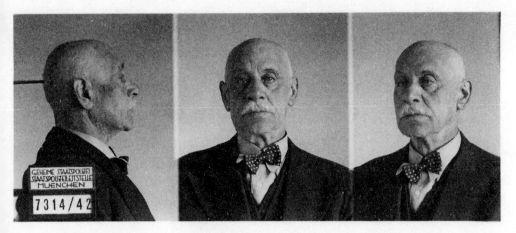

Benno Neuburger in Gestapo custody, 1942. Bruises are visible on the right side of his face. (Federal Archive of Germany, R 3018/2999, vol. 3, fol. 5)

Ultimately, Benno admitted to mailing fourteen postcards. Undeterred and right to the face of the Gestapo officers, he called the "evacuations" of often ill and sick Jews to the occupied eastern territories "murder." He wanted to make the German population aware of the Jewish suffering. Since he believed an open battle would be futile, Benno decided to fight Hitler with anonymous messages. In his confession, he explained that he called Hitler an "idiot" for thinking Jews are stupid, a "robber" for taking their money, a "criminal" for unjustly making their life unbearable, and a "son of a bitch" for enacting restrictions against the Jews that one would not even apply to animals. A week later, in its final report to the investigating judge at the Munich courthouse, the Gestapo blamed Benno Neuburger for defaming Hitler and advocated charging him under the Treacherous Attacks Law of 1934. Moreover, the Gestapo argued that Neuburger wanted to change the minds of Germans about Hitler and incite them to change the government, which counted as treason. On his civil registry card, under the date of his internment, a note indicates that the officer thought a return seemed unlikely.[26]

Benno Neuburger appeared in court on April 4. He openly admitted again that he had sent more than a dozen postcards with hateful comments about Hitler. Astonishingly, he also underscored his main motive, namely his outrage about Hitler's announcement about the annihilation of the

Jews. The investigating judge, named Zeller, issued an arrest warrant for the crime of preparing treason and for treacherous attacks on Hitler. He did not grant bail for three reasons: the suspect's status as a Jew, the gravity of the alleged crimes, and the public's—that is, political—interest in his case.[27]

A week later, the Special Court in Munich informed the People's Court in Berlin about the arrest warrant for "preparation of treason." The People's Court had been founded in 1934 and served the Nazi state as a quasi-judicial tool against alleged and real enemies. By 1942, the slightest suggestion of a regime change was considered treason, which included even acts of propaganda. Thus, almost any opposition to the Nazis was punishable by the People's Court. On the Reich main prosecutor's indictment letter of May 6, the first words written in large letters were "Jew!" and "Arrest!" He dropped the lesser charges for treacherous attacks against Hitler and focused on "preparation for treason," for mailing fourteen postcards with grave insults of Hitler, which allegedly aimed at inciting the German people against the "Führer" and the National Socialist government. The Reich main prosecutor listed all of the scolding messages on the postcards and laid out the supposed motives, repeating some of the explanations Benno had given, such as his rage about Hitler's speeches and the "evacuation" of the Jews. The prosecutor emphasized Benno's desire to stop the Nazi policy against the Jews and alleged that he must have been aware that this could only be achieved by overthrowing Hitler and his government.[28]

From prison, Benno wrote to his wife Anna: "I am terribly sorry that I cause you so much distress. I hope that this will change for you. . . . I regret everything I did, especially since everything one does has no effect. That almost all our relatives and friends were taken away and, as I heard yesterday, 14 days after we moved out, Erna Lohmann . . . took her own life. Such things upset me a lot . . . I got angry when I heard about the extermination and annihilation of the Jews—it can't be tit for tat, hence, I did something which I should not have done etc. Now you know what I did, indeed. In fact, I never involved myself in politics—everybody who knows me is aware of this. . . . Don't worry so much. Hopefully, some of the damage can be undone and the court will deal with me in a humane manner."[29] Two days after writing the letter, Benno ended up in the hospital ward of the Stadelheim prison.

Anna Neuburger never received her husband's hearfelt confession. Since it supposedly contained unwanted references, the People's Court mandated its confiscation. Because she had no clue what happened to her husband, she sought legal help. On June 30, Felix Koenigsberger, a former lawyer, now called "legal adviser," sent an inquiry about Benno Neuburger to the Munich court. He pointed out that the old man had been in custody for months and his wife had no information about the reasons for his incarceration. She feared that she might soon be deported from Munich, as so many others had, without being able to see him again. Koenigsberger asked the authorities to consider the defendant's advanced age and crime-free life and permit him to join his wife on a transport instead of serving time, in case he was sentenced for a lighter crime.[30]

The Jewish lawyer could not know that Neuburger's fate lay in the hands of the People's Court in Berlin. On May 27, the Second Senate president appointed Berlin lawyer Dr. Heinz Bergmann as Benno's public defense counsel and revealed the charges to Neuburger. Three weeks later, Bergmann declared that he would respond to the accusations, but he never did. Benno was transferred from Munich to Berlin-Moabit prison to stand trial at the People's Court. The vice president of the German People's Court and head of its Second Senate, Karl Engert, served as the main judge for the trial. A Nazi party member since 1921, he presented his task as follows: "just as the Wehrmacht has to safeguard the external existence of the state, the People's Court has a similar obligation for inner security in collaboration with the Gestapo." Engert was an unforgiving judge. For resistance activities, he punished Germans younger than eighteen with the death penalty, which was not legal under the Nazis.[31]

Benno Neuburger's trial began on July 20 at 9 a.m. In addition to Engert and chamber judge (*Kammergerichtsrat*) Granzow, three Nazi party officials functioned as judges: Nazi party district office leader (*Gauamtsleiter*) Fischer, Nazi party Gau judge (*Gaurichter*) Kapeller, and Nazi party county leader (*Kreisleiter*) Plankensteiner. Dr. Meier represented the Reich main prosecutor. By this time, it must have been clear to Benno that he was facing capital punishment or at least life in prison. Engert asked Benno for his explanation of the alleged crimes. Fearless, Neuburger again boldly admitted that he had authored and mailed the postcards because he was embittered by the endless attacks of the Nazis against the Jewish people. His children had lost their jobs and left Germany. He was forced to move out of his apartment. Explaining his remark of "Murderer of 5,000,000" on postcard number 9, he pointed out that about 10 million Jews were living in Europe and half of them were in danger of eradication. He insisted, however, that he never intended to commit high treason. He had just been out of his mind. The court questioned this line of defense; supposedly, Neuburger could not claim inaccountability for his actions, since he had not shown any mental deficiency since his arrest. Dr. Meier requested the ultimate punishment, while the defense lawyer asked for a milder sentence. After a brief retreat, Engert announced the verdict of the People's Court: Benno Neuburger was "guilty of treason" and was to receive the death penalty. Furthermore, he had to pay for the costs of the trial. Engert adjourned the court session at 10:55 a.m.[32] Within a mere two hours, Benno's fate was sealed.

The judgment claimed that with the postcards, the accused initiated resistance against the person and the institution of the Führer, ultimately aiming to change its anti-Jewish policy. According to the People's Court, "enemy powers" would make every effort to weaken the confidence of the German people in their government in order to achieve the end goal: overthrow National Socialism. Hence, the defendant sought to defile the Führer's personality with shameless scoldings, aiming at the collapse of the German people and their authority during a fateful war. The court saw proof in the phrase "Hail the new God of 1933–1943" on the postcard from January 14, which suggested that Hitler, whom Benno sarcastically called the new God, would disappear in 1943. Thus, in the eyes of the People's Court, Benno Neuburger had prepared high treason by producing and distributing these writings, which went through many hands until they arrived at the Munich central post office and were turned over to the police. Benno and allegedly the entire Jewish population prepared for the removal of the Führer. For such a crime, the court saw only the death penalty as the appropriate punishment.[33]

The next morning, the police transferred Benno to the now notorious Plötzensee prison in Berlin, where many anti-Nazi resisters were cruelly murdered. Two weeks later, the Reich main prosecutor sent copies of the official judgment to the Reich minister of justice. The Reich ministry requested to expedite the punishment, assigned headman Hehr from Hanover to carry out the execution, and ordered the subsequent transfer of the corpse to the Anatomical Institute of Berlin University. In the meantime, the People's Court asked all involved institutions for reasons for a potential pardon. The director of the Munich-Stadelheim prison responded that Benno behaved well, but his work diligence was questionable. Nothing came to mind that would speak for clemency. The prison director in Berlin-Moabit outright refused to advocate for any act of mercy. He characterized Neuburger as a "stubborn Jew" who had no regrets. Purportedly, Neuburger had avowed in an impertinent way: "Since the state had already harassed me in the most flagrant way for the last ten years, the death penalty for me was a given anyway."[34]

On September 3, the Reich minister of justice, Otto Thierack, declared that, based on his authorization by Hitler, he was declining clemency to Benno Neuburger and ordering that justice should take its course. The People's Court scheduled the execution by guillotine at the Berlin-Plötzensee prison for September 18. The body would not be handed over to the family and no information about the procedure would be offered to the public. As an announcement of the death penalty, sixty posters were to be printed on bright red paper and—after a discussion—hung only in Munich, where Neuburger was from. The notorious president of the People's Court, Dr. Roland Freisler, signed a letter mandating that Vice President Engert, judge Granzow, and *Ministerialrat* Singer, who was an SS officer, needed to be on standby for potential appeals by the death row inmate.[35]

On the evening before the execution, a group of men, including prosecutor Wittmann and a civil servant from the Reich main prosecutor's office at the People's Court, a representative of the prison director, and the prison's doctor visited Neuburger's cell. At 8:18 p.m., Wittmann, responsible for the execution of the death penalty, verified the identity of the convict and explained to him that he represented the Reich main prosecutor. He read aloud the relevant parts from the People's Court's judgment and the Reich minister of justice's letter denying clemency. He then disclosed that the execution of the death sentence had been scheduled for the next morning at

4:48 a.m. Wittmann advised the prisoner to be prepared for his final hour and express last wishes to the prison guards. Benno appeared calm during the visit, albeit not totally, as the prosecutor noted.[36]

In his "last will," handwritten on prison letterhead and signed "Benno Israel Neuburger," Benno requested that his body "will be allowed to be laid to rest by the Jewish community in Berlin. [Jewish burial]" in the presence of a rabbi. He asked for "an inexpensive grave stone or a memorial slab to be mounted on the grave," which he wanted to pay for from his own bank account. The Jewish community in Munich should receive his last possessions, including his watch, and inform his wife. Benno begged that his "last wishes be fully granted."[37]

The next morning, while the city was still cloaked in darkness, prosecutor Wittmann, a justice official, and the prison representative Schmidt appeared in the execution chamber. Pale electrical light illuminated the front part of the room that was furnished with a table. On the black cloth-covered table, one could see a crucifix and two lit candles. A dark curtain hid the rear part of the execution chamber that housed the guillotine. Executioner Hehr, standing in front of the black fabric, reported that he and his assistants were ready to proceed. The prosecutor and the other two officials took their places behind the table. At 4:48 a.m., two prison guards brought Benno Neuburger in with his hands tied behind his back. They shut the door of the chamber. After the prosecutor, as the head of the execution, confirmed Benno's identity once again, he ordered the headman to proceed with the execution. One of Hehr's assistants opened the curtain revealing the guillotine. The prison guards handed Benno over to the executioner. Benno remained silent and mainly stayed calm, according to the record of the execution. He did not resist, when the executioner led him to the guillotine and untied his hands. Benno took off his shirt and lay down. Quickly, Hehr released the guillotine and, with a coarse noise, the cold blade cut off the head and ended the life of the seventy-one-year-old German-Jewish man. Only twenty-seven seconds had passed from the time Neuburger entered the execution chamber until the announcement of his death by the henchman. On the same day, at least a dozen other rebellious Germans, including one woman, lost their lives in Plötzensee.[38]

The cruel procedure was not the end of Benno Neuburger's story. After his death, the German state requested an execution fee of 300 Reichsmarks. This money plus the full trial costs—fees for the defense lawyers, the 167 days of imprisonment (1.5 Reichsmarks per day), his last wish (2.15 Reichsmarks), and the printing and distribution of the posters that would publicly announce his execution—accumulated to the remarkable amount of 1,065.55 Reichsmarks owed by the survivors of the Neuburger family. In addition, bright red posters distributed by the German Municipal Advertisement Agency (*Deutsche Städtereklame*) announced Neuburger's death penalty and execution at public places everywhere in Munich. The German press also published a short notice about the execution, arguing that Neuburger had denigrated Hitler and the government in the most horrible way.[39]

The very last letter Benno had written was not sent to either his wife or his children. Before his execution, Benno was informed that Anna had been deported. Because his children lived in an enemy country, his only chance to address his family was to write to his niece and the remainder of the family in Munich. The letter read, "Dear relatives, Hope that you dear Ilse and Hermann are healthy and your father in Theresienstadt is well. Today I want to tell you that tomorrow I will not be on this earth anymore, because I will be executed on account of my mistakes—this I have never believed, but it cannot be changed. . . . You or some of yours will make that known to my wife, if that is possible, because it may once again be possible to hear from Jews who were evacuated into foreign countries. I greet you All heartfully and wish that you All have a Good Future and you keep me in your memory. . . . Uncle Benno."[40]

Anna never learned about Benno's tragic fate. A few days after her husband's trial, she sent a last postcard to her family in Munich about her upcoming "evacuation" and told them it was terrible leaving alone. She mentioned a letter from Benno but said, "Don't ask what he wrote." The very same day, on July 23, the Gestapo forcibly relocated Anna and fifty other Jews from camp Milbertshofen to Theresienstadt. In September, one day after the henchman had murdered Benno in Berlin, Anna and other elderly German Jews left the ghetto in the first of several transports to the extermination camp Treblinka, where all traces of her were lost.[41]

Other Stories of Written Protest Against the Persecution

Benno Neuburger's scolding of Hitler with postcards is a bold example of written protest, but distributing anonymous leaflets and postcards was rather rare in the Third Reich. Other forms of such protest were more widespread, such as criticizing the Nazi persecution of the Jews in letters and more often by penning petitions.

Countless petitions authored by Jewish individuals gather dust on shelves in archives across Germany. Petitions were a legitimate form to air griev-ances in Nazi Germany, even for Jews. For them, it was the only political means left after losing their civil rights. Thousands of Jewish men and women sent such petitions to local, regional, or ministry officials; to Hitler and other high-ranking Nazi functionaries; and sometimes to private com-panies and organizations. With these entreaties, they criticized Nazi laws, violent attacks, racial classification, and local segregation. They reclaimed their rights as workers, citizens, and Germans.[42]

In 1933, Frieda F. appealed to President von Hindenburg to stop "the public incitement to pogroms and violent attacks on Jews." And in 1934, Julius Fromm, a well-known entrepreneur in Berlin, successfully protested in a petition to the police president against the revocation of his citizenship. He insisted on his Germanness and underlined that he had more than ful-filled his duty to his country. With their petitions, Jews targeted discrimina-tory national laws as well as local measures; some criticized violent attacks against their businesses.[43]

From May through July 1935, Storm Troopers, Hitler Youth, and other Berliners targeted Jewish stores in several districts of the German capital, defacing store windows and sidewalks in front of shops with humiliating slogans and physically attacking Jews and foreigners. Max Loewy sent a pe-tition on July 29, 1935, to the president of the Berlin Police, his third letter in a week, and complained about frequent attacks by three young SA men leading a group of teenagers. They had entered his patisserie, "Hansa," in Berlin-Tiergarten six times and violently drove out his customers, demol-ished interior furnishings, and vandalized the front yard. Despite Loewy's repeated requests, the police did not protect his business. According to his appeal, the attacks not only ruined his Jewish family, they also harmed his employees, his landlord, the suppliers—even the tax office, since he would be unable to pay his taxes. Finally, he requested that the police president prevent further attacks, referring to the police chief's own decree of July 27 prohibiting any individual actions against Jews.[44]

Petitioning became a common practice over the next years. Even during the war, Jews continued sending their grievances in the form of entreaties to various authorities. In January 1940, the Munich police rejected ten petitions from Jews, who requested exclusion from the discriminatory marking of their ration cards and the obligation to buy only in stores permitted for Jews. After the beginning of the war, only twelve such grocery shops had been assigned for 4,500 Jews in the Bavarian capital. In Vienna, many Jews complained in letters to the Reich commissar and Nazi Gauleiter Josef Bürckel about the effects of radicalized persecution. They contested prohibitions on visiting public parks, restrictions regarding food provision, and relocations from certain areas. Especially numerous were the petitions challenging the eviction from their homes. In March 1940, for example, Adolf Fleischmann protested in a petition to the Vienna Gauleiter his eviction from the rental apartment where he had lived for twenty-five years. Because petitions even from Jews were an accepted medium for airing grievances, they did not face consequences. By contrast, the Gestapo did incarcerate Käthe Kern in Vienna on September 17, 1940, because she commented in a private letter on the evictions. She wrote that the Gestapo forced the eviction notice upon those Jews, who disobeyed the order of the city housing office. She spent two weeks in jail.[45]

As with Benno Neuburger's postcards, the Nazi state treated critical comments in regular mail as treacherous acts aimed at the erosion of the trust of the German people in the Nazi state. Most of them were discovered through Nazi authorities' surveillance of private letters, which blurred the lines between public and private spaces. Emilie Kohn, who lived in Munich and lost her livelihood—her café—wrote a letter to her children in December 1933 describing the situation of the Jews in Germany as unbearable. For her remarks, she was punished by the Special Court in Munich with two months in jail. Josef Löwy sent letters from Munich to France in December 1935 in which he complained about unemployment and poverty in Germany and how all doors were shut. Interestingly, when the Gestapo discovered and investigated the issue, the prosecutor conceived it as a characterization and not an insult and decided not to proceed with an indictment.[46]

Fear of censorship, however, meant that critical comments were rare. Not many Jews had the courage to write openly, although in private they would severely criticize the way the Nazi state treated German Jews. Throughout the second half of the 1930s, Paul Malch, a leather product merchant from Düsseldorf, exchanged hundreds of letters with his son, who had emigrated to the United States. None of those letters sent from Germany contained the slightest critique of the Hitler government and the Nazi persecution. Yet, in 1937, Malch used two business trips to Venlo in the Netherlands, which was close to his hometown, to send letters full of fierce invectives to his son. In one of them, Malch condemned the opening of the propaganda exhibition "The Eternal Jew" in November 1937 and scolded Nazi leaders. He wrote: "The German Reich is the organizer of the show! Hence, this is quite an official exposition. The content is an insult, offense, derision, and mortification of the German Jews and the Jews of the world. A planned protest of German rabbis was immediately prevented by threatening them with concentration camp in case there would be protest inside Germany, with prison in case protest would come from abroad. . . . This malignant blackguard and mudslinger Streicher, the companion of the Führer. . . . Only Hitler could and would defile defenseless people!"[47]

Hence, the neutral apolitical tone and the absence of criticism in so many letters mailed from Nazi Germany did not result from a lack of concern, critique, or opposition, but rather from a widespread fear of censorship and punishment. There are some exceptions, though. During the summer of 1938, Paul Wahle, thirty-three, penned letters from Munich to his lover, often referring to Germany as a dictatorship and underlining that his situation as a Jew meant being a disenfranchised person and second-class citizen. Wahle wrote that he hoped for the looming war to be the end of the "system." Since his lover was a non-Jewish woman, he was punished with three years in prison for "race defilement" and, in a separate trial, sentenced to an additional ten months under the Treacherous Attacks Law.[48]

As time went on, more and more Jews became desperate. They started to express criticism in letters to relatives abroad, even though they were aware of censorship. In a letter dated December 1938, a seventy-eight-year-old, Therese Wassermann, complained to her son Willy, who had emigrated to Amsterdam in 1933, about the increasing attacks on Jewish property. She denounced the violence during the November pogrom, after she had heard from her former housemaid that Jews were forced to march through the town Bautzen, Saxony, with signs around their necks marked with the word "Jew." Although the envelope had no return address, the letter was traced back to her. When Wassermann stood by her words during the Gestapo interrogation, ironically, the prosecution dropped the case in April 1939 because it could not prove that she had deliberately lied.[49]

At the end of 1939, in a letter to Emmy Rabow in Shanghai, sixty-two-year-old Paul Cohn complained that the labor office had sent 150 Jewish women to work as forced laborers in potato fields outside Berlin. Describing his time as a forced laborer at the potato harvest, he wrote, "The work was terribly hard; the biggest disgrace was that these dogs did not give us any dime, just room and board. The food was bad, but with us Jews they can do it." Since he called the labor officials "dogs," he was investigated for an offense against the Treacherous Attacks Law. Unexpectedly, the prosecutor dropped the case and recommended that the labor office file a complaint of libel, although that did not happen.[50]

During the war, Jews increasingly complained about new anti-Jewish measures. In March 1941, the Special Court in Berlin sentenced Walter Friedmann, a doctor of law, under the Treacherous Attacks Law to four months in prison. Writing to Georg Lilienthal in Sweden, Friedmann criticized the legal system in Nazi Germany and complained about the food restriction for Jews. Jakob Mann, thirty-seven, an unmarried disability pensionist, had worked as an insurance clerk but in 1934 retired with benefits because of his 75 percent disability stemming from a battlefield injury in the war of 1914–1918. Since 1938, Mann had sent more than sixty letters to his lover Elsa König, who had emigrated to England, via his cousin in Switzerland. He wrote three of the letters in cipher using lemon as ink. The censorship office in Frankfurt intercepted one of them in December 1939, in which Mann complained about the special ration cards for Jews that limited the amount of food they were permitted to purchase, which was less than what non-Jews received during the war. He wrote that he expected any change to come only from outside Germany, but that he was sure "his soff"—that is, Hitler's end (*sof*, in Hebrew, means end)—was coming eventually. This thought provided Mann with the strength and courage to live through this ordeal, he wrote to his lover. Ironically, a few days after he was detained for treacherous attacks against the state, the same state awarded him the honorary cross for battlefield veterans. Indicted by the Special Court in 1940, Mann defended himself against the accusations by claiming that what he said was true, and by "his soff," he did not mean Hitler's end, but the end of the war. The judges at the Special Court did not believe him and punished him with eight months in prison.[51]

Rarer even than critical comments in private letter exchanges were written public displays as well as anonymous letters, postcards, and leaflets protesting acts of persecution. Some Jewish individuals combined such written protest with a demonstration of their Germanness. In the spring of 1933, Heinrich and Erich Leyens printed a poster addressing Hitler. While denouncing the Nazi boycott of their shop, they emphasized their own patriotic contributions as German soldiers in the World War as well as those of twelve thousand Jews who had given their lives for Germany.[52] When the police failed to stop the organized summer riots in Berlin for weeks, anonymous protest flyers started popping up in mailboxes of businesses. On July 17, 1935, the manager of the Scherl publishing house's Friedrichstrasse branch in Berlin's city center brought a business-card-sized flyer to the police. The message read: "Germany is a cultural disgrace today. I am a German Jew and loyal to the emperor. Indeed, the Germans should expel the foreigner Hitler. My father and I were born in Hamburg. I fought as a private in the world war. Down with HITLER."[53] Ironically, the protest bore a pseudonym signature of King Cohn. Cohn, a common Jewish family name, traditionally was used in German anti-Semitic poems or songs.

Various administrative Nazi reports for July and August of 1935 stressed the Jews' self-confidence and their impudent attitude. In September, the Nazi government introduced the infamous Nuremberg Laws, which provided the legal foundation for the segregation of the Jews, stripped them of their political rights, forbade them to marry non-Jews, prohibited their using non-Jewish housekeepers, and banned Jews from flying the Nazi flag or displaying the colors of the German Reich. While a number of German Jews chose to respond with petitions, some drafted and distributed protest flyers, such as those found in Berlin in September and December 1935. One flyer called on all Jewish women to demonstrate their disapproval by dismissing their non-Jewish domestic help before the racist laws could take effect. Another flyer detailed the Jewish contributions to German historical achievements.[54]

During the next two years, German Jews did not stop protesting anonymously against anti-Jewish measures introduced by the Nazi government or by local administrations. In January 1936, the Gestapo arrested Sally Baum, a merchant from Wanne-Eickel, for distributing leaflets. Baum had been arrested once before for insulting a local Nazi party leader in September 1935. A court sentenced him to pay a hefty fine of 1,500 Reichsmarks because the leaflets could potentially disturb the public order. In Berlin-Prenzlauer Berg, the police reported that a person had dropped leaflets with "Jewish agitation" at private apartment doors. The forty-nine-year-old Alfred M. from Mühlheim wrote defamatory letters to the Nazi government and frequently threw flyers signed "We Jews" from a train near Düsseldorf. The flyers called Hitler "the demon of Germany." The Gestapo, upon taking him into custody, discovered that in 1933, after the SA had beaten him and painted anti-Jewish slogans at his home, he had sent letters to Göring protesting his treatment.[55]

Siegfried Heumann, fifty-six, had served in the same regiment as Hitler during the earlier war. He had written various patriotic war songs, such as "The Bavarian Lions!" He even wrote the "The Old Banners" in Bavarian dialect, emphasizing his pride in "being a German in Bavaria land." As a national conservative living in Munich, he became more and more upset with the Nazi oppression of the Jews. Starting in spring 1935, Heumann mailed anonymous letters to twenty high-ranking army officers in Munich. The envelopes contained copies of the Jewish war veterans' newspaper, *The Shield*, and, in some cases, handwritten notes like "Commemorate the Jewish Front Soldiers." His letter in June 1936 to Generalmajor Otto Tscherning enclosed a handwritten note that read, "Léon Blum, the Frenchman a[nd]

Jew, respects and honors Adolf Hitler as a front-line soldier. Adolf Hitler despises, dishonors, humiliates Jewish front-line soldiers!" In the margin, he added, "German culture." Tscherning and another officer handed the letters over to the police. After the Gestapo identified Heumann's handwriting and arrested him, he explained that he felt offended by the constant stream of press articles attacking Jews. On trial in February 1937, he argued that as a war veteran he felt particularily humiliated. Several defense witnesses testified to his patriotism and war service. Notwithstanding his honorary record, the Special Court in Munich sentenced him to three months in jail under the Treacherous Attacks Law for his critique of Hitler.[56]

During the November pogrom in 1938, Jews used pen and paper to document the crimes. In Berlin, Jews wrote down the names and addresses of destroyed Jewish stores. Under the pretext of activities hostile to the German state, the police arrested Heinz Goldstandt, Alfred Petersdorff, Herbert Fuchs, and Kurt Löwenthal and transferred them to the Gestapo. Edith Wolff, who later formed her own resistance group, mailed out postcards calling National Socialism the biggest cultural outrage, signed "The Eternal Jew." In Hamburg, Walter G. wrote, copied, and distributed by mail a fourteen-page protest letter with the title "J'accuse," predicting the doom of 500,000 Jews.[57] After the pogrom, in one of its daily reports, the Vienna Gestapo said it had received a number of anonymous letters disparaging "with genuine Jewish impudence the Führer and the party." One such letter read, "Dear sweet Gestapo. We will soon beat your ass. Until the German mutt race will arrive in our ghetto alley, Hosanna to our Greenshpan, the hero boy from Paris. Where now the murder frenzy unfolds, there you will soon come into a big fuss. Gun down the dog, the Hitler!"[58]

The traumatic experience of the violent pogrom led many Jews to commit suicide. Some proudly donned their decorations from the World War before taking their own lives, while others left protest notes to be discovered by neighbors or the police; as Hedwig Jastrow, seventy-six, wrote in her last letter, "I am leaving life as someone whose family has had German citizenship for 100 years and has always remained loyal to Germany. I have taught German children for 43 years and have helped them through all their trials and tribulations. I have done charity work for the German *Volk* for even longer, both in times of war and times of peace. I don't want to live without a Fatherland, without a homeland, without an apartment, without citizenship rights, ostracized and reviled."[59]

More Jews commited suicide after the announcement of the deportations in 1941. On January 15, 1941, the university professor and medical doctor Heinrich Joseph commited suicide with his wife Edith and his mother-in-law Charlotte Müller in their Vienna apartment. The police found a letter in which he called out the Nazi persecution of the Jews and the upcoming "relocation" as reasons for the family suicide. Martha W., a sixty-year-old homemaker in Rathenow, Brandenburg, took her own life when she was ordered to appear at a police station in January 1943. She was being investigated for sending out letters calling Hitler a crook and a gangster.[60]

Anonymous protests did not cease during the war, either. In 1941, the Vienna Gestapo discovered that Emil Deutsch had not only listened to foreign broadcasts, which was prohibited for every German during the war under the new radio crimes law, but had mailed defamatory letters to an anti-Semitic Nazi store owner between September 1940 and April 1941. In almost a dozen of these anonymous letters, Deutsch had criticized the persecution of the Jews and the recent mass deportations to Nazi-occupied Poland. He insisted that the thefts during the pogrom would not be allowed to be repeated. He also enclosed propaganda photographs. These images were collectors' items used as advertisements for an Austrian cigarette company. He wrote invidious comments on the backs calling Hitler and the Nazis "bandits" and "plunderers." On the back of a Hitler group photograph was written: "This somebody wants to mess with Churchill" and "This image best characterizes this criminal riff-raff." Deutsch received an extra harsh sentence of seven years in prison for "radio crimes" under the 1939 law and "treacherous attacks" under the 1934 law.[61]

Even from prison, Jews sent anonymous messages. In November 1939, the Special Court in Berlin had sentenced the former tailor Alfred Lewithan to nine months in jail for public comments "harming the German state." However, the harsh sentence did not silence him. While preparing Neckermann mail order catalogues to be sent out from the jail, Lewithan put letters in some of the packages. These contained negative comments about Hitler and his cronies. In addition, on some of the catalogue pages he wrote bitter complaints about recently introduced food and clothing restrictions for Jews. On other

Emil Deutsch's handwritten comments on the back of a propaganda photograph of Hitler and other Nazi party members (cigarette album collector item), circa Spring 1941. (Vienna City and State Archive, Sondergericht, SHv Strafakten, A1: 6002/47, fol. 1210)

pages, he hinted that a big change was coming, and soldiers would fight for the reestablishment of the monarchy. It all culminated in the sentence: "Because we persecuted the Jews, we are doomed. This was wrong!!!" Two mail order catalogue subscribers from Dresden reported the hidden messages, and the Gestapo identified Lewithan as the author. On January 27, 1941, the Special Court in Berlin sentenced him as a frequent offender under the Treacherous Attacks Law to five years in prison. Long before his sentence ended, on June 13, 1942, the Gestapo deported Lewithan to the occupied East; a week earlier, his wife Hildegard was also deported from prison but to a different extermination site. Alfred Lewithan died in Majdanek.[62]

These stories show that German and Austrian Jews of all ages and genders protested in writing against the Nazi persecution. Their actions ranged from distributing anonymous leaflets to leaving suicide notes. They also wrote critiques in letters to family and petitions to Nazi authorities. Jews disparaged the Nazi leadership and their policies, individual laws, and local anti-Jewish restrictions.

Although many Jews wrote entreaties against anti-Semitic measures, critical remarks in private letters were rarer because of fear of interception. In both cases, Jewish men and women contested anti-Jewish policies. However, although countless authors of critical petitions, who insisted on their Germanness and their contributions to the fatherland, received responses from local and central Nazi institutions, the Gestapo arrested the authors of private letters, and courts punished them with jail time for very similar comments. Despite many letters to friends and families in Germany or abroad that were intercepted, there were presumably volumes of messages that did reach their intended recipients and provided hope, community, and solace by sharing dissent and criticism.

Many undiscovered writings might be lost, while others wait to be detected in private collections and state archives. Among the many protests penned by "impudent Jews" between 1933 and 1945, Benno Neuburger's postcards stand out not only because of their boldness emanating from his anger and courage, but because of his chilling foresight when he called Hitler the murderer of five million Jews.

FIVE

Acting in Physical Self-Defense

Daisy Gronowski in Urfeld and Others

On November 10, 1938, the assembly bell rang in the main camp building in the small German village of Urfeld between Bonn and Cologne at the Rhine River. In the camp, Jewish teenagers were getting agricultural training to prepare them for their future emigration to Palestine. That day, the bell sounded different, more alarming than usual. Daisy Gronowski, a sixteen-year-old with brown eyes and reddish-brown hair, wondered why they were being summoned.[1]

When she came down the stairs, she stopped abruptly: "And here they were. They had some sort of sticks in their hands, like clubs. They had guns. And they were not in uniforms." During Kristallnacht in some places members of the Sturmabteilung did not wear uniforms, since they were supposed to be reflecting the outrage of the people. The "hoodlums," as she called them, started smashing things. They kicked over the stove and broke every chair, every table, everything inside the building. Then they formed two rows and made the young boys, and even girls, run between them; as they did, the Storm Troopers on both sides struck them with clubs. "The boys, they were bleeding," Daisy remembered; and when her turn came, she stubbornly decided: "Hell, I am not gonna run."[2]

Daisy Gronowski was born in Königsberg, the capital of East Prussia, on March 6, 1921. Her father, Bruno Gronowski, earned a living as a merchant and manufacturer. The family owned several businesses. One of the properties was a bed and breakfast in a small spa town by the Baltic Sea, where the family would often vacation. For his brave fighting in the World War, Bruno Gronowski had earned two Iron Crosses, first and second degree. Daisy's mother Ellen, née Philipp, was an actress. Inez, Daisy's younger sister by four years, completed the family. Although they belonged to a conservative temple, the family only observed the high holidays. As Daisy pointed out in retrospect, "We were Germans [first] and Jews next."[3]

When Daisy turned five, the family moved to Berlin. Her mother could not stand the provincial atmosphere in Königsberg, and not only because she had grown up in the German capital. As an aspiring actress, she had been used to an independent cosmopolitan life. Living in the East Prussian house with her father-in-law, a very controlling patriarch, had been challenging for Ellen. After the move to Berlin, Daisy followed in her mother's footsteps and became a child actress. She befriended Marlene Dietrich's daughter, who went to the same school. Sometimes they even carpooled with their respective chauffeurs. The Gronowski family lived a good life in Berlin. In addition to their home in the capital, they owned a summer cottage in the Spreewald, two hours southeast of Berlin. On weekends, they would go by car and visit this area and its picturesque canals.[4]

Her parents enrolled Daisy at a public elementary school in Berlin-Charlottenburg, between Savignyplatz and Kurfürstendamm, in April 1927. The impressive five-story building, designed by the architect Paul Bratring in 1888, featured red bricks and black tiles. Today the school is named after the artist Joan Miró and offers a German-Spanish bilingual education. Daisy was supposed to attend this school for primary and secondary education until eighth grade.[5]

However, times changed dramatically in 1933. With the "big boycott" on April 1, things started to go bad for many Jews, as Daisy remembered. Although she later recalled "being kicked out" of her school, there are no records of Berlin schools expelling Jewish pupils that early. Rather, it seems her parents reacted to an increasingly hostile and racist environment and transferred Daisy to another public school in the fall. Other concerned Jewish parents also removed their children from the same school for the same reason in the same year.[6]

In addition to parents reacting to racist attitudes of Nazi teachers and administrators by enrolling their children at public schools that were more protective or at Jewish private schools, Jewish students left their public schools in Germany for another reason: many families emigrated. In 1933 alone, 13,000 Jews fled from Berlin to other countries. That same year, 1,650 of 6,264 Jewish students left Berlin elementary schools (*Volksschulen*). The total number of Jewish students in all Berlin public schools decreased from 12,746 to 7,696. In 1934, Jews were still eligible for reduced school fees if they were from needy families. Over the following years, Berlin introduced more than eighty anti-Jewish restrictions affecting education, welfare, and businesses. In 1938, only 1,346 Jews still studied at Berlin public schools, while the number of students in Jewish private schools had more than tripled since 1933. Right after the pogrom in November 1938, Berlin forbade Jews to attend public schools. Two weeks later, the Reich Ministry of Education expelled Jewish pupils from public schools across Nazi Germany.[7]

Daisy's new school was located in a different direction, but still only about a twelve-minute walk away. The Fürstin-Bismarck-Schule, which Daisy started to attend in fifth grade in 1933, had been established as the first Berlin High School for Girls in 1857. The school building, less than twenty years old, featured modern classrooms and even had labs to teach natural sciences for more than a thousand female students. The Jewish principal, Dr. Robert Burg, pursued a reform agenda. During the first Nazi years, the school still provided a protective environment, according to the recollections of a number of Jewish survivors.[8] By contrast, the vocational school at which Daisy enrolled after finishing eighth grade, in March 1936, seemed more like a place of Nazi indoctrination. Only two Jews attended that school, learning the "female craft" of sewing, among other things. This experience, along with the increasing number of local and national restrictions, impacted Daisy's daily life. It felt like constant harassment.[9]

The Gronowski family's synagogue was led by Rabbi Dr. Joachim Prinz. Daisy "loved that man."[10] So did many other teenagers, especially girls. In his early thirties, he seemed unusually young, liberal, and unconventional for a rabbi. He enjoyed Berlin's social and cultural life, including parties. Teenagers admired him for his informal attitude, his charisma, and his courage, while some of the elderly generation made his life difficult. As some other rabbis did in synagogues throughout Nazi Germany, Prinz openly opposed Nazi politics in sermons and prayers, despite Gestapo agents sitting in the audience and listening. Rabbi Prinz even gave critical talks in public, describing the dramatic impact of the widespread discrimination against the Jewish population in Nazi Germany: "For us, outside is the ghetto. In the marketplaces, on the country roads, in the restaurants, the ghetto is everywhere. It has an emblem. The emblem means: neighbourless. . . . We would not find it all so painful if we did not have the feeling that we once *did have* neighbors." A Jewish newspaper published his chilling assessment under the headline "Attempt of a first analysis. Ghetto 1935."[11]

Prinz urged the German Jews to leave the country. Looking back later, he said, "I was doing the most outrageous things, violating every law of the land and dancing on a volcano." The Gestapo arrested and interrogated him several times before finally forcing him and his family to leave Germany in 1937. They immigrated to the United States, where Prinz later became president of the American Jewish Congress and strongly supported the civil rights movement. Drawing on his experience with the persecution of the Jews in Nazi Germany, he gave moving remarks at the Lincoln Memorial right before Dr. Martin Luther King Jr. made his historic "I have a dream" speech in 1963.[12]

The fearless Berlin rabbi was more than just talk. An outspoken Zionist, he aimed at protecting his brethren. At the age of eleven, Daisy joined Hashomer Hatzair, a Zionist youth group. One day, she and twenty other group members visited Rabbi Prinz in his synagogue during the holiday Simchat Torah. Suddenly, a gang of Nazis entered the building and raised clubs to smash things. Although he was not a tall man, as Daisy observed, Prinz calmly approached them: "Gentlemen, is there anything at all that I can do for you?" His confident attitude made the young Nazis lower their sticks and back out. Undoubtedly, Prinz's courage left a mark on Daisy. During the mid-1930s, she spent much time with her Hashomer Hatzair group. To defend themselves, the older teenagers received jiu-jitsu training and learned how to use knives, practiced their strokes with sandbags, and had target practice with guns in a basement. The youth group leader even provided them with brass knuckles to carry on them all the time.[13]

Two members of a Hashomer Hatzair group from Berlin during an excursion, 1935–1938. (United States Holocaust Memorial Museum, Photograph 22211, courtesy of Marion House)

The leftist Zionist youth group leaders also taught the Jewish adolescents to adopt fake identities and mimic Nazi rhetoric and attitudes. The Berlin group was "somehow connected to the Communist party," according to Daisy. In her retrospective view, the Communists were the only ones resisting the Nazis. In order to gather information for the underground, Daisy attended Nazi youth meetings disguised in a stolen Hitler Youth uniform that she had been provided with by their anonymous contacts: "Hell, my idea was: Ya, perhaps they're gonna get me, perhaps they even going to kill me. But, I am not gonna sit down and wait and be shaken with fear."[14] Daisy was not alone. Several thousand German Jewish men and women participated in such organized underground activities against the Third Reich. By doing so, they faced a doubled risk of severe punishment as both racial and political enemies of the Nazi state. Many lost their lives. Those courageous Jews pursued two goals at once: to end the dictatorship and to abolish anti-Jewish persecution.[15]

Soon, Daisy could not tolerate the situation in Nazi Germany any longer and decided to leave her home country. To be prepared, she enrolled at a Jewish agricultural training camp in Urfeld, most likely in the spring of 1938 when she was seventeen. Daisy believed that this was her only way out: "Without money, without connections. . . . I had to try anything." At this point, according to Daisy, the Nazi state had confiscated all the family's money, as well as two paintings, furs, jewelry, and furniture. Although it is unclear when and how exactly the Gronowskis lost all their possessions, they found themselves depending on the support of the Jewish community in Berlin.[16]

Since the 1920s, Jewish organizations had developed vocational training programs. In reaction to Nazi persecution, they vastly expanded them, particularly so-called "re-training" in agriculture to teach farming, cattle breeding, and gardening. The *Hachscharah* (Hebrew for preparation) was aimed at training young Jews for emigration. Many countries where Jews hoped to emigrate—Palestine as the prime destination for most Zionists, but also Latin America—were more receptive to Jewish migrants with agricultural qualifications. The reactions to the training camp expansion were mixed in Germany. When the Zionist organization Hechaluz established the agricultural camp in Urfeld, the local officer of the Nazi-controlled German Labor

Front panicked, because of the potential influx of Jews into the little hamlet, and sought advice. However, SS officials did not thwart the plans because such training sites supported their interest in getting Jews out of Germany, and as a result they only recommended that local authorities in Urfeld prohibit the Jewish teenagers from leaving the camp in groups.[17]

When Daisy arrived, approximately sixty Jews resided at Urfeld camp. The teenagers worked on a farm owned by a German who was opposed to the Nazis. For a while, the boys and girls, mostly between fifteen and seventeen years old, lived there happily, according to Daisy. In their leisure time, they went swimming in the Rhine or went boating across the river. They visited nearby cloisters, where the monks made wine and the youngsters tried "this awful tasting stuff." Nevertheless, soon she felt stuck in the camp. She could not imagine the life in Palestine she was preparing for. Yet, Daisy was hesitant to leave for good. By writing letters, she kept in contact with her family in Berlin. One time, she was able to travel back home for vacation. Daisy knew that once she left Germany, she would not see her parents for a long time. She was very concerned about how life was changing for them.[18]

On November 10, 1938, the teenagers in the camp heard the news about violent incidents in Cologne and Bonn, two cities ten and eighteen kilometers away from Urfeld. This was a nationwide Nazi pogrom against the German Jews, and soon a gang of men in civilian clothes raided the camp facilities, smashing the furnishings and beating up the boys. When Daisy's turn came to run between the two lines of violent men with clubs, she told herself: "Hell, I am not gonna run. I am gonna walk . . . Here, I am. . . . 5 foot nothing. . . . And, I am a skinny little girl. And, all of the sudden . . . I remember gettin' one on the back. And that was it." Interviewed in 1995, she touched her right shoulder with her left hand and grimaced, vividly remembering how it had hurt. But it didn't stop her. "I just walked slowly through, looking at all of them. Now, here, big tough guys. You want to hit a little girl? What can I do about it."[19]

At the end of the gauntlet, one of the attackers waited for her. He approached Daisy and pointed her to another side of the room. He grabbed her right hand and started to saw into it with a rusty pocketknife. She twisted her body to see what she could do and then started fighting. She kicked his legs. She was tiny, but he was not very big either. And he was young, too. After some wrestling, she used "a little trick" that she had learned back during the Hashomer Hatzair training in Berlin. She moved forward and pushed her head hard into his stomach. Taking advantage of the assailant's surprise, she twisted the knife out of his hand and stabbed him.[20]

Blood soaked out of the wound. Although her attacker lost consciousness, he was not dead. Fortunately, the rest of the intruders did not notice the incident; they were still busy beating some of the Jewish boys at the other end of the lobby. A couple of Daisy's friends, however, saw it and came to help. They dragged the unconscious intruder to the side and hid him under a sofa, which was still intact despite the earlier vandalism. At this moment in her interview, after so many years, Daisy breathed a heavy sigh of relief: "Anyway, this is when we took off!" She and some of the teenagers ran out of the house and into the fields. The perpetrators tried to catch the group but gave up after a while.[21]

In many other camps, Jewish teenagers did not get so lucky. Gestapo and Storm Troopers arrested male trainers and trainees. The Gross-Breesen camp in Silesia was destroyed and everyone over eighteen was taken to a concentration camp. After demolishing a camp building in Bomsdorf, a Storm Trooper asked for the whereabouts of two of the forty trainees. When one teenager was too scared to respond, the enraged attacker shot the boy in the head. During the next days, the Reich Representation of the Jews in Germany petitioned the Gestapo headquarters to release the teachers, "because of their activities to promote emigration." At the end of November, the SS freed all "leaders of the retraining camps," as well as trainees, from the concentration camps.[22] In Urfeld, the intruders left the camp partly destroyed, and training had to be suspended. Some camps closed temporarily; others had to be put up for sale. Of the twenty-nine Jewish retraining camps existing before the pogrom, only twenty sites with 1,190 training slots reopened. Later, during the war, such places were only permitted to exist when trainees could be redeployed for compulsory labor at any time. The Hachscharah camp in Urfeld ceased to exist in October 1939.[23]

After Daisy and her friends escaped the raid of their camp, they went to the farm where they used to work. The owner invited them to hide in his cellar, and to protect the Jewish teens, he sent his sons with two German shepherds to patrol the property. When the Nazi gang approached, the dogs set out to attack them and they withdrew. Daisy and the other teenagers stayed at the farmer's house overnight; however, the perpetrators returned the next morning and forced the farmer to give them up. They were marched through Urfeld several times. The unusual sight made some villagers angry. This was a Catholic area, after all. As Daisy described it, some farmers emerged from their houses with pitchforks and shovels: "Leave 'em alone. They're just kids!" The Nazis shouted back: "We're taking them to Palestine." Clubs versus pitchforks, they fought off the villagers. The Nazis marched the teenagers to the outskirts of Bonn and locked them up in an abandoned cold and dirty building full of rats and bats.[24]

The teenagers tried everything to get out. They were able to remove some loose bricks and flee through the wall opening. With nowhere else to go, they decided to march back to Urfeld. When they found their camp trashed, their only hope was getting "to the cloisters." Four of them decided to cross the Rhine River. "You haven't lived until you have gotten in November into ice-cold water in Germany with all your clothes on," Daisy remembered, laughing. The four clung to a boat moving slowly through the freezing water. After their arrival at the other side of the river, the shivering boys went to a monastery, and the girls approached a nearby women's cloister. When they rang the doorbell, the mother superior looked at them and said, "Well, get them in." Daisy would never forget that moment. The nuns helped them out of their cold and wet clothes. They even treated the cut on Daisy's hand, which she had frequently sucked on during the two-day odyssey, to avoid infection from the rusty knife. Yet even though they were safe, there was a downside. Hiding in the cloister meant the Jewish girls had to learn the Catholic rituals. For Daisy, this felt "boring as anything, but we learned it. We are very grateful to them. They were good to us."[25]

After several weeks, the Jewish girls thought their stay was getting too dangerous for the nuns. But where could they go? The group decided to go back to the training camp in Urfeld. But they were captured. This time, the Nazis brought them to a "holdover-camp" in Euskirchen, more than thirty kilometers from Urfeld. In a big hall, everyone slept on the floor with some blankets. The camp, secured with barbed wire, had no bathrooms. Because of the unsanitary conditions, Daisy contracted lice and some type of typhoid, as did many inmates. She developed a high fever and lost hair and weight. Somehow, all but one of the inmates survived the disease. After her recovery, Daisy secretly planned another escape with some camp inmates. One night, they lifted up the rusty barbed wire and crawled underneath it. In spite of their ragged appearances, they found a ride to Cologne. At the Jewish Community, an official told Daisy that they could not sleep there, but she snapped, "the hell I can't." Her obstinacy paid off; they were allowed to stay. An official told them that Great Britain was offering visas for "people to work on the land." Daisy immediately enlisted. As desperate as she was, she would have signed up "to clean the streets of London with a toothbrush."[26]

Only two members of the group received the necessary papers from England, but luckily, Daisy was one of them. She and the other teen had to wait two long days for their passports. When they arrived, they were only valid for twelve hours, but the Jewish community had already purchased travel tickets. A spelling error on her papers meant her girlfriend had to stay. With a Jewish boy who replaced her friend, Daisy went to the train station. She carried nothing with her on this journey into the unknown, literally leaving everything behind.[27]

After the train had left Cologne, something felt wrong. Daisy had "this funny instinct." Even though some soldiers were drinking outside her compartment at the end of the train, she opened the door, snuck past them, and took her companion to the second-class car, and then to first class. In one of the compartments, a kind-looking elderly man with glasses was sitting alone reading a newspaper. It must have been perfectly obvious that Daisy and her friend did not have first-class tickets. Nonetheless, she entered and greeted the man in a friendly manner; he smiled back but did not respond. Suddenly, the train stopped. It was the German border, and the first-class car came to a halt in Dutch territory. German police passed outside the window, and when Daisy accidentally locked eyes with the officers, they smiled and turned around. A short while later, they opened the compartment door. Suddenly, the elderly man stood up, placed himself in front of Daisy and her friend, and said with authority, "Just a moment, gentlemen, not so fast."[28]

Daisy remembers that he introduced himself as the Swiss ambassador to Germany. However, during and after the war, the Swiss ambassador Hans Frölicher was heavily criticized for his friendly behavior toward the Nazis. His reports from Berlin, which are now accessible in Swiss archives, confirm his pro-Hitler attitude—so it is unlikely that the man in the first-class compartment was Frölicher. But considering his age, his critical legacy, and his actions, the man in the train could have been Franz Rudolf von Weiss, the Swiss consul in Cologne, whose reports contained poignant remarks about Nazi persecution politics. Most remarkable was his vivid description of the November pogrom in Cologne, which he concluded with a clear denunciation of the German government for this "inhuman action against the Jews."[29]

The diplomat told the police officers that the compartment was under Swiss jurisdiction. The German officers tried to ignore this, arguing that they wanted the teenagers out since they were German. The Swiss diplomat countered that Germany had stripped them of their citizenship. When the officers insisted that both must leave, now because they did not possess first-class tickets, the diplomat responded that he would take care of it. After endless minutes for Daisy and her companion, the Germans withdrew. Then the train started to move and pulled slowly forward, farther into the Netherlands. Finally, Daisy was free.[30]

From the Dutch port of Rotterdam, Daisy and her companion crossed the channel in a boat. On March 28, 1939, they stepped on shore in England, and from there they took a train to London. As they stood in front of the Liverpool Street station with nowhere to go, Daisy and her friend saw a truck pull up, sent by the Bloomsbury House to pick up refugees from Germany. There was no question about these two: "We looked like the walking dead." At the Bloomsbury House, the Jewish Refugee Committee and other Anglo-Jewish and Christian aid organizations worked to find homes for German-Jewish children. After the November pogrom, Great Britain had agreed to take in unaccompanied Jewish children and teenagers from the German Reich in the program known as Kindertransport (children's transport), and eventually welcomed more than ten thousand of these young refugees. The aid organizations also sought accommodations and jobs for escaping adolescents and adults. Daisy, who was still sick, stayed at the Bloomsbury House, sleeping on a chair, until a wealthy British Jewish couple who needed help with eight other refugee children invited her to live and work with them. Finally, she had a bed with linen, towels, food, and shelter.[31]

By this time Daisy was eighteen years old. When the Nazis invaded Poland in September 1939 and Great Britain declared war on Germany, she lost contact with her parents. After a long time, she finally received messages from her family through the Red Cross that everything was okay. However, in October 1941, a big wave of deportations hit the Jewish population in Germany. Daisy's father, Bruno Gronowski, fell victim to the second wave in November. His transport with 1,053 men, women, and children was the first sent to occupied Latvia. On November 30, 1941, the train arrived in Riga, and the deportees were marched to a forest called Rumbula. They were exhausted. Some lost their luggage; others were beaten along the way to the woods, where all Berlin Jews, including Daisy's father, were shot and killed. The Riga transport was one of the first deportations of German Jews subjected to a massacre. When Himmler, the head of the SS, heard rumors that Berlin Jews would be included in a large massacre, he ordered: "Jew transport from Berlin: No liquidation," but the order came too late. Himmler's late intervention has led to a heated discussion among historians about whether the massacre was just a local misstep or the actual beginning of the systematic murder of European Jewry.[32]

Daisy's mother Ellen was not on this train. She had divorced Daisy's father and married Walter Eppenstein. On March 28, 1942, the Gestapo deported Daisy's mother, stepfather, and sister. After the Gestapo informed the Jewish community about impending transports, the community notified the victims. They could take up to fifty kilograms of belongings with them. At the assembly point—synagogue Levetzowstrasse 7–8 in Berlin-Tiergarten— Gestapo officers forced the Jews to hand over the keys to their homes as well as all valuables and cash. Sometimes more than a thousand people waited for days to be deported, sleeping on the synagogue floor on sacks filled with straw. After a winter pause due to military necessities, their train was the first in a new deportation wave stretching until July that would forcibly relocate more than 45,000 Jews from Germany, Austria, and the Protectorate to transfer ghettos in Nazi-occupied Poland.[33]

Daisy's family went with a transport of more than 980 Jewish men, women, and children to Piaski, a small town twenty kilometers southeast of Lublin, in occupied Poland, where they arrived two days later. From the train station, the Jews had to walk twelve kilometers to the Piaski ghetto. Before the arrival of four thousand German Jews in the spring of 1942, the SS had emptied the ghetto by removing three thousand Polish Jews and murdering them at the Belzec extermination camp. The exact fate of Daisy's mother and sister after their arrival remains unclear. In June 1942, deportations from the Piaski ghetto resumed, but now to the Sobibor extermination site. Authorities closed the ghetto and transferred the last Jews to a death camp in February 1943.[34]

A letter Daisy had sent to her family via the Red Cross came back unopened. In the meantime, the young woman, now twenty-one, had begun to work in a defense plant in London during the day; at night, she waited on tables in a hotel. She also worked as an English-German translator, and in this capacity, she met a man who later turned out to be an officer with the KGB, the Soviet secret service. When he planned a trip to East Prussia, Daisy begged him to look for her family. Returning from Germany, the officer told Daisy that only an aunt, her father's sister, remained alive. Daisy told him that the aunt had married a Nazi and denounced her three brothers; in this way, she took revenge on her "evil" aunt, and the Soviets supposedly sent her to Siberia. Daisy could not trace any other member of her extended family and realized she might be the only survivor.[35]

Given the hardships she had endured to this point, Daisy believed that someone owed her a life, and this life was not going to happen where she was. Like many foreigners, she never felt welcome in Great Britain. She had her eyes set on the United States. A romantic relationship, which later failed, enabled her emigration. In 1947, almost eight years after she had escaped from Germany to England, she arrived in New York. At twenty-six, she wanted to start an entirely new life. She chose a new name for herself: Diane Peters. A few weeks later, she followed the daughter of family friends to California. She took architecture classes at UCLA and attended a beauty school. After five years of residency, the United States granted her citizenship. She had been stateless since the Nazi government withdrew her German citizenship when she left for England.

In Los Angeles, she worked as a cosmetologist for thirty years and developed an interest in politics. She claimed, "Politics are for everybody. I think you are political when you get up in the morning, when you fill your gas tank, when you go to the market, when you pay your bills, when you pay your mortgages; you are always political. Politics roots everything. It was politics that destroyed [the] first part of my life." First, she leaned toward the Democrats, later toward the Republicans. She was elected vice president of the Beverly Hills Republican Assembly. In this capacity, she befriended the governor of California and met several presidents of the United States.[36]

In 1955, she married Dr. Alfred Jacobs, in her eyes, the most wonderful man on earth: "He has made up for every rotten thing that ever happened to me in the past." Yet, despite her very happy marriage, she suffered from nightmares and frequently woke up screaming. Since the end of the war, she has tried desperately to find out exactly what happened to her family. She repeatedly inquired at the International Tracing Service—in 1945, 1947/48, 1952, 1979, and 1996—but to no avail.[37] Physically petite, Daisy/Diane has been a strong, resilient, driven woman all her life, but never having closure regarding the fate of her mother, father, and sister did cast a long shadow on her new, successful life in the United States.

Other Stories of Physical Self-Defense

The story of Daisy defending herself during Kristallnacht is astonishing, but her action did not stand alone. Quite a few episodes of individual resistance against physical attacks emerged from our new set of sources. Jews defended themselves against verbal insults and physical assaults, as the USC Shoah Foundation Visual History Archive confirms with rich evidence.

Among the 170 interviews of German Jews that include discussion of some acts of defiance, 32 survivors talk about physically defending themselves during their adolescent years in the Third Reich. Before, during, and after school, they fought off attacks by classmates or students from other schools, as well as assaults launched by neighbors' children or Hitler Youth members. Even more interesting, 11 of the 32 survivors who talk about defending themselves against attacks were girls. A group of boys had constantly harassed the twelve-year-old Fanny Lust for being Jewish, and one day she confronted an especially aggressive boy and punched him, knocking out one of his teeth, as she tells the interviewer, still smiling after so many years.[38]

Survivors also describe Jewish adults getting into brawls with co-workers, Nazi neighbors, and SA men, both when they were attacked on the street and when the SA intruded in their homes. Men defended their families as well as Jewish neighbors. Joan Winter's father knocked down a neighbor after he forbade Jews to use the elevator in their apartment house. In Breitenbach, an adolescent Lothar Roth beat up a local Nazi who had made a dirty remark to him a day after his father was buried. The local mayor warned the family that the Nazis were looking for revenge. So Roth left town on a bicycle and escaped over the German border to Switzerland.[39]

Notably, it was almost impossible to find evidence about physical altercations in the official Nazi documentation, and only a few instances left traces in the archives. In March 1935, in a small town in Hesse called Schlüchtern, a Jewish merchant defended himself against three SA men. The county commissioner wrote in his official report that the Jew started the brawl by beating a Storm Trooper. He added that this incident demonstrated that the Jews were regaining lost confidence and were becoming more and more impudent. In his report for May–June 1935, the district president (*Regierungspräsident*) for the state of Hesse complained that the Jews became overbearing again. He referred to an incident at a local cattle market where, during an altercation, a Jew used a stick to beat a Storm Trooper over his head from behind.[40]

One case survived in the Main state archive in Wiesbaden. One late morning in October 1936, the Jewish merchant Erich Junghans was riding his bicycle in his hometown. At Dominikaner Square, he saw four boys, fourteen years old, with slingshots. They were shooting stones at Jews leaving a synagogue after service. Passing by, he yelled at them to stop. Later, on his way back, he noticed that the teenagers were still harassing Jews at the synagogue. He stopped and confronted them. Three boys ran away, but the fourth, Adalbert Schäfer, did not move. Junghans slapped him on his cheek and the boy fell. Junghans got up on his bicycle again and made his way to a nearby restaurant for lunch. When he left the establishment later, he saw the boy giving a signal to his waiting father, Karl Schäfer, an office clerk, who approached Junghans, grabbed his arm, and told him to come with him to the police station. Junghans responded that only the police had the right to make an arrest. Yet Schäfer claimed he had all the rights, being an old party comrade. Because Schäfer would not let go, Junghans beat him several times. Dozens of people gathered around observing the altercation. Schäfer's son came back with a policeman, who took both adults to the nearby precinct. Schäfer complained to the officers that the "Jew Junghans" had beaten his son, who, as a result, hit his head on the pavement. He insisted that his son would never aim at people with his slingshot. He told the police that when he tried to arrest the culprit, Junghans beat him several times against the chest. Schäfer also claimed that Junghans's brother Oskar had intervened and also hit him several times. According to Schäfer, after he mentioned that he was an SA member, Oskar Junghans supposedly started to laugh and made derogatory remarks about the Storm Troopers.

Subsequently, there was a trial, in which several witnesses supported Junghans, denying the alleged derogatory remarks about the SA, and countered Schäfer's version of the story. They all reported that Schäfer had exclaimed that when you help the Jews, you are a Communist. In front of the judge, Schäfer declared that a Jew had no right to educate or punish a "Christian child." In a surprising turn of events, the son suddenly admitted to having shot the Jews with his slingshot and lied about Junghans knocking him to the ground. Nonetheless, the judge sided with the old Nazi comrade. He sentenced Erich Junghans to three weeks in jail and Oskar Junghans to two weeks in jail for defamation. His verdict on February 20, 1937, emphasized that even though it was a minor incident, the punishment needed to be harsh since the "Jews become more impudent again." The judge alleged that Junghans's motivation was "hatred toward Aryans." The Junghans brothers contested the ruling, albeit only somewhat successfully: the appellate court acquitted Oskar and reduced Erich's sentence for beating the teenager to ten days in jail.[41]

In another case, Max Cohn, fifty-nine, a Jewish merchant and widower who lived in Mörfelden, boarded a local train at Frankfurt's main station at the end of 1937. In the train car, he saw Wilhelm Markert, a gardener, reading *Der Stürmer*, the anti-Semitic newspaper. After some time, Markert stood up, walked around, and showed everyone an article with the headline "Assassination Attempt," which accused a Jew of promising a bounty of 10,000 Reichsmarks for the murder of a Nazi party county leader. Markert told the passengers repeatedly, "See how bad the Jews are." Cohn was getting agitated and angry; he told Markert to stop or he would beat him up. Markert approached Cohn and tried to kick him; Cohn kicked back, and the gardener lost his balance and fell; Cohn hit him over the head several times with his umbrella. Passengers intervened and stopped the altercation. Subsequently, Markert, an SA man and Nazi party member, pressed charges. The prosecution requested ten weeks in jail. On trial, Cohn defended himself by emphasizing that he had only reacted to Markert's repeated claims of how bad Jews are. He received six weeks for battery.[42]

Altercations like these with Junghans and Cohn were recorded only because the physical attacks were denounced and treated as politically motivated against the Nazis.

During the pogrom of November 1938, Jews defended themselves in various ways against the nationwide attack, and like Daisy Gronowski, some physically resisted assailants. In Krefeld, the local synagogue was burning, and Rabbi Dr. Arthur Bluhm, forty-nine, went there and pleaded desperately with the fire department chief to save important emigrant papers from the endangered building, to no avail. A man approached Bluhm and assaulted him, while nearby Storm Troopers "howled and incited the attacker." The rabbi asked a passing police officer to protect him, but the man "took no notice." In testimony written shortly after his arrival in the United States, the rabbi said the attacker's face "was that of a criminal. If I were to meet him, I would recognize him. I defended myself as well as I could." Minutes later, four SS officers approached the two men and ordered the "criminal" to let go. Bluhm was detained and brought to Dachau. After his release from the concentration camp, he fled Germany immediately.[43]

In Peine, Lower Saxony, a group of SS men invaded approximately twenty family homes, destroying the interiors. When three SS men broke into the Marburger family apartment and started beating his father, Hans, seventeen, tried everything to fight them off and help him. Unfortunately, he stood no chance. They overwhelmed him, dragged him to the local syn-

After being forced to clean the street, a Jewish victim of Nazi harassment resists two
uniformed men forcing him to push a supply cart down the street, January 27, 1939.
(Courtesy of the United States Holocaust Memorial Museum, Photograph 85340)

agogue, and locked him in a room. One man shot the Jewish teenager to
death before they set the synagogue ablaze with gasoline.[44]

Ruth Winick, née Weil, eight, lived in Steinsfurt, Baden, and grew up in
a Jewish farmer's household. In an interview for the Shoah Foundation, she
described how a group of armed men had attacked her family's home during
the pogrom. They knocked down the door with axes, hurled bricks into windows, and began to destroy everything. The assailants threw feather pillows
and linens out of the windows, and left neither a bed nor a chair remaining
in the home. Toward the end of the attack, one of them urinated on top of

all the mess in the kitchen. When one of the young men went after her little sister, her grandmother Mathilde attacked him with a kitchen knife.[45]

In Berlin, the Nazis destroyed a big synagogue in Hardy Kupferberg's neighborhood, and the night after the pogrom the ashes were still smoldering. Kupferberg, sixteen, saw approximately ten Hitler Youth members standing on the pedestal of the synagogue entrance and throwing stones into the ruins. Hidden behind trees, "I took this stone in my right hand and I threw it against this boy who was standing on the pedestal. . . . With all my might." When she realized the stone had hit the boy, she thought, "My god what have I done. So, I went; he fell down." Under cover of darkness, Kupferberg escaped, and did not reveal the incident until many decades later.[46]

Even after the violent Kristallnacht attacks, Jews did not stop physically defending themselves or others. Frank Theyleg, nineteen, beat up two SA men who had frequently terrorized the two elderly Jewish women who owned their apartment building in Berlin. At the elevator, he first provoked them with words and then beat the men with some tools from his job. A sympathetic police officer saved Theyleg from prosecution by urging him to emigrate immediately. The family made it to Shanghai. There, Theyleg learned Mandarin and Shanghainese from his new Chinese friends. They helped find work for him at a factory. Once Japanese troops took over the factory and commanded the workers to manufacture hand grenades, Theyleg and a friend conspired to assemble defective products that would not explode.[47]

After the start of mass deportations to occupied Poland, many Jews decided to go underground or live under false identities, sometimes on their own and sometimes with the help of courageous non-Jewish Germans. At the end of February 1943, the Gestapo launched a "factory action" (*Fabrikaktion*) in order to deport the remaining Jewish forced laborers from Nazi Germany to Auschwitz. During the brutal raid, more than four thousand Berlin Jews escaped over the course of only one day; this was every third man and woman of the targeted group. Many Jews made this decision in a split second, some when Gestapo appeared at their workplaces and others after warnings by coworkers, managers, and even police officers. Even though there was no coordination between them, their hiding constituted the largest mass resistance action against Nazi plans in Germany. In response to this mass act of non-compliance, the Gestapo orchestrated an unrelenting search, which entailed forcing Jews to spy on fellow Jews during the following weeks and months.[48]

Martin Friedmann was a forced laborer in a plumbing workshop when he escaped deportation. He lived in hiding for two months. One fateful day, the police spotted him on the street. Friedmann valiantly resisted arrest by beating up a police officer and managed to flee again. However, another police officer caught him a short while later. The Gestapo deported Friedmann to Auschwitz on June 28, 1943.[49]

Of the several thousand German Jews in hiding in Berlin, some prepared to resist with arms in case of discovery. The Berlin labor office had deployed Kurt Jacobson, fifty-two, as a forced laborer to the Waxoline chemical company. Otto G. Barth, who only recently had acquired the factory, lacked managing experience. As soon as Barth learned that Jacobson had been a businessman, he convinced him to work for him in a different capacity. Jacobson began running the factory under the forged name Jansen, and even started to pour money into the firm, since it was in dire financial straits. Jacobson's wife worked as his secretary, also under a false name. Barth provided the couple with a secret apartment in the factory. In the hidden, freshly renovated space, discovered by coincidence during a random factory inspection, Gestapo officers found two handguns and live ammunition. According to the entry in a police precinct logbook, they also discovered food, suitcases, and identification papers of other Jews—clear evidence of the existence of an informal Jewish network to support the survival of hidden Jews. The officers detained Jacobson's wife and issued a warrant for Kurt Jacobson, who was not at the factory.[50]

On the evening of August 30, 1943, police spotted Kurt Jacobson with his son Wolfgang walking on a street in the center of the capital of the Nazi Empire. The officers tried to arrest the two men, but they started to run. An officer called Jacobson by name, and when Kurt turned around and reached into his pocket, the police officer assumed he had a handgun and shot him. Kurt Jacobson collapsed. Guarded by Gestapo, he died in the Jewish hospital the next day. The police caught his son soon after the shooting.[51]

For Jews in Nazi Germany, who were so vulnerable under constant persecution, it took courage to defend themselves or other Jews against verbal and

Lfd. Nr.	Bezeichnung der Angelegenheit	Was ist darauf veranlaßt?	Wann und durch wen abgegeben?
	[handwritten entry]		
785.	*[handwritten entry]*		30/8.

Police log book entry about the Gestapo raid and Kurt Jacobson, August 30, 1943. (Landesarchiv Berlin, A Rep. 408, No. 4, no fol.)

physical attacks from students, neighbors, Storm Troopers, and other Nazis who harassed them, their families, or their neighbors. For physical altercations and self-defense, age mattered, as did previous self-defense training. Most Jews who physically defended themselves and others against attacks were young or, at most, middle-aged adults. Some Jewish teenagers had training in jiu-jitsu or boxing from Zionist youth organizations, and in other cases, rage or anger alone led Jews to ignore the risk of serious injury and arrest.

This form of individual resistance emerges less frequently in police and court records than protest, contestation of Nazi propaganda, and defiance of the laws, probably because the Nazi state did not view physical confrontations as "political offenses." The few cases that have left traces in the German archives were connected to actual or imagined anti-Nazi arguments. Moreover, personal assaults against anybody, including Jews, were punishable under German law, so there was not much interest in investigating and prosecuting such altercations.

Hence, the majority of the examples stem from stories survivors told in their written or video testimonies. Still, most survivors mentioned these altercations as an afterthought. For Daisy Gronowski, the real heroes were the survivors of the death camps. By contrast, she called her odyssey "a Sunday picnic." Her message for the world was that everyone needs to care about politics. For her, politics can make the difference between living and dying: "It was politics that brought Hitler to power. It was politics that killed over 20 million people, . . . six million Jews, . . . plus all the people dying in World War 2. . . . Who knew it would happen in Germany. . . . Nothing is for granted in life. . . . You have to be the captain of your own ship."[52]

Conclusion

Three weeks after Nazi Germany invaded Poland in September 1939, Edith Britz wrote a letter. It was intercepted. She had already been denounced for "race defilement" and political conversations with non-Jewish Germans. Fortunately, witnesses vouched for her, and she escaped repercussions. In the confiscated letter, the Jewish woman from Berlin described how two police officers knocked on her door one morning at 6 a.m. In that moment, she felt that she would do anything to prevent them from arresting her. However, it turned out that they were just picking up her radio, which all Jews were obliged to hand over to the German state once the war started. Still, Edith Britz thought, "I am so upset that I could attack anybody who wants to enter my pad. . . . I will go crazy, if there will be more; they stole my sleep, they stole everything from me."[1]

Her words reveal the level of anxiety, anger, and repulsion that many Jews seemed to feel after experiencing years of anti-Jewish policies and personal persecution. It is not too far-fetched to assume that such emotions might have triggered many of the actions of the Jewish resisters who challenged the Nazi state through attacks on Nazi propaganda, defiance of Nazi laws, oral and written protest against Nazi policies, and physical defense of themselves and others. Even after years of extreme persecution, Jewish women and men in Greater Germany refused to obey, submit, or surrender, and instead resisted in myriad ways. The frequent references to the "impudent Jews" in Nazi sources need to be appreciated as a contemporary response to a truth that has been long neglected.

With the inclusion of individual acts in the new broad definition of Jewish resistance, our perspective changes dramatically. Under the new lens, a wealth of evidence has emerged that radically challenges the prevailing view of a lack of Jewish responses to persecution.

The stories in this book constitute only a fraction of the probable number of incidents in which individual Jews contested Nazi persecution in Greater Germany. The material in the archives is unfortunately incomplete. Everywhere in Germany, police destroyed documents at the end of the war. Those that did survive are only fragments or cover limited time periods. Documents such as the Berlin precinct logbooks do not exist anywhere else; police reports about "political incidents" survived for only a few other cities. Special Courts files exist in many archives, but they are incomplete. In Berlin, only two thousand of approximately ten thousand Special Court cases for the period between 1933 and 1945 have survived, and most of those case files contain only indictments or judgments, but no court proceedings. Researchers face similar problems with regular court documents in regional and local archives. Important archives of big cities with a sizable Jewish population, such as Hannover, Breslau/Wroclaw, Stuttgart, Nuremberg, Stettin/Szczecin, and Prague, still need to be scrutinized.

Many acts of individual Jewish resistance will be never known, however. They left no traces in the archives, because (fortunately, for the historical actors involved) they were never denounced, and therefore never prosecuted, as some incidents mentioned in postwar testimonies tell us. The majority of those courageous people perished in the Holocaust, and we will never know about them and what they did. Many Jewish men and women who survived would not talk about their small acts of resistance, whether because of their traditional understanding of resistance as solely armed and organized efforts or because of their general reluctance to speak about their personal experiences.

Considering these points, it is only fair to conclude that individual acts of resistance were far more widespread in the Jewish population than we ever imagined, proving that the traditional assumption of Jewish passivity in Nazi Germany was utterly wrong. Every month during the 1930s, local police and the Gestapo arrested hundreds of Jews in cities and small towns for "political offenses." In 1942, after nine years of Nazi oppression, twelve hundred Jewish men and women served prison sentences for scolding Hitler and other "crimes." At the time, they were 2 percent of the remaining German Jewish population, which included many elderly people and children. During the factory raid in 1943, a third of the targeted Jewish Berliners went into hiding. To appreciate and commemorate the courageous efforts of countless German and Austrian resisters, our standard Holocaust narrative needs to be thoroughly updated by integrating the stories of their many individual actions against Nazi policies, both in Greater Germany and all Nazi-occupied countries.

The sheer number of individual acts is staggering. Moreover, every Jewish man and woman developed particular responses as an outcome of their own personal experiences of persecution policies on the local, regional, and national levels. These reactions should be treated not as isolated incidents, but collective contestation of diverse, changing, and sometimes contradictory national and local persecution in the Third Reich. Despite their great variety, the forgotten stories of individual Jewish resistance against Nazi persecution can be divided into five groups: German and Austrian Jews contested Nazi and anti-Jewish propaganda by destroying Nazi symbols, flags, and posters and anti-Jewish signs and posters. Jews verbally protested on the streets and in offices, restaurants, and their houses, criticizing violent attacks, business boycotts, exclusionary measures, and anti-Jewish legislation. Jewish men and women also protested in letters, petitions, anonymous postcards, and leaflets scolding the Nazi regime and its leaders, rejecting their policies, and reclaiming their rights and their Germanness. Jews disobeyed the growing number of anti-Jewish laws and local measures, for example by sabotaging forced labor, not handing over precious metals, rejecting racist taxonomies, visiting prohibited spaces, and escaping camps and deportations. Finally, Jews defended themselves or fellow Jewish Germans from verbal insults and physical attacks by Storm Troopers, Hitler Youth members, and Nazi neighbors.

In particular, Jews actively responded to waves of anti-Jewish violence and even international political crises with peaks of individual resistance. In June–July 1935, for example, when SA, Hitler Youth, and other Berliners defaced Jewish stores and physically attacked Jews and foreigners, dozens of

Jews protested, verbally and in writing, in the Nazi capital. The danger of a potential war during the Sudeten crisis in 1938 emboldened Jews across Germany to criticize the regime, as did the brutal experience of the pogrom in November 1938, exemplified by Henriette Schäfer's objections to her neighbors and relatives about the violent persecution. The increasing segregation and the start of deportations led to a large number of Jews escaping and forging their identities in 1942–1943, yet also to renewed efforts to protest, as the case of Benno Neuburger demonstrates.

Besides rebelling against specific anti-Jewish measures and attacks, Jews also felt compelled to break general laws because of their persecution. During the war, for example, the Nazi state forbade the whole population to listen to foreign broadcasts and to trade with rationed goods. As did other Germans, Jews broke these wartime rules. However, for them it was different. First, they did not enjoy the same political and legal protections as other Germans. Second, specific aspects of the persecution drove Jews to neglect these war decrees. The prohibition on Jews obtaining newspapers in 1938, for example, triggered more hunger for information, which led them to commit so-called radio crimes after the war started; harsher food rationing for Jews led to illicit trade activities; and hiding from mass deportations produced a dependence on the black market.

Big cities, such as Berlin, Vienna, and Frankfurt, saw a similar amount of verbal protest against the general persecution as well as a comparable variety of contestations of particular laws and local restrictions. In spite of previous scholarly claims that cities like Berlin provided better anonymity and therefore better chances for Jewish women and men to act more freely, numerous cases of individual resistance also emerged in small towns and villages, where everyone knew each other.

These stories also reshape our previous perception that resistance might be predominantly a male affair. When all individual actions against the Nazis and their collaborators are understood as resistance and of equal value, it balances our gendered view and highlights the many ways in which Jewish women resisted during the Holocaust.

Similarly, no patterns of a particular generation, class, socialization, or education among the resisting Jews have materialized. This tentatively seems to confirm a disputed claim by Philip Zimbardo from decades ago that "individual behavior is largely under the control of social forces and environmental contingencies rather than personality traits, character, willpower or other empirical unvalidated constructs."[2] Jewish women and men of all ages and from all educational and professional backgrounds defied Nazi measures or raised their voices in protest.

Only a few tendencies seemed noticeable. Slightly more women than men seem to have publicly criticized the persecution. More men than women engaged in physical self-defense. The elderly, more than younger Jews, seem to have actively challenged the Nazi humiliation of the forced name changes.

Even more interesting is that a number of Jewish women and men resisted more than once. Many committed several offenses, especially after the beginning of the war, and often simultaneously, such as protesting in public, not wearing the star, and breaking the curfew; or breaking the curfew, visiting forbidden spaces, and destroying anti-Jewish signs. In other cases, the same people were punished multiple times for repeated public protests or for hiding their "racial identity" for years and committing other "offenses."

Resistance did not always end with capture and trial. Some Jews escaped arrest or from camps, like Daisy Gronowski. Other Jews still resisted when already incarcerated by not admitting guilt or confirming lesser "crimes" that they actually committed, like Hans Oppenheimer. Others spoke up in jail in front of guards and other inmates. Some Jews stood by their protests, unwavering, even on trial, like Benno Neuburger at the intimidating public stage of the People's Court in the Nazi capital. Those Jewish men and women developed what could be called "resistance careers."

Individual Jewish resistance did not occur only in Germany and Austria. The Sudeten territory newspaper *Leitmeritzer Tagblatt* published a frequent column titled "The complaining Jew." In 1941, officials in the office of the Reich Protector for Bohemia and Moravia discussed growing problems with the defiant attitude of Czech Jews, and perceived draconian measures as the only remedy for the situation. During December 1941 alone, the Gestapo in Olmütz (Olomouc) and Prossnitz arrested more than a dozen Jews for not obeying anti-Jewish laws.[3]

Such widespread individual behavior did have some effect on the anti-Jewish persecution. In some cases, the Nazis adjusted their policies; in others they radicalized their measures in response to individual resistance. After introducing restricted shopping hours for Jewish consumers in Berlin in summer 1940, for example, the Berlin police president had to issue several threatening follow-up decrees, because Jews did not obey and tried to circumvent the new rule.[4]

The German and Austrian Jews who were punished by the Special Courts for a variety of political offenses, including protest and criticism, found themselves with a criminal record. Because of this, all those Jewish men fell victim to the raid against "asocial Jews" in June 1938. Historians were already aware that during the "asocial action," minor offenses, such as a fine for smoking in the forest during the wildfire season, led to imprisonment of Jewish males in a concentration camp, but in addition, all the German Jews who had served prison sentences under the Treacherous Attacks Law for resisting the Nazi regime and its persecution of the Jews also suffered the same fate. Quite a few of those rebellious Jews endured months and years of incarceration in concentration camps. Some even lost their lives because of beatings, excessive labor, and malnutrition. Those who made it out of the concentration camps immediately left the country, as David Bornstein did.

Once released from prison or a concentration camp, many Jews escaped Nazi Germany as soon as they could, at least until the war. Hence, while few lost their lives, for many, ironically, their early resistance saved their lives. Those captured after the beginning of the war missed their chance because of closed borders, and from 1941 onward, the Gestapo often immediately included Jews in the mass deportations to the occupied East after they served their prison time. At the end of 1942, following an agreement between the minister of justice and Himmler, the head of the SS, the judiciary handed prisoners over to the SS even before their sentences ended. As in the case of Hans Oppenheimer, they were concentrated in Auschwitz, where they often perished. The longer the war progressed, the more their chances of survival diminished.

The stories of Jewish defiance surprisingly reveal frequent unexpected behavior of non-Jews, including some Nazis; for example, acts of solidarity by helpful neighbors, co-workers, and former fellow frontline soldiers or supportive testimonies of sympathetic trial witnesses. The same archives that house acts of individual Jewish resistance also offer evidence of criticism and protest by non-Jewish Germans against the Nazi leadership and their policies, and, more unexpected, against the persecution of the Jews, particularly in 1938. This challenges older notions of a progressing conformism, as well as general passivity and indifference among non-Jewish Germans, and confirms trends in recent research that point to more complicated stories of individual behavior.[5]

In addition, assumptions of a steady Nazification of the courts and a full erosion of the legal system in Germany after 1933 are too simplistic. In court, Jews would encounter a majority of judges sticking to legal standards in managing proceedings and sentencing according to the law; some judges were even sympathetic and demonstrated an understanding of the difficult situation facing Jews as late as during the mass deportations. This was equally true for regular and Special Courts trying Jews for offenses regarding the penal code or a variety of other laws. The Special Courts are often seen as chiefly Nazi institutions that were supposed to quell resistance and punish political offenses by employing specific legislation, such as the Treacherous Attacks Law. However, some Jews received lesser sentences than the prosecution had requested in indictments.

More surprising is the fact that courts acquitted quite a number of Jews when they denied or disputed accusations. In some instances, courts acquitted Jews of all charges even during the war, or included them in Hitler's wartime amnesty for minor offenses, which seems rather ironic and was probably not what the Nazi leader intended. In some cases, courts did not proceed with pursuing charges after inconclusive investigations. Individual judges deemed some witnesses or denunciators as unreliable, or expressed sympathy with the persecuted. In other cases, judges acted compassionately when Jewish defendants said they had acted out of despair or brought up a history of mental illness. However, even being freed or acquitted unexpectedly meant that these Jews had already spent weeks or months in police custody during the investigation and trial proceedings, which took a heavy toll on people's lives, livelihoods, families, and futures.

Notably, even during the war, Jews tried to use the German legal system to fight discrimination. Such opposition could yield a positive result; for example, Jewish forced laborers sued two private enterprises to pay them for work on Nazi holidays. A Berlin labor court ruled in favor of these Jews.[6]

On the opposite end of the spectrum, we find a horrific number of denunciations by SA, SS, police, passers-by, neighbors, and workmates. These consequential actions were motivated by many reasons: anti-Semitism, loyalism, material interests, personal grudges, revenge. Nazi party members and Gestapo officers as well as prosecutors and judges displayed anti-Jewish attitudes, resulting in arrests and trials for even a few critical words in public or private settings. Often, Jewish defendants received particularly harsh prison sentences, and during the war these sentences got longer and were followed by imprisonment in concentration camps, or deportation to ghettos and extermination sites. In almost all of these cases the perpetrators still acted based on legislation and legalized policies, but in 1941–1942 the Vienna Gestapo, as an exception, skipped legal procedures and incarcerated rebellious Jews without trial in concentration camps or included them in transports to the Nazi-occupied East.[7]

Everything that Jews did and the German state perceived as a threat to the imagined Nazi people's community was persecuted and punished as resistance. It mattered only what the Nazis thought about the "impudent Jews" and what they perceived as resistance. The smallest act of Jewish defiance could trigger ruthless punishment. The former merchant Nachmann Wilzig sat a bit intoxicated in a Berlin beer pub one late morning in 1937. His welfare benefits had just been cancelled, and he exclaimed loudly: "I am an old German Jewish boy and we will get back our rights one day." The court claimed that as a Jew he should have behaved with restraint. The cancellation of his welfare benefits would not justify him "to vociferate against the racial legislation of the Third Reich in such an impudent and audacious manner." For his words, even spoken in a drunken state, the seventy-five-year-old man received a sentence of three months in prison.[8]

If so many German and Austrian Jews rebelled, why have these acts been forgotten until today? Various factors contributed to the omission of individual Jewish resistance in the historical accounts during the decades since the end of the Second World War, such as the misguided opinion that resistance meant only groups with arms and the traditional assumption that Jews never fight back. In 1935, the prominent author Kurt Tucholsky wrote a letter from Sweden about the situation of the Jews in Nazi Germany to the novelist Arnold Zweig, who had fled to Palestine. Citing a long history of passive Jewish suffering, Tucholsky complained extensively about the alleged lack of self-defense among German Jews after 1933 and a dearth of courageous leadership who would stand up for Jewish rights. He judged harshly: "Judaism is defeated, as much defeated as it deserves—and, it is just not true that Judaism is fighting for thousands of years. It just does not fight."[9]

After the war, Jews would or could not tell their stories of defiance. During the Holocaust, many of the German Jews who resisted were murdered or perished. Those who survived the ghettos and camps had seen too much horror to value their small acts of opposition. The magnitude and systematic nature of the Nazi murder of European Jews—almost six million lives extinguished—must have discouraged any meaningful discussions about resistance, let alone seemingly small deeds such as public protest or disobeying Nazi laws. Postwar debates in Berlin newspapers centered on the monstrosity of Nazi crimes in Europe, particularly after the Nuremberg Trials started. The fate of the German Jews, and even more their resistance, took a back seat in favor of gruesome details from the extermination sites in Nazi-occupied eastern Europe.[10]

The Jewish community in Berlin alone shrank from 160,000 people in 1933 to barely 8,000 in 1945. The destitution of the remainder of the once large and proud Jewish community, daily worries about food and shelter, the search for emigration destinations, and the fight against Nazis, anti-Semites, and Jewish collaborators still living among the survivors filled the meeting schedules of the representatives of the Berlin Jewish community until at least 1947. Those concerns, along with the search for surviving family members and the quest for recompensation, also dominated the pages of the Jewish weekly *Der Weg*.[11] All of this left no opportunity to discuss or remember individual Jewish resistance.

Some German Jews themselves flat out denied the existence of any resistance, however. *Der Weg* published an article commemorating the 1938 pogrom in November 1946, in which the author answered the "familiar question" of why Jews did not respond with violence to the violence. Astoundingly, he claimed, "Except for some desperate resistance from a few individuals and small groups in later years, all responsible minded men agreed that every violent resistance would be futile and would just present the Nazis with a welcome reason for the persecution and eradication of everybody."[12] A year earlier, the Jewish journalist Leo Menter had made a similar claim but gave a different explanation. Referring to the reactions of German Jews to the "yellow star," he asserted: "Ire was not foreign to them, but it had already burned down, had become dull from many stitches by those cynical measures executed over and over for years, immediately when a scar had healed. No, there was no resistance. Already our fathers had learned how to obey."[13]

This book proves otherwise. All Jewish individuals, however, who indeed resisted, did never act in a vacuum; they always behaved in a web of relationships and were nothing without their families, friends, neighbors, and co-workers. Think about David Bornstein, his wife, and his parents-in-law; Benno Neuburger, his wife, his adult children abroad, and his relatives living with them; Hans Oppenheimer and his parents; Daisy Gronowski and her Zionist youth community; or Henriette Schäfer, her non-Jewish husband, and their neighbors. In the future, researchers need to address how personal relationships influence, support, and encourage or perhaps discourage and curtail the decision making of individual resisters. They also want to look at the role of informal groups and networks of friends, acquaintances, colleagues, or neighbors, and how individual resistance oscillates into collective opposition.[14]

The case of a petition against the exclusion from municipal contracts, for which Heinrich Haber organized the signatures of two hundred Berlin Jewish textile merchants, speaks to this. As does the case of Edith Wolff, who first protested with postcards against the 1933 boycott, then against the pogrom violence in 1938, the introduction of the yellow star in 1941, and finally the execution of Jewish representatives at the end of 1942. Facing the "factory action" in 1943, she co-founded a Jewish underground group, "Chug Caluzi," that supported Jews in hiding. Jews also participated in non-Jewish resistance groups. Twenty-year-old graphic artist Cioma Schönhaus, who lived in hiding in Berlin since 1942, forged papers for a rescue network operated by the Confessing Church. Between 1933 and 1945, around three thousand German Jews were involved in one way or another in organized anti-Nazi opposition, mostly participating in left-wing workers' resistance groups.[15]

Similarly, it will be worth exploring what organized social and political support of the local Jewish community meant for individual self-assertion. Representatives and staff of Jewish political organizations, religious communities, and other institutions defied or protested Nazi policies and orders. Since the beginning of the dictatorship, they worked hard to defend the Jewish population against the impact of the persecution. Moreover, they intervened with appeals to political parties and state officials, sometimes successfully, as in the case of some Prussian districts in Upper Silesia, the former plebiscite area, when they invoked the German-Polish Geneva Convention of May 15, 1922, to stop the application of anti-Jewish laws in summer 1933.[16] Jewish officials developed strategies to manipulate Nazi institutions, such as pitting the Gestapo against labor offices or ministries against municipalities and vice versa.[17]

The forgotten stories of the many Jewish resisters restore agency to ordinary men and women in extraordinary circumstances. Many German and Austrian Jewish men and women emerge as courageous historical actors; however, many were terrified before, during, and after their often bold actions, which underscores the danger they faced.[18] The documentation and analysis of their individual acts of resistance, however grand or small, deepens our general understanding of the Nazi persecution of the Jews and their responses. The stories about the individual resistance of Hans Oppenheimer and many Jewish men and women like him are an essential, yet neglected, part of this history. We need to apply a broader lens to other Nazi-occupied countries in order to tell a richer story of Jewish individual and community responses during the Holocaust. We can take this further to look at the behavior of persecuted minority groups in other authoritarian regimes to better understand individual responses in global instances of systematic mass violence and genocide. The status of the persecuted can be elevated from oppressed victims to courageous historical actors, speaking to the power of seemingly small deeds that mighty dictators and genocidaires perceive as existential threats.

When ordinary Jews under the most repressive regime imaginable were bold and brave enough to criticize Nazi and racist ideology, defy humiliation, break laws, oppose local restrictions, and defend themselves against physical attacks, resisting individually in large numbers without any substantial support, it affirms that everyone is able under any circumstances—and, thus, also has a responsibility—to resist racist or oppressive ideologies and policies anywhere in the world, especially now.

This memorial of stories not only illuminates the bold actions of so many "impudent Jews," but gives a voice to all of those who bravely resisted, including those whose actions cannot be acknowledged because they were never discovered, did not leave traces in the archives, were kept under a veil of silence, or because they perished during the Shoah. As Rabbi Max Nussbaum from Berlin aptly put it after the war: "We . . . were besieged . . . in a hundred different manners, and therefore we fought back in a hundred different manners."[19]

NOTES

Abbreviations

BA Berlin	Bundesarchiv Berlin
BLHA Potsdam	Brandenburg State Main Archive
CJA Berlin	Centrum Judaicum Archiv-Stiftung Neue Synagoge
DÖW Vienna	Dokumentationsarchiv des Österreichischen Widerstands Wien
HHStA Wiesbaden	Hesse Main State Archive Wiesbaden
ISA Jerusalem	Israel State Archives Jerusalem
LA Berlin	Landesarchiv Berlin
RGVA Moscow	Russian State War Archive Moscow
SStA Leipzig	Saxonian State Archive Leipzig
StA Chemnitz	State Archive Chemnitz
StA Freiburg i. Br.	State Archive Freiburg i. Br.
StA Hamburg	State Archive Hamburg
StA Munich	State Archive Munich
StadtA Bad Segeberg	City Archive Bad Segeberg
StadtA Kelkheim	City Archive Kelkheim
USC SF/VHA	USC Shoah Foundation Visual History Archive
USHMM Washington	United States Holocaust Memorial Museum Washington
WSuLA Vienna	Wiener Stadt- und Landesarchiv
YVA Jerusalem	Yad Vashem Archives Jerusalem

Introduction

1. Translations of this and the following quotations are by the author. In this book, the terms "Jew" and "Jewish" refer to the people the Nazis perceived and persecuted as Jewish, which included Germans of Jewish origin who were practicing Protestants, Catholics, or atheists. Hertha Reis was denounced, detained, and indicted for treacherous attacks against the Nazi state under the 1934 law; LA Berlin, A Rep. 355, no. 5697, no fol.: Copy of indictment, Generalstaatsanwalt beim Landgericht als Leiter der Anklagebehörde beim Sondergericht an das Sondergericht Berlin, June 7, 1941, 1–4.

2. For an in-depth discussion of this perception's origins and endurance, see Richard Middleton-Kaplan, "The Myth of Jewish Passivity," in *Jewish Resistance Against the Nazis*, ed. Patrick Henry (Washington, D.C.: Catholic University of America Press, 2014), 3–26.

3. Max Mannheimer, *Spätes Tagebuch: Theresienstadt–Auschwitz, Warschau–Dachau* (Munich: Pendo, 2009), 37.

4. USC Shoah Foundation Visual History Archive (USC SF/VHA), Interview Max Mannheimer, December 5, 1996, tape 1–6.

5. Konrad Kwiet and Helmut Eschwege, *Selbstbehauptung und Widerstand: Deutsche Juden im Kampf um Existenz und Menschenwürde, 1933–1945*, 2nd ed. (Hamburg: Christians, 1986); Marion Kaplan, *Between Dignity and Despair: Jewish Life in Nazi Germany* (New York: Oxford University Press, 1998); David Engel, *Daring to Resist: Jewish Defiance in the Holocaust* (New York: Museum of Jewish Heritage, 2007). See also Ştefan Cristian Ionescu, *Jewish Resistance to Romanianization, 1940–1944* (Basingstoke, U.K.: Palgrave Macmillan, 2015); Guy Miron, " 'Lately, Almost Constantly, Everything Seems Small to Me': The Lived Space of German Jews Under the Nazi Regime," *Jewish Social Studies* 20 (Fall 2013), no. 1, 121–149, here 127. Similar for general anti-Nazi resistance: Wolfgang Neugebauer, *The Austrian Resistance, 1938–1945*, translated by John Nicholson and Eric Canepa (Vienna: Edition Steinbauer, 2014).

6. Wolf Gruner, " 'The Germans Should Expel the Foreigner Hitler': Open Protest and Other Forms of Jewish Defiance in Nazi Germany," *Yad Vashem Studies* 39 (2011), no. 2, 13–53, here 18; Wolf Gruner, "Defiance and Protest: A Comparative Micro-Historical Re-evaluation of Individual Jewish Responses Towards Nazi Persecution," in *Microhistories of the Holocaust*, ed. Claire Zalc and Tal Bruttmann (New York: Berghahn, 2017), 209–226, here 210. For Bauer's definition, see Yehuda Bauer, "Forms of Jewish Resistance," in *The Holocaust: Problems and Perspectives of Interpretation*, ed. Donald L. Niewyk, 3rd ed. (Boston: Wadsworth, 2002), 116–132, here 117; Yehuda Bauer, *The Jewish Emergence from Powerlessness* (Toronto: University of Toronto Press, 1979), 27.

7. Report Elisheva Lernau, April 1, 2003, Jewish Museum Berlin, 2004/127/29; Christoph Kreutzmüller, "Bilder der Bedrohung: Von Juden aufgenommene Fotos der Verfolgung," in *Medaon* 12 (2018), no. 23, 1–6, here 2. On Stuttgart: Information by Judith Samuel, Los Angeles, in email to author, June 15, 2020.

8. The sign read, "Ich werde mich nie wieder bei der Polizei beschweren." It is readable in a different photograph from the same series as the one in this book; commons.wikimedia.org/wiki/File:Bundesarchiv_Bild_183-R99542,_M%C3%BCnchen,_Judenverfolgung,_Michael_Siegel.jpg (accessed May 14, 2018). See Douglas G. Morris, "The Lawyer Who Mocked Hitler, and other Jewish Commentaries on the Nuremberg Laws," *Central European History* 49 (2016), no. 3–4, 383–408.

9. For the case of the latter, see Marion Detjen, *"Zum Staatsfeind ernannt":* *Widerstand, Resistenz und Verweigerung gegen das NS-Regime in München* (Munich: Buchendorfer Verlag, 1998), 255–256.

10. Kreutzmüller, "Bilder der Bedrohung," 2–3; Angelika Schleindl, *Verschwundene Nachbarn: Jüdische Gemeinden und Synagogen im Kreis Gross-Gerau* (Gross-Gerau: Kreisausschuss Gross-Gerau, 1990), 123.

11. For other cases of such defiant behavior in Vienna and Berlin: USC VHA/SF, Erika Absil (b. 1926 in Vienna), tape 1, seg. 25; USC VHA/SF, Miriam Klothen (b. 1925 in Berlin), Segment 15 (Thanks to Teresa Walch, Greensboro, for pointing this interview out to me).

12. USC SF/VHA, Elena Marx, tape 1, min. 25; USC VHA/SF, Lea Aronson, tape 1, min. 27–31; LA Berlin, B Rep. 020 Acc 1201, no. 6949, fol. 441–442: Logbook Police precinct, Berlin-Schöneberg, entry no. 330 and 331, November 10, 1938; Gruner, "Defiance and Protest," 215–216.

13. Bericht von Henry (Heinz) Bauer, o. D. (1990), in: Leo Baeck Institute, New York, AR 6347; Fotos von Henry (Heinz) Bauer, 1938, Museum of Jewish Heritage, New York, 1901.90; Kreutzmüller, "Bilder der Bedrohung," 4; Alexander Schmidt, "Scheinbare Normalität: Drei Skizzen zur Geschichte der Nürnberger Juden 1918 bis 1938," in *Geschichte und Kultur der Juden in Nürnberg,* ed. Andrea Kluxen and Julia Krieger (Würzburg: Ergon Verlag, 2014), 285–314. On the destruction of homes: Wolf Gruner, " 'Worse than Vandals': The Mass Destruction of Jewish Homes and Jewish Responses During the 1938 Pogrom," in *New Perspectives on Kristallnacht: After 80 Years, the Nazi Pogrom in Global Comparison (Casden Annual),* ed. Wolf Gruner and Steven Ross (West Lafayette, Ind.: Purdue University Press, 2019), 25–49.

14. YVA Jerusalem, M55/JM 20756, StA Würzburg, Gestapo Würzburg, no. 11338, fol. 77RS-78: Note Gestapo Würzburg, August 1, 1940. On denunciation and its importance as a political tool to enforce Nazi laws in the Third Reich, see Robert Gellately, *The Gestapo and German Society: Enforcing Racial Policy, 1933–1945* (Oxford: Oxford University Press, 1991), 130–184; Inge Marsolek, "Denunziation im Dritten Reich: Kommunikationsformen und Verhaltensweisen," in *Überleben im Untergrund: Hilfe für Juden in Deutschland, 1941–1945,* ed. Beate Kosmala and Claudia Schoppmann (Berlin: Metropol, 2002), 89–107; Gisela Diewald-Kerkmann, *Politische Denunziation im NS-Regime oder die kleine Macht der "Volksgenossen"* (Bonn: Dietz, 1995); Stefan Christian Böske, *Denunziationen in der Zeit des Nationalsozialismus und die zivilrechtliche Aufarbeitung in der Nachkriegszeit* (Dissertation, Bielefeld University, 2008).

15. For example: "Trotz der harten Schläge, die Juden in Berlin erhalten, sind sie immer noch frech und aufsässig"; Joseph Goebbels, *Tagebücher, 1924–1945,* vol. 4, edited by Ralf Georg Reuth (Munich-Zürich: Piper, 1992), 1792, entry for May 11, 1942. The antisemitic term is still used today by neo-Nazis in Germany: Monika

Schwarz-Friesel and Jehuda Reinharz, "Das Echo der Vergangenheit: 'Der freche Jude hetzt wieder gegen Deutsche!'," in *Die Sprache der Judenfeindschaft im 21. Jahrhundert* (Berlin/Boston: De Gruyter, 2013), 174–193.

16. Otto Dov Kulka and Eberhard Jäckel, eds., *Die Juden in den geheimen NS-Stimmungsberichten, 1933–1945* (Düsseldorf: Droste, 2004) (CD version), doc. no. 163: Gendarmerie Steinach/Saale, report for second half of June, Steinach an der Saale, June 28, 1934. (The English version of the book, containing excerpts of 752 documents out of 3,744 total documents, is Otto Dov Kulka and Eberhard Jäckel, eds., *The Jews in the Secret Nazi Reports on Popular Opinion in Germany, 1933–1945* [New Haven: Yale University Press, 2010]). In the notes that follow, the German version is cited (as *Die Juden*) when there is no English translation of the original document or the translated excerpts do not contain the particular citation; otherwise the English version is cited (as *The Jews*). For more examples of "Jewish impudence" in official reports from 1934, see Kwiet and Eschwege, *Selbstbehauptung*, 224–227. Kulka and Jäckel, eds., *Die Juden*, doc. no. 690: Stapostelle Regierungsbezirk Aachen, report for March 1935, April 5, 1935; Kulka and Jäckel, eds., *Die Juden*, CD-no. 831: Landrat Schlüchtern, report for March and April 1935, Schlüchtern, April 23, 1935; Kulka and Jäckel, eds., *Die Juden*, doc. no. 972: Regierungspräsident Wiesbaden, report, July 1, 1935; Kulka and Jäckel, eds., *Die Juden*, doc. no. 998: Gestapo Arnsberg, report for July 1935; Kulka and Jäckel, eds., *Die Juden*, doc. no. 1078: Report Gendarmerie Steinach/Saale for July 1935.

17. Kulka and Jäckel, eds., *Die Juden*, CD-no. 1004: Stapostelle Landespolizeibezirk Berlin, report for July 1935 (n.d.). For more details on the arrests, see Gruner, "The Germans," 32. Kulka and Jäckel, eds., *Die Juden*, CD-no. 1596: report Gestapo, state police district Berlin for January 1936 (n.d.); see also Kulka and Jäckel, eds., *The Jews*, 190–191. Cited in Wolf Gruner, *Persecution of the Jews in Berlin, 1933–1945: A Chronology of Measures by the Authorities in the German Capital* (Berlin: Topography des Terrors, 2014), 25. When people entertained such relationships, the Nazi authorities perceived the fact as Jewish defiance. For example, the state of Hesse prosecuted Raimund Ullmann (b. 1904) for several "crimes," including "race defilement" in summer 1935: HHStA Wiesbaden, Abt. 461/7416, Raimund Ullmann, fol. 2a: Note Police president, with clipping, July 19, 1935. Although countless German Jews ended up in jail for "race defilement," this book focuses on cases of Jewish opposition to the general persecution or specific laws.

18. Eleven defendants came from Breslau, six from Frankfurt, five from Cologne, the others from various cities, including Berlin. From those living in Breslau, several fled across the border to Czechoslovakia before their respective trials; RGVA Moscow 500-1-240, fol. 19–23: List of Jews, who committed treason, no date (approximately April 1936). Thanks to Christoph Kreutzmüller for this document.

19. Kulka and Jäckel, eds., *Die Juden*, doc. no. 2081: Bürgermeister Gambach report for December 1936 and January 1937, Gambach, January 19, 1937. The Gestapo

arrested Ludwig and Lothar Hermann (b. 1899 and 1901), in Ludwigshafen am
Rhein, Max Seligmann (b. 1888), Bernhard and Isidor Traubel (b. 1887 and 1900),
and Max Nussbaum (b. 1875), in Würzburg, Ernst Horn (b. 1897) in Munich, Ernst
and Fritz Loew (b. 1906 and 1907), in the hamlet Kirchheimbolanden; StA Munich, Gestapo-Leitstelle Munich, no. 5, fols. 1–34: Daily reports, Bavarian Police,
January 1936. In February, they detained Moritz Schindel (b. 1913) in Munich,
Josef Gutmann (b. 1879) in Würzburg, Louis Hirschmann (b. 1877) in Nuremberg,
and in the month of March, Max Meyer (b.1888) and Oskar Laredo (b. 1878) both
in Würzburg, Isidor Behr (b. 1867) in Nuremberg, and Berthold Schweissheimer
(b. 1898) in Nördlingen, and in April, Isaak Liebenstein (b. 1872) in Kitzingen;
StA Munich, Gestapo-Leitstelle Munich, no. 5, fols. 79–143: Daily reports, Bavar-
ian Police, February, March, and April 1936. In July 1936, police detained Josef
Löwenthal (b. 1904) in Aschaffenburg, in Weissenburg Max Gutmann (b. 1885),
and in August Kurt Siegel (b. 1908) in Würzburg and in September Julius Strauss
(b. 1902) in Nuremberg, and in October Willy Schwab (b. 1889) in Kitzingen,
Leopold and Gustav Grünbaum, born 1879 and 1905, in Würzburg; StA Munich,
Gestapo-Leitstelle Munich, no. 5, fols. 244, 256, 286, 307, 342, 347: Daily reports,
Bavarian Police, July, August, September, and October 1936; Kulka and Jäckel,
eds., *Die Juden*, CD-no. 2327: SD-Oberabschnitt Nord II 112, report for 1937, Stettin
[1937]. In February 1938, the Gestapo arrested Max Cohn (b. 1896 in Hamburg)
and Siegfried Lion (b. 1872 in Cassel) for "atrocity propaganda"; YVA Jerusalem,
O2/1160.1, fol. 166 and 222; RGVA Moscow, 500-1-216, fol. 7: Security service of the
SS, II 212, report for II 1, October 31, 1938 (Thanks to Christoph Kreutzmüller
for this document).

20. StA Munich, Staatsanwaltschaften, no. 3277, fol. 1–4RS: Gestapo letter to prosecutor State Court Munich, November 19, 1937. *Der Stürmer*, the notorious anti-
Semitic newspaper, picked up the story, calling it a Jewish murder attack, although
the prosecution had dropped the case, since nothing had happened and the witness
was not deemed reliable; StA Munich, Staatsanwaltschaften, no. 3277, fols. 21–67:
Notes about interrogations, November 1937 and clippings from *Der Stürmer*, no.
49, December 1937. Kulka and Jäckel, eds., *The Jews*, 308–309: Report Gestapa
[Gestapo headquarters] II A 2 Berlin, June 27, 1938. See also Kulka and Jäckel, eds.,
Die Juden, CD-no. 2461.

21. On October 4, 1938, the police took Alfons Flatow (b. 1869) into custody and
handed him over to the Gestapo after police records revealed that in 1932 he had
declared possession of one knife, thirty-one brass knuckles, a revolver, and twenty-
two live rounds of ammunition; LA Berlin, A Pr.Br.Rep. 030, no. 21620, fol. 6–7RS:
113th Police precinct, report about a political offense, October 3, 1938, to Gestapo;
LA Berlin, A Pr.Br.Rep. 030, no. 21620, fol. 9–10RS: 106th Police precinct, report
about a political offense, October 4, 1938, to Gestapo. See also the arrest of Julius
Gold (b. 1893), who had registered a Walther handgun with six bullets in 1932; LA

Berlin, A Pr.Br.Rep. 030, no. 21620, fol. 11–12RS: 106th Police precinct, report about a political offense, October 4, 1938, to Gestapo; Gruner, *Persecution of the Jews in Berlin*, 118. *Verordnung gegen den Waffenbesitz der Juden, 11 October 1938*; Reichsgesetzblatt (RGBl.), 1938 I, 1573. On German gun laws before 1933 and the actions to disarm Jews, see Stephen P. Halbrook, "Nazi Firearms Law and the Disarming of the German Jews," *Arizona Journal of International and Comparative Law* 17 (2000), no. 3, 483–537, here 519–537.

22. Kulka and Jäckel, eds., *Die Juden*, doc. no. 2669: Landrat Herford, report about November 10, 1938, Herford, November 21, 1938.

23. LA Berlin, A Pr.Br.Rep. 030, no. 21620, fol. 156: 296th Police precinct, report about a political offense, Reinickendorf December 13, 1938, to Gestapo; *Die Verfolgung und Ermordung der europäischen Juden durch das nationalsozialistische Deutschland, 1933–1945*, vol. 3, *Deutsches Reich und Protektorat, September 1939–September 1941*, edited by Andrea Löw (Munich: De Gruyter, 2012), doc. no. 5, 92–93; YVA Jerusalem, O2/1160.1, fol. 252; Kulka and Jäckel, eds., *The Jews*, no. 3094: RSHA, Amt III (SD), report "Meldungen aus dem Reich Nr. 75," Berlin, April 10, 1940; see *Meldungen aus dem Reich, 1938–1945: Die geheimen Lageberichte des Sicherheitsdienstes der SS*, 17 vols., edited by Heinz Boberach (Herrsching: Pawlak, 1984), 975–979. The Jewish widow and landlady Rosa Braun (b. 1870) was arrested for "impudent" and "asocial" behavior toward tenants and authorities in Munich; StA Munich, Gestapo-Leitstelle München, no. 54, fol. 261RS: Daily reports, Munich, June 22, 1940. In Vienna, the Gestapo arrested Elsa Färber (b. 1887 in Böhmisch-Leipa) for ten days as well as the former physician Wilhelm Fischer (b. 1869 in Krasna, Bukowina) for twenty-one days, who both had visited premises forbidden for Jews; DÖW Vienna, Gestapo-leitstelle Wien daily report, no. 1, October 1 and 2, 1940.

24. USC SF/VHA, Gunner Lukas, tape 2, min. 6; USC SF/VHA, Paula Lindemann, tape 1, min. 22; USC SF/VHA, Heinz Langer, tape 2, min. 17; USC SF/VHA, Irene Hofstein, tape 1, min. 28; USC SF/VHA, Efrayim Vagner, tape 1, min. 42; USC SF/VHA, Edith Sternfeld, tape 1, min. 22; USC SF/VHA, Anita Siegel, tape 2, min. 45; USC SF/VHA, Martha Friedmann, tape 3, min. 1–5; USC SF/VHA, Kurt Liffmann, tape 2.

25. Wolf Gruner, *The Holocaust in Bohemia and Moravia: Czech Initiatives, German Policies, Jewish Responses* (New York: Berghahn, 2019), 235–236; Kulka and Jäckel, eds., *Die Juden*, CD-no. 3271: SD-Aussenstelle Bielefeld, report "Stimmung in der Bevölkerung," Bielefeld, July 23, 1941.

26. *Polizei-Verordnung über die Kennzeichnung der Juden, 1 September 1941*; RGBl., 1941 I, 547. See also Gruner, *The Holocaust in Bohemia and Moravia*, 234–236.

27. YVA Jerusalem, M38/120 (DÖW). The Gestapo arrested four members of the Jewish Seckl family in Wiener Neustadt (Austria) and another Jewish woman for inciting behavior toward the German population in January 1942. All were transferred to

an assembly camp in Vienna for deportation; YVA Jerusalem, M38/122 (DÖW), fol. 18. In Berlin, a divorced convert to Protestantism, Leo Borstein (b. 1899), was indicted for having frequently expressed hostile and insulting opinions about the Nazi state in public and having hidden his "race" to avoid forced labor deployment; LA Berlin, A Rep. 355, no. 4225 Bornstein, Leo, no fols.: Indictment Main Prosecutor to Special Court Berlin, February 3, 1942, 1–3; DÖW Wien, Gestapo-Leitstelle Wien, daily reports October–December 1940, no fols.: Gestapo-Leitstelle Wien, daily report, no. 9, October 19–21, 1940, 5. Within four weeks in fall 1941 alone, the Siemens factory security handed over Gilga Basch, Elfriede Götz, and Helmut Borchardt to the Gestapo for their refusal to work. In addition, Borchardt was not wearing the notorious "yellow star," introduced in September 1941; LA Berlin, B Rep. 020, Acc. 1124, no. 6939, Police Siemensstadt, no fols.: entry no. 207, September 5, 1941, entry, no. 225, September 22, 1941, entry, no. 237, October 1, 1941, entry, no. 266, December 9, 1941. Cf. Gruner, "The Germans Should Expel." Jewish forced laborers also defied the Nuremberg race laws. For example, a Jewish forced laborer forged a sexual relationship with a non-Jewish female worker and was punished with four years in a penitentiary; StA Hamburg, 213-11, no. 66094.

28. See for example: Zwi Aviram, *Mit dem Mut der Verzweiflung: Mein Widerstand im Berliner Untergrund, 1943–1945*, ed. Beate Kosmala and Patrick Siegele (Berlin: Metropol Verlag, 2015), 40–41.

29. Protocol Reich Justice Ministry about meeting with RFSS on September 18, 1942, in *Der Prozess gegen die Hauptkriegsverbrecher vor dem Internationalen Militärgerichtshof, 14. November 1945–1. Oktober 1946*, vol. 26 (Nürnberg: IMT, 1948), doc. no. PS-654, 200–203; see H. G. Adler, *Der verwaltete Mensch: Studien zur Deportation der Juden aus Deutschland* (Tübingen: Mohr-Siebeck, 1974), 251–252; Peter Longerich, *Holocaust: The Nazi Persecution and Murder of the Jews* (Oxford: Oxford University Press, 2012), 324.

30. Some accounts on organized Jewish resistance in Nazi Germany: John M. Cox, *Circles of Resistance: Jewish, Leftist, and Youth Dissidence in Nazi Germany* (New York: Peter Lang, 2009), 81–143; Eric Brothers, *Berlin Ghetto: Herbert Baum and the Anti-Fascist Resistance* (Stroud, U.K.: Spellmount, 2012); Christine Zahn, " 'Nicht mitgehen, sondern weggehen!': Chug Chaluzi—eine jüdische Jugendgruppe im Untergrund," in *Juden im Widerstand: Drei Gruppen zwischen Überlebenskampf und politischer Aktion, 1939–1945*, ed. Werner Vathke and Wilfried Löhken (Berlin: Hentrich, 1993), 159–205. See also Kaplan, *Between Dignity and Despair*, 212–313; Ferdinand Kroh, *David kämpft: Vom Jüdischen Widerstand gegen Hitler* (Reinbek bei Hamburg: Rowohlt, 1988), 38–47, 92–102. In most general histories of resistance in Nazi Germany and its occupied countries, even organized Jewish resistance either seems neglected or appears marginalized; see Neugebauer, *The Austrian Resistance, 1938–1945*; Laurent Douzou, "A Perilous History: A Historiographical Essay on the French Resistance," *Contemporary European History* 28 (2019), no. 1, 96–106.

31. See, for example, Alan S. Zuckerman, "The Limits of Political Behavior: Individual Calculations and Survival During the Holocaust," *Political Psychology* 5 (1984), no. 1, 37–52, here 48–51. See the discussion in Middleton-Kaplan, "The Myth of Jewish Passivity," 3–26.

32. Avi Patt points out the irony that the early and continuous attention to the Warsaw Ghetto uprising as a unique and rare act of resistance reinforced the notion of passivity; Avinoam Patt, *The Jewish Heroes of Warsaw: The Afterlife of the Revolt* (Detroit: Wayne State University Press, 2021), 1–2. See also Yael S. Feldman, " 'Not as Sheep Led to Slaughter'?: On Trauma, Selective Memory, and the Making of Historical Consciousness," *Jewish Social Studies: History, Culture, Society* 19 (2013), no. 3, 139–169, here 142, 149, and 157.

33. Laura Jockusch, *Collect and Record!: Jewish Holocaust Doucmentation in Early Postwar Europe* (New York: Oxford University Press, 2012). The Black Book chapter presents examples of resistance according to country and, in the case of Poland and occupied Soviet territory, according to city; The Jewish Black Book Committee, *The Black Book: The Nazi Crime Against the Jewish People* (New York: American Book–Stratford Press, 1946), 414–464, especially 432–433; discussion of resistance activities also appears elsewhere in the book, such as at 406; Marie Syrkin, *Blessed Is the Match: The Story of Jewish Resistance* (Philadelphia: The Jewish Publication Society, 1947).

34. Raul Hilberg, *The Destruction of the European Jews* (London: W.H. Allen, 1961), 662; Raul Hilberg, *Perpetrators, Victims, Bystanders: The Jewish Catastrophe, 1933–1945* (New York: Aaron Asher, and HarperCollins, 1992), 170–185. See for this discussion, Michael Marrus, "Jewish Resistance to the Holocaust," *Journal of Contemporary History* 30, no. 1 (1995), 83–110, here 86–88; Konrad Kwiet, "Problems of Jewish Resistance Historiography," *Leo Baeck Institute Yearbook* 24 (1979), 37–57, here 37. Robert Rozett added Bettelheim to the common picture of Arendt and Hilberg, both of whom neglected the existence of Jewish resistance; see Robert Rozett, "Jewish Resistance," in *The Historiography of the Holocaust*, ed. Dan Stone (Houndmills, U.K.: Palgrave Macmillan, 2004), 341–363, here 343. Cf. Gruner, "The Germans," 14–17.

35. Saul Friedländer, *Nazi Germany and the Jews*, vol. 1, *The Years of Persecution, 1933–1939* (New York: HarperCollins, 1997); Saul Friedländer, *Nazi Germany and the Jews*, vol. 2, *The Years of Extermination, 1939–1945* (New York: HarperCollins, 2008). See also Moshe Zimmermann, *Deutsche gegen Deutsche: Das Schicksal der Juden, 1938–1945* (Berlin: Aufbau, 2007).

36. Friedländer, *Nazi Germany and the Jews*, 2: xv.

37. YVA Jerusalem, M55/2145.2 (Special Court Freiberg/Saxony 4412796-1), fol. 1–75.

38. *Gesetz gegen heimtückische Angriffe auf Staat und Partei und zum Schutz der Parteiuniformen*; RGBl., 1934 I, 1269. For the punishment of insults using the "Treacherous Attacks Law" of 1934 and the details of that procedure, including the

necessary approval by the Reich Ministry of Justice, see in detail, Bernward Dörner, *"Heimtücke": Das Gesetz als Waffe; Kontrolle, Abschreckung und Verfolgung in Deutschland, 1933–1945* (Paderborn: Schöningh, 1998), 20–25, 67–84, 120–127, 169–170; however, this work only mentions that Communists and "asocial" defendants received more severe sentences. Dörner based his research mainly on cases from West German archives; Jewish defendants are mentioned in only one case. See also Peter Hüttenberger, "Heimtückefälle vor dem Sondergericht München, 1933–1939," in *Bayern in der NS-Zeit,* vol. 4, *Herrschaft und Gesellschaft im Konflikt, part C,* ed. Martin Broszat, Elke Fröhlich, and Anton Grossmann (Munich-Vienna: Oldenbourg, 1981), 435–526.

39. Decree of the Reich Government regarding the Jurisdiction of the Special Courts, December 20, 1934; StA Munich, Polizeidirektion München, no. 6958, no fols.: Dienstliche Nachrichten der Polizeidirektion München, February 18, 1935, Special issue (Front page). On the judicial and political practice at various local Special Courts: Bernd Schimmler, *Recht ohne Gerechtigkeit: Zur Tätigkeit der Berliner Sondergerichte im Nationalsozialismus* (Berlin: Wissenschaftlicher Autoren-Verlag, 1984); Christiane Oehler, *Die Rechtsprechung des Sondergerichts Mannheim, 1933–1945* (Berlin: Duncker & Humblot, 1997); Herbert Schmidt, *"Beabsichtige ich die Todesstrafe zu beantragen": Die nationalsozialistische Sondergerichtsbarkeit im Oberlandesgerichtsbezirk Düsseldorf, 1933 bis 1945* (Essen: Klartext, 1998); Oskar Vurgun, *Die Staatsanwaltschaft beim Sondergericht Aachen* (Berlin: Duncker & Humblot, 2017); Freia Anders-Baudisch, " 'Rechts'-Praxis nationalsozialistischer Sondergerichte im 'Reichsgau Sudetenland,' 1940–1945," *Bohemia* 40 (1999), no. 2, 331–366.

40. Anders-Baudisch, " 'Rechts'-Praxis nationalsozialistischer Sondergerichte," 348; Manfred Zeidler, *Das Sondergericht Freiberg: Zu Justiz und Repression in Sachsen, 1933–1940* (Dresden: Hannah-Arendt Institut für Totalitarismusforschung, 1998), 44–45. See, for example, Wolfgang Form and Theo Schiller, eds., *Politische NS-Justiz in Hessen: Die Verfahren des Volksgerichtshofs, der politischen Senate der Oberlandesgerichte Darmstadt und Kassel, 1933–1945, sowie Sondergerichtsprozesse in Darmstadt und Frankfurt/M. (1933/34),* 2 vols. (Marburg: Historische Kommission für Hessen, 2005); Hannes Ludyga, *Das Oberlandesgericht München zwischen 1933 und 1945* (Berlin: Metropol, 2012).

41. Philip Friedman, "Outline of Program for Holocaust Research," in *Roads to Extinction: Essays on the Holocaust,* ed. Ada June Friedman (New York: The Jewish Publication Society of America, 1980), 571–576, here 575; cited by Sari Siegel, *Between Coercion and Resistance: Jewish Prisoner-Physicians in Nazi Camps, 1940–1945* (Dissertation, University of Southern California, 2018), 288–289.

42. Meir Dworzecki, "The Day to Day Stand of the Jews," in *Jewish Resistance During the Holocaust: Proceedings of the Conference on Manifestations of Jewish Resistance, Jerusalem, April 7–11, 1968* (Jerusalem: Yad Vashem, 1971), 152–181, here 153. See

also Boaz Cohen, "Dr Meir (Mark) Dworzecki: The Historical Mission of a Survivor Historian," *Holocaust Studies* 21 (2015), no. 1–2, 24–37, 28; and Siegel, *Between Coercion and Resistance,* 288.

43. The Amidah concept is most often cited from Bauer's publication, but in a limited way focusing on spiritual and cultural resistance; Yehuda Bauer, "Forms of Jewish Resistance During the Holocaust," in *The Jewish Emergence from Powerlessness* (Toronto: University of Toronto Press, 1979), 26–40. See also Yehuda Bauer, *They Chose Life: Jewish Resistance in the Holocaust* (New York: The American Jewish Committee, 1973); Yehuda Bauer, *Jewish Reactions to the Holocaust* (Tel Aviv: MOD, 1989).

44. See for example, Rebecca Rovit, *The Jewish Kulturbund Theatre Company in Nazi Berlin* (Iowa City: University of Iowa Press, 2012); Michael Brenner, "Jewish Culture in a Modern Ghetto: Theater and Scholarship Among the Jews of Nazi Germany," in *Jewish Life in Nazi Germany: Dilemmas and Responses,* ed. Francis Nicosia and David Scrase (New York: Berghahn, 2010), 170–184.

45. Kwiet and Eschwege, *Selbstbehauptung,* 18–19. See also Kwiet, "Problems," 41.

46. Detlef Peukert, *Inside Nazi Germany: Conformity, Opposition, and Racism in Everyday Life* (New Haven: Yale University Press, 1987), esp. 246–247; Martin Broszat, "A Social and Historical Typography of German Opposition to Hitler," in *Contending with Hitler: Varieties of Resistance in the Third Reich,* ed. David Clay Large (Cambridge: Cambridge University Press, 1991), 25–34; Alf Lüdtke, *Eigen-Sinn: Fabrikalltag, Arbeitererfahrungen und Politik vom Kaiserreich bis in den Faschismus* (Hamburg: Ergebnisse Verlag, 1993); Alf Lüdtke, ed., *Herrschaft als soziale Praxis: Historische und sozialanthropologische Studien* (Göttingen: Vandenhoeck & Ruprecht, 1991). See more recently, *Germans Against Nazism: Nonconformity, Opposition, and Resistance in the Third Reich: Essays in Honour of Peter Hoffmann,* edited by Francis R. Nicosia and Lawrence D. Stokes (New York: Berghahn, 2015).

47. James C. Scott, *Weapons of the Weak: Everyday Forms of Peasant Resistance* (New Haven: Yale University Press, 1985); James C. Scott, *Domination and the Arts of Resistance: Hidden Transcripts* (New Haven: Yale University Press, 1990). See also Rose Weitz, "Women and Their Hair: Seeking Power Through Resistance and Accommodation," *Gender and Society* 15 (2001), no. 5, 667–686, here 668–669.

48. See the chapter "On Resistance" in Eugene D. Genovese, *Roll, Jordan, Roll: The World the Slaves Made* (New York: Vintage, 1976), 597–660; James H. Sweet, "Slave Resistance," Freedom's Story, TeacherServe, National Humanities Center (nationalhumanitiescenter.org/tserve/freedom/1609-1865/essays/slaveresist.htm; www.digitalhistory.uh.edu/disp_textbook.cfm?smtid=2&psid=3045#:~:text=%22Day%2Dto%2Dday%20resistance,was%20another%20form%20of%20resistance, all accessed August 9, 2020).

49. *Nonviolent Social Movements: A Geographical Perspective,* edited by Stephen Zunes et al. (Malden, Mass.: Blackwell, 1999); Kristina Thalhammer et al., ed.,

Courageous Resistance: The Power of Ordinary People (New York: Palgrave Macmillan, 2007); Martin Butler et al., *Resistance, Subjects, Representations, Contexts* (Bielefeld: Transcript-Verlag, 2017).

50. Most recently: Judy Batalion, *The Light of Days: The Untold Story of Women Resistance Fighters in Hitler's Ghettos* (New York: William Morrow, 2021); Rachel L. Einwohner, *Hope and Honor: Jewish Resistance During the Holocaust* (New York: Oxford University Press, 2022). Finkel wants to return agency to the Holocaust victims by challenging the notion of their alleged passivity, and analyzes several victims' strategies, but in the end adopts a very narrow definition of resistance as only organized activity aiming to harm the perpetrators physically or materially; Evgeny Finkel, *Ordinary Jews: Choice and Survival During the Holocaust* (Princeton: Princeton University Press, 2017). See also Jiří Kosta et al., eds., *Tschechische und slowakische Juden im Widerstand, 1938–1945* (Berlin: Metropol, 2008); Barbara Epstein, *The Minsk Ghetto, 1941–1943: Jewish Resistance and Soviet Internationalism* (Berkeley: University of California Press, 2008); Michael Berger and Gideon Römer-Hillebrecht, eds., *Jüdische Soldaten-Jüdischer Widerstand in Deutschland und Frankreich* (Paderborn: Ferdinand Schöningh Verlag, 2011).

51. Yehuda Bauer, *Rethinking the Holocaust* (New Haven: Yale University Press, 2000), 119–166; Rozett, "Jewish Resistance," 341–363; Dan Michman, *Holocaust Historiography: A Jewish Perspective* (London: Vallentine Mitchell, 2003); Henry, *Jewish Resistance*.

52. Frank Bajohr, " 'Arisierung' als gesellschaftlicher Prozess: Verhalten, Strategien und Handlungsspielräume jüdischer Eigentümer und 'arischer' Erwerber," in *"Arisierung" im Nationalsozialismus: Volksgemeinschaft, Raub und Gedächtnis*, ed. Irmtrud Wojak and Peter Hayes (Frankfurt/Main: Campus, 2000), 15–30; Christoph Kreutzmüller, *Ausverkauf: Die Vernichtung der jüdischen Gewerbetätigkeit in Berlin, 1930–1945* (Berlin: Metropol, 2012); in English, *Final Sale in Berlin: The Destruction of Jewish Commercial Activity, 1930–1945* (New York: Berghahn, 2015).

53. Jürgen Matthäus, "Evading Persecution: German-Jewish Behavior Patterns After 1933," in *Jewish Life in Nazi Germany*, ed. Nicosia and Scrase, 47–70.

54. A few petitions are mentioned in Saul Friedländer, *Nazi Germany and the Jews*, vol. 1.

55. On the hitherto neglected importance of petitions, see Thomas Pegelow-Kaplan and Wolf Gruner, eds., *Resisting Persecution: Jews and Their Petitions During the Holocaust* (New York: Berghahn, 2020).

56. For all, see Kwiet and Eschwege, *Selbstbehauptung*, 141–215. See also Wolfgang Altgeld and Michael Kissener, "Judenverfolgung und Widerstand: Zur Einführung," in *Widerstand gegen die Judenverfolgung*, ed. Michael Kissener (Konstanz: Universitätsverlag, 1996), 9–40, here 31–36; Kwiet, "Problems," 55. Paucker calls the flight from deportation transports resistance, although this would have been not a political activity, but a defiance of Nazi orders; Arnold Paucker,

"Widerstand von Juden und Hilfen für Verfolgte," in *Widerstand gegen die nationalsozialistische Diktatur, 1933–1945*, ed. Peter Steinbach and Johannes Tuchel (Bonn: Bundeszentrale für politische Bildung, 2004), 285–306, here 301.

57. YVA Jerusalem, O2/1160.1, fol. 89 and 197; StA Munich, Gestapo-Leitstelle München, no. 132, fol. 6: Circular Gestapo Munich, February 20, 1942. A Jewish woman (b. 1888) escaped the General Government and hid in Vienna. Another woman left Vienna without permission. Nine more Jews were arrested who wanted to escape to Hungary. The Gestapo brought them to Vienna to be deported to occupied Poland. During the same month, a Jewish couple, both over sixty years old, was caught leaving Vienna and not wearing the "yellow star." Both were deported to the East; YVA Jerusalem, M38/122 (DÖW), fol. 2–28. Abraham Weinberger (b. 1886) and his wife Olga (b. 1893) were captured trying to cross the border to Hungary or Yugoslavia. The Weinbergers had lived in hiding in Vienna since October 1941. The Gestapo also arrested a family of three for ignoring the decree about the "yellow star" and for trying to flee Vienna. The same month, forty-year-old Arthur Kanzenhofer and thirty-year-old Paula Laufer tried unsuccessfully to cross the Hungarian border. In August 1942, the Gestapo arrested Ignaz Schnürer (b. 1918), who had hidden in Vienna for months fearing deportation; YVA Jerusalem, M38/122 (DÖW), fol. 25–28; YVA Jerusalem, M69/3492 (Öst. Staatsarchiv Wien), fol. 3.

58. Cited by Robert Rozett, *Conscripted Slaves: Hungarian Jewish Forced Laborers on the Eastern Front During the Second World War* (Jerusalem: Yad Vashem, International Institute for Holocaust Research, 2013), 27.

59. Tanja von Fransecky, *Escapees: The History of Jews Who Fled Nazi Deportation Trains in France, Belgium, and the Netherlands* (New York: Berghahn, 2019).

60. BLHA Potsdam, Rep. 41/272, fol. 87: Decree (secret), Head of Order Police, April 6, 1943; LA Berlin, Pr.Br.Rep. 30 Berlin CV, Tit. 198 a2 Juden, no. 62, no fols.: Arrest form, criminal police Berlin, May 6, 1943; LA Berlin, A Rep. 408, no. 4 Tätigkeitsbuch Kripo 17 Revier, no fols.: Entry no. 971, November 4, 1943.

61. Paucker, "Widerstand von Juden," 301; Wolf Gruner, *Widerstand in der Rosenstrasse: Die Fabrik-Aktion und die Verfolgung der "Mischehen" 1943* (Frankfurt am Main: S. Fischer-Verlag, 2005), 205. Marion Kaplan called "hiding" a courageous act defying the fate the Nazis had prepared for the Jews. On survival strategies such as obtaining false papers, ration cards, or food from the black market, see Kaplan, *Between Dignity and Despair*, 201–212. For the data for Germany and a comparison, see Marnix Croes and Beate Kosmala, "Facing Deportations in Germany and the Netherlands: Survival in Hiding," in *Facing the Catastrophe: Jews and Non-Jews in Europe During World War II*, ed. Beate Kosmala and Georgi Verbeeck (Oxford: Berg, 2011), 97–158.

62. Research on rescuers: Mark Roseman, *A Past in Hiding: Memory and Survival in Nazi Germany* (New York: Picador USA, 2002); Mark Roseman, *Lives Reclaimed: A Story of Rescue and Resistance in Nazi Germany* (Oxford: Oxford University Press,

2019); Wolfgang Benz and Juliane Wetzel, eds., *Solidarität und Hilfe für Juden während der NS-Zeit*, vols. 1–4 (Berlin: Metropol Verlag, 1996–2003); *Resisting Genocide: The Multiple Forms of Rescue*, edited by Claire Andrieu, Sarah Gensburger, and Jacques Semelin (New York: Columbia University Press, 2011); Susanne Beer, *Die Banalität des Guten: Hilfeleistungen für jüdische Verfolgte, 1941–1945* (Berlin: Metropol Verlag, 2018).

Local studies on hiding: Gunnar S. Paulsson, *Secret City: The Hidden Jews of Warsaw, 1940–1945* (New Haven: Yale University Press, 2002); Susanna Schrafstetter, *Flucht und Versteck: Untergetauchte Juden in München; Verfolgungserfahrung und Nachkriegsalltag* (Göttingen: Wallstein Verlag, 2015); Susanna Schrafstetter, "The Geographies of Living Underground: Flight Routes and Hiding Spaces of Fugitive German Jews, 1939–1945," in *Lessons and Legacies 14: The Holocaust in the 21st Century: Relevance and Challenges in the Digital Age*, ed. Tim Cole and Simone Gigliotti (Evanston, Ill.: Northwestern University Press, 2020), 111–138; Richard N. Lutjens Jr., *Submerged on the Surface: The Not-So-Hidden Jews of Nazi Berlin, 1941–1945* (New York: Berghahn, 2019).

63. Croes and Kosmala, "Facing Deportations," 115; Beate Kosmala, "Zwischen Ahnen und Wissen: Flucht vor der Deportation (1941–1945)," in *Die Deportation der Juden aus Deutschland*, ed. Birthe Kundrus and Beate Meyer (Göttingen: Wallstein, 2004), 135–159, here 139.

64. Wolf Gruner, "Die Reichshauptstadt und die Verfolgung der Berliner Juden, 1933–1945," in *Jüdische Geschichte in Berlin: Essays und Studien*, ed. Reinhard Rürup (Berlin: Hentrich, 1995), 246–251; Beate Meyer, "Gratwanderung zwischen Verantwortung und Verstrickung: Die Reichsvereinigung der Juden in Deutschland und die Jüdische Gemeinde zu Berlin, 1938–1945," in *Juden in Berlin, 1938 bis 1945*, ed. Beate Meyer and Hermann Simon (Berlin: Centrum Judaicum, 2000), 291–337, here 309–312.

65. Schrafstetter, *Flucht und Versteck*, 125–140; Lutjens Jr., *Submerged*, 207.

66. Victor Klemperer, *I Shall Bear Witness: A Diary of the Nazi Years, 1942–1945*, translated by Martin Chalmers (New York: Random House, 1999); Marie Jalowicz Simon, *Untergetaucht: Eine junge Frau überlebt in Berlin, 1940–1945* (Frankfurt am Main: S. Fischer, 2014); Cioma Schönhaus, *The Forger: An Extraordinary Story of Survival in Wartime Berlin* (Cambridge, Mass.: Da Capo, 2008); Zenon Neumark, *Hiding in the Open: A Young Fugitive in Nazi-Occupied Poland* (Chicago: Vallentine Mitchell, 2006).

67. The following historians discuss Jewish suicides as acts of defiance or resistance: Konrad Kwiet, "The Ultimate Refuge: Suicide in the Jewish Community under the Nazis," in *Leo Baeck Institute Yearbook* 29 (1984), 135–167; Kwiet and Eschwege, *Selbstbehauptung*, 194–215; Christian Goeschel, *Suicide in Nazi Germany* (Oxford: Oxford University Press, 2009), esp. 96–118; Zimmermann, *Deutsche*, 174. Most recently: Elie Fagan, *Choosing to Die: Elective Death of German-Speaking Jews*

During the Holocaust (Dissertation, Gratz College, 2022). Arnold Paucker questions the labeling of suicides as individual resistance, while acknowledging it was a form of protest; Paucker, "Widerstand von Juden," 286. For the opinion that it was mere desperation, see Christine Hartig, " 'Conversations about taking our own lives—oh, a poor expression for a forced deed in hopeless circumstances!': Suicide Among German Jews, 1933–1943," in *Leo Baeck Institute Yearbook* 52 (2007), 247–265; David Cesarani, *Final Solution: The Fate of the Jews, 1933–1949* (London: Pan, 2016), 225.

68. LA Berlin, A Rep. 408/38, no fol.: Log book Criminal police precinct no. 285 Weissensee entry no. 16, January 13, 1942.

69. Note, November 29, 1938, printed in *Jewish Responses to Persecution*, vol. 1, 1933–1938, ed. Jürgen Matthäus and Mark Roseman (Lanham, Md.: AltaMira, 2010), 369. For the German original, see *Die Verfolgung und Ermordung der europäischen Juden durch das nationalsozialistische Deutschland, 1933–1945*, vol. 2, *Deutsches Reich, 1938–August 1939*, edited by Susanne Heim (Munich: De Gruyter, 2009), doc. no. 181, 512. See also Goeschel, *Suicide*, 103.

Chapter 1. Contesting Nazi Propaganda

1. StA Hamburg, 213-11 Staatsanwaltschaft Landgericht–Strafsachen, no. 54253 (prev. 213-11_01410_38), fol. 1–9+RS: Reichspost directorate to prosecutor in Hamburg, August 15, 1936, Copy of note, Richard Kalkreuter, Post office Bad Segeberg, August 13, 1936, Copy of note, Schümann, Post office Ulzburg, August 13, 1936, protocol, interrogation Richard Kalkreuter, police Bad Segeberg, September 8, 1936, and Note about complaint, Schümann, police station 55, Hamburg, August 13, 1936.

2. StA Hamburg, 213-11, no. 54253, fol. 1–5: Reichspost directorate to prosecutor in Hamburg, August 15, 1936, Copy of note, Richard Kalkreuter, Post office Bad Segeberg, August 13, 1936, and protocol, interrogation Richard Kalkreuter, police Bad Segeberg, September 8, 1936.

3. StA Hamburg, 213-11, no. 54253, fol. 1–9: Reichspost directorate to prosecutor in Hamburg, August 15, 1936; Copy of note, Kalkreuter, Post office Bad Segeberg, August 13, 1936, Copy of note, Schümann, Post office Ulzburg, August 13, 1936, protocol, interrogation Richard Kalkreuter, police Bad Segeberg, September 8, 1936, Note about complaint, Schümann, Police station 55, Hamburg, August 13, 1936, with Gestapo stamp of August 14, 1936.

4. ISA Jerusalem, Mandatory Palestine Naturalization Applications, 1937–1947, Government of Palestine, Department of Migration, Uscher-David Bornstein Application; www.archives.gov.il/en/archives/Archive/0b07170680034dc1 /File/0b07170680bf9f00 (last accessed March 11, 2022; thanks to Karen Franklin, New York, for pointing me to this file). Hamburg Phone Book 1926, 64; Hamburg

Phone Book 1927, 63: agora.sub.uni-hamburg.de/subhh-adress/digbib/view?did=c1:1
540202&p=67&z=175"; Hamburg Phone Book 1928, 82: agora.sub.uni-hamburg.de
/subhh-adress/digbib/view?did=c1:1516598&p=82&z=250; Hamburg Address directory 1936, 1559: agora.sub.uni-hamburg.de/subhh-adress/digbib/view?did=c1:869559
&p=1571&z=175; Hamburg Address directory 1937, 292: agora.sub.uni-hamburg.de
/subhh-adress/digbib/view?did=c1:962649&p=2089&z=150; Hamburg Phone
Book 1938, 81: agora.sub.uni-hamburg.de/subhh-adress/digbib/view?did
=c1:1351917&p=88; Hamburg Address directory 1938, 108: agora.sub.uni-
hamburg.de/subhh-adress/digbib/view?did=c1:875173&p=259&z=150 (all accessed
on February 28, 2018).

5. StA Hamburg, 213-11, no. 54253, fol. 13 and fol. 44RS. First, in 1930, Bornstein had
   rented an apartment at Neumünsterstrasse (today called Neumünstersche Strasse),
   no. 32, second floor, in Eppendorf, the northern part of the city; Hamburg Address
   Book 1930, II, 121: agora.sub.uni-hamburg.de/subhh-adress/digbib/view?did=
   c1:854384&p=282&z=275; Hamburg Address Book 1930, IV, 639; Hamburg
   Address directory 1936, 1559; Hamburg Phone Book 1938, 81; Hamburg Address
   directory 1938, 108: agora.sub.uni-hamburg.de (all accessed on February 28, 2018);
   BA Berlin, Residentenliste, Margarete Bornstein general entry, accessed via
   USHMM; Information according to: StadtA Bad Segeberg Abt. 18 Geburtenbuch
   1898 no. 21. Abt. 18; Dr. Georg Asmussen, City Archive Bad Segeberg, email to
   author, June 6, 2018; ISA Jerusalem, Mandatory Palestine Naturalization
   Applications, 1937–1947, Government of Palestine, Department of Migration,
   Uscher-David Bornstein Application, 5 and 11; www.archives.gov.il/en/archives/
   Archive/0b07170680034dc1/File/0b07170680bf9f00 (last accessed March 11,
   2022).
6. Avraham Barkai, *From Boycott to Annihilation: The Economic Struggle of the
   German Jews, 1933–1943* (Hanover, N.H.: Brandeis University Press, 1989), 127–129.
   For the scope and details of this process in Berlin, see Kreutzmüller, *Final Sale*.
   For Hamburg, see Bajohr, *Aryanization*.
7. StA Hamburg, 213-11, no. 54253, fol. 20: Nazi party Eppendorf-Süd to Gestapo
   Hamburg, November 19, 1936.
8. StA Hamburg, 213-11, no. 54253, fol. 9+RS and 10: Note about complaint, Schümann, police station 55, Hamburg, August 13, 1936, with attachments, protocol,
   Kalkreuter, and protocol, Schümann, and note of criminal police officer Frank,
   August 14, 1936.
9. StA Hamburg, 213-11, no. 54253, fol. 10: note of criminal police officer Frank,
   August 14, 1936.
10. StA Hamburg, 213-11, no. 54253, fol. 1+RS: Reichspost directorate to prosecutor in
    Hamburg, August 15, 1936. Later, the Reich Post Directorate filed their own charges
    for criminal property damage; StA Hamburg, 213-11, no. 54253, Reich Post direction
    to Prosecutor office at the State Court Hamburg, September 26, 1936.

11. StA Hamburg, 213-11, no. 54253, fol. 4: Draft letter, Main prosecutor in Hamburg to Gestapo Kiel, August 20, 1936.

12. The next day, the Gestapo sent the file with the statements over to the prosecutor office in Hamburg; StA Hamburg, 213-11, no. 54253, fol. 10+RS and 12+RS: note of criminal police officer Frank, September 2, 1936, and note of September 3, 1936.

13. StA Hamburg, 213-11, no. 54253, fol. 5: protocol, interrogation Richard Kalkreuter, police Bad Segeberg, September 8, 1936.

14. StA Hamburg, 213-11, no. 54253, fol. 18: Handwritten note, Main Prosecutor, Special Court, Hamburg office at the State Court Hamburg, September 26, 1936.

15. StA Hamburg, 213-11, no. 54253, fol. 18–19: Gestapo to Main Prosecutor with Statement Kalkreuter, November 19, 1936.

16. StA Hamburg, 213-11, no. 54253, fol. 19–20: Gestapo to Main Prosecutor, November 19, 1936; Nazi party Eppendorf-Süd to Gestapo Hamburg, November 19, 1936.

17. StA Hamburg, 213-11, no. 54253, fol. 21+RS: Handwritten note, Main Prosecutor, Hamburg, January 5, 1937.

18. StA Hamburg, 213-11, no. 54253, fol. 21–22: Handwritten note, Main Prosecutor, Hamburg, January 5, 1937; Handwriting on form, local court Hamburg, January 11, 1937.

19. StA Hamburg, 213-11, no. 54253, fol. 23: Letter, David Bornstein to local court Hamburg, January 12, 1937.

20. StA Hamburg, 213-11, no. 54253, fol. 27+RS: Handwritten protocol of the trial proceedings, court Hamburg, January 15, 1937.

21. StA Hamburg, 213-11, no. 54253, fol. 28–29RS: Handwritten protocol of the trial proceedings, court Hamburg, January 15, 1937.

22. StA Hamburg, 213-11, no. 54253, fol. 30–34: Handwritten protocol of the trial proceedings, court Hamburg, January 15, 1937; Handwritten protocol of the trial proceedings, court Hamburg, January 22, 1937.

23. StA Hamburg, 213-11, no. 54253, fol. 30–31 and 34–35RS: Handwritten protocol of the trial proceedings, court Hamburg, January 15, 1937; Handwritten protocol of the trial proceedings, court Hamburg, January 22, 1937.

24. StA Hamburg, 213-11, no. 54253, fol. 36–40: Judgment, court Hamburg, no date (February 1937), 1–9.

25. StA Hamburg, 213-11, no. 54253, fol. 44: Note, Gestapo, February 26, 1937.

26. StA Hamburg, 213-11, no. 54253, fol. 44–45: Notes, Gestapo, February 26 and 27, 1937.

27. BA Berlin, Residentenliste, BornsteinDavidA12423503_0_1, accessed via USHMM; Hamburg Phone Book 1938, 81: agora.sub.uni-hamburg.de/subhh-adress/digbib /view?did=c1:1351917&p=88 (accessed on February 25, 2018); ISA Jerusalem, Mandatory Palestine Naturalization Applications, 1937–1947, Government of Palestine, Department of Migration, Uscher-David Bornstein Application, 6–7 and 18; www .archives.gov.il/en/archives/Archive/0b07170680034dc1/File/0b07170680bf9f00 (last accessed March 11, 2022).

28. StA Hamburg, 213-11, no. 54253, fol. 50: Letter, Prosecutor office, State Court Hamburg, to Bernhard David, April 24, 1937.

29. BA Berlin, Residentenliste, BornsteinDavidA12423503_0_1, accessed via USHMM; Hamburg Phone Book 1938, 81: agora.sub.uni-hamburg.de/subhh-adress/digbib /view?did=c1:1351917&p=88 (accessed on February 25, 2018); ISA Jerusalem, Mandatory Palestine Naturalization Applications, 1937–1947, Government of Palestine, Department of Migration, Uscher-David Bornstein Application, 6–7 and 18; www .archives.gov.il/en/archives/Archive/0b07170680034dc1/File/0b07170680bf9f00 (last accessed March 11, 2022).

30. Information according to Dr. Georg Asmussen, City Archive Bad Segeberg, email to author, June 6, 2018.

31. YVA Jerusalem, International Tracing Service (ITS) Arolsen, 20170628_09521 David Bornstein; BA Berlin, Residentenliste, David Bornstein general entry, accessed via USHMM.

32. YVA Jerusalem, 051/OSOBI, no. 88 (Moscow 500/1/261), fol. 30: memo SD-Dept. for Jewish Affairs, June 8, 1938, on meeting in Security Main Office, June 1, 1938. See Wolf Gruner, *Der Geschlossene Arbeitseinsatz deutscher Juden: Zwangsarbeit als Element der Verfolgung, 1938–1943* (Berlin: Metropol-Verlag, 1997), 43. In total more than 1,200 "asocials" died; Nikolaus Wachsmann, *KL: A History of the Nazi Concentration Camps* (New York: Farrar, Straus and Giroux, 2015), 151 and 671 fn. 115, and 177–179. Gruner, *Persecution of the Jews in Berlin*, 3 and 108.

33. BA Berlin, Residentenliste, BornsteinDavidCC4091658_0_1B, accessed via USHMM. At the moment of his release, the camp had registered 9,100 inmates. From this number, the SS marked 6,152 men as "asocials," among them 781 Jews and 442 so-called Gypsies; BA Berlin, Residentenliste, BornsteinDavidEE4093792 _0_1, accessed via USHMM. BA Berlin, Residentenliste, BornsteinDavidA12423503 _0_1 (SS-Doc, July 24, 1938), accessed via USHMM on February 1, 2018.

34. Max Domarus, ed., *Hitler: Reden und Proklamationen, 1932–1945*, vol. 1/II, *1935–1938* (Munich: Süddeutscher Verlag, 1965), 890–891.

35. His wife, Margarete, is noted with an emigration date to Palestine of June 1936 in her general entry at the residentenliste. However, she was a witness at her husband's trial in February 1937, hence she emigrated later; BA Berlin, Residentenliste, BornsteinMargarete, Entry Residentenliste accessed via USHMM on February 1, 2018. That she emigrated with her husband and her daughter is confirmed by her naturalization record; ISA Jerusalem, Mandatory Palestine Naturalization Applications, 1937–1947, Government of Palestine, Department of Migration, Uscher-David Bornstein Application.

36. See Wolf Gruner, "Von der Kollektivausweisung zur Deportation der Juden aus Deutschland: Neue Perspektiven und Dokumente (1938–1945)," in *Die Deportation der Juden*, ed. Kundrus and Meyer, 21–62.

37. Gruner, *Persecution of the Jews in Berlin*, 33–35 and 118–119.

38. Hamburg Address Book 1940, IV, 439: agora.sub.uni-hamburg.de/subhh-adress/digbib/view?did=c1:654910&p=2887&z=200; Hamburg Address Book 1941, IV, 444: agora.sub.uni-hamburg.de/subhh-adress/digbib/view?did=c1:898557&p=289 1&z=225; Hamburg Address Book 1943, IV, 447: agora.sub.uni-hamburg.de/subhh-adress/digbib/view?did=c1:458357&p=2942&z=250; Hamburg Phone Book 1943, 298: agora.sub.uni-hamburg.de/subhh-adress/digbib/view?did=c1:1356762&p=302&z=325 (all accessed on January 28, 2018). Only in 1942, when the mass deportations of the German Jews had been in full swing, Walter Maltzahn, a sales representative for the "Mineral Oil Works Albrecht & Co.," rented Bornstein's former space. Maltzahn still ran his business at the Wallhof in the mid-1950s; Hamburg Address Book 1943, IV, 447: agora.sub.uni-hamburg.de/subhh-adress/digbib/view?did=c1:458357&p=2942&z=250; Hamburg Phone Book 1943, 298 agora.sub.uni-hamburg.de/subhh-adress/digbib/view?did=c1:1356762&p=302&z=325; Hamburg Address Book 1947, II, 241: agora.sub.uni-hamburg.de/subhh-adress/digbib/view?did=c1:465592&p=258&z=300; Hamburg Phone Book 1947, 68: agora.sub.uni-hamburg.de/subhh-adress/digbib/view?did=c1:1549009&p=70; Hamburg Address Book 1947, II, 241: 973: agora.sub.uni-hamburg.de/subhh-adress/digbib/view?did=c1:680437&p=1034&z=125 (all accessed on January 28, 2018).

39. ISA Jerusalem, Mandatory Palestine Naturalization Applications, 1937–1947, Government of Palestine, Department of Migration, Uscher-David Bornstein Application, 3, and 31; www.archives.gov.il/en/archives/Archive/0b07170680034dc1/File/0b07170680bf9f00 (last accessed March 11, 2022).

40. For example, see USC SF/VHA, Pesach Schindler, tape 1, min. 36; Ester Scheiner, tape 1, min. 23.

41. Michael Geheran, *Comrades Betrayed: Jewish World War I Veterans Under Hitler* (Ithaca: Cornell University Press, 2020), 65–66; Kaplan, *Between Dignity and Despair*, 22–23.

42. Law for the Protection of German Blood and German Honor, September 15, 1935, RGBl., I 1935, 1147.

43. SStA Leipzig, 20114 Landgericht Leipzig, 5510 Natho, Moritz.

44. USC SF/VHA, Joachim Boin, tape 1, min. 16:35–17:05. Thanks for pointing out this testimony go to Nicole Nocon, Cottbus/Germany.

45. YVA Jerusalem, M55/2150, fol. 52–60 and 70–72: Judgment, Special Court Freiberg (Saxony), August 28, 1936; Main prosecutor, State Court Dresden, arrest warrant, October 21, 1935.

46. YVA Jerusalem, M55/2150, fol. 52–60, 70–72, 188–189, 204–235: Judgment, Special Court Freiberg (Saxony), August 28, 1936; Main prosecutor, State Court Dresden, arrest warrant, October 21, 1935; Confiscated handwritten letter Paul Wolff to Wilhelm Stapel, April 1 (5?), 1936; Opinion about Wolff's mental health, State Health office Freiberg, July 29, 1936; de.wikipedia.org/wiki/Wilhelm_Stapel (accessed July 10, 2018).

47. StA Hamburg, 213-11_01242/36, Jacob Heilbut, fol. 1–7, 32; www.dhm.de/datenbank
    /dhm.php?seite=5&fld_0=PLI24373 (accessed January 28, 2018); DNB report,
    August 6, 1935, in " 'Das haben wir nicht gewusst!': Was aufmerksame Leser im
    Dritten Reich aus ihrer Tageszeitung erfahren konnten. Eine katholische Klein-
    stadt im Spiegel des Sauerländischen Volksblattes, 1930–1941." Zusammengestellt
    von Rolf Müller, in *Olpe in Geschichte und Gegenwart*, vol. 16–19 (2008–2011); here
    cited from www.google.com/url?sa=t&rct=j&q=&esrc=s&source=web&cd=1&ved
    =0ahUKEwjioLjFg_fYAhVW8WMKHRh4BBUQFggsMAA&url=https%3A%2F%2
    Fwww.olpe.de%2Fmedia%2Fcustom%2F2513_541_1.PDF%3F1452677742&usg=AO
    vVawoNdOyxZtA3Li19pWPXO5Mt (accessed January 26, 2018). Letter Walldorf
    (Werra) to the Thuringian government, August 22, 1935, in *Quellen zur Geschichte
    Thüringens*, Halbband 1, "Arisierung" in *Thüringen, Entrechtung, Enteignung
    und Vernichtung der jüdischen Bürger Thüringens, 1933–1945*, ed. Monika
    Gibas, 2nd revised ed. (Erfurt: Landeszentrale für Politische Bildung Thüringen,
    2008), 67.
48. Cordula Tollmien, *Nationalsozialismus in Göttingen (1933–1945)* (Dissertation,
    Georg-August-University Göttingen, 1998), 182.
49. StA Hamburg, 213-11_01242/36, Jacob Heilbut, fol. 1–7, 32, 6–25, 1–5 (II).
50. YVA Jerusalem, ITS Arolsen, Jacob Heilbut TD; StA Hamburg, 213-11_01242/36,
    Jacob Heilbut, fol. 6–35, 1–5 (II).
51. Letter Walldorf (Werra) to the Thuringian government, August 22, 1935, in *Quellen
    zur Geschichte Thüringens*, Halbband 1, 67. Non-Jewish Germans also tore down
    the anti-Catholic poster. In Lingen, Dr. Beckmann received a punishment of 150
    Reichsmarks or fifteen days in jail for it. He later lost his job as the head physician at
    the local hospital, www.tourismus-lingen.de/veranstaltungen_4/kultureinrichtungen
    /das_st._bonifatius_hospital.html (accessed January 28, 2018). Another case is
    recorded for Hannoversch Münden: Heidi Rosenbaum, *"Und trotzdem war's 'ne
    schöne Zeit": Kinderalltag im Nationalsozialismus* (Frankfurt: Campus, 2014), 565;
    USC SF/VHA, Henry Schuster, tape 1, min. 26–28.
52. SStA Leipzig, 20031 Polizeipräsidium, PP-S 5004, no fols.: Report Abschnittskom-
    mando Süd to Order police, June 30, 1939.
53. DÖW Vienna, Gestapo-Leitstelle Wien, Tagesrapporte September–December
    1940, no fols.: Gestapo-Leitstelle Vienna, daily report, no. 8, 17.-18.2.1941, S. 3.
54. The Main prosecutor could not charge her under the Treacherous Attacks Law,
    since the letter was directed to a foreign country and thus would not undermine
    the trust of the German people to Hitler. From the court jail, she was handed
    back to the Gestapo; WSuLA Vienna, Sondergericht, SHv Strafakten, no. 522
    Marie Schmidt, fol. 1, 3 and 14: Gestapo to Main prosecutor Vienna, November 18,
    1941; Abwehrstelle Wehrmacht Vienna to Gestapo Vienna, October 24, 1941; Note,
    Main Prosecutor Vienna, December 12, 1941. See also YVA Jerusalem, M38/120
    (DÖW), fols. 22–23.

Chapter 2. Verbal Protest Against the Persecution

1. HHStA Wiesbaden, Abt. 409/6 Haftanstalten, no. 73, no fols.: Form Prison Frank-furt-Höchst, September 13, 1939; ibid., Abt. 461 Staatsanwaltschaft Frankfurt /Main/7925, fol. 5–7: Gestapo summons form, April 17, 1939.

2. *The Persecution and Murder of the European Jews by Nazi Germany, 1933–1945,* vol. 1, *German Reich, 1933–1937,* edited by Wolf Gruner (Berlin: De Gruyter Oldenbourg; Jerusalem, Israel: Yad Vashem, 2019), doc. no. 15 and 52, 114–116 and 197; Wolf Gruner, "Local Initiatives, Central Coordination: German Municipal Administration and the Holocaust," in *Networks of Nazi Persecution: Bureaucracy, Business, and the Organization of the Holocaust,* ed. Gerald D. Feldman and Wolfgang Seibel (New York: Berghahn, 2005), 269–294.

3. See recently Gruner and Ross, *New Perspectives on Kristallnacht.*

4. HHStA Wiesbaden, Abt. 461 Staatsanwaltschaft Frankfurt/Main, no. 7925 Henriette Schäfer, fol. 2: Gestapo note, April 14, 1939; cited by Gruner, "Defiance and Protest," 216.

5. HHStA Wiesbaden, Abt. 461/7925, fol. 10+RS: NSDAP Blockleiter to Ortsgruppe Bockenheim, March 30, 1939.

6. HHStA Wiesbaden, Abt. 461/7925, fol. 13: Wilhelm Schäfer to Gestapo Frankfurt, March 30, 1939.

7. HHStA Wiesbaden, Abt. 461/7925, fol. 1: Gestapo note, April 1, 1939. A few days later, the Nazi party county office in Frankfurt sent the report of party block leader (Zellenleiter) Kollmer to the Gestapo: HHStA Wiesbaden, Abt. 461/7925, fol. 10: NSDAP Kreisleitung to Gestapo, April 6, 1939.

8. HHStA Wiesbaden, Abt. 461/7925, fol. 2: Gestapo note, (April) 14, 1939.

9. HHStA Wiesbaden, Abt. 461/7925, fol. 3: Gestapo note, April 14, 1939.

10. HHStA Wiesbaden, Abt. 461/7925, fol. 4+RS: Gestapo note, April 14, 1939.

11. HHStA Wiesbaden, Abt. 461/7925, fol. 14–17: Wilhelm Schäfer to Gestapo, April 16, 1939.

12. HHStA Wiesbaden, Abt. 461/7925, fol. 5–7: Gestapo summons form, April 17, 1939.

13. HHStA Wiesbaden, Abt. 461/7925, fol. 8: Gestapo note, April 17, 1939.

14. HHStA Wiesbaden, Abt. 461/7925, fol. 18+RS: Gestapo note, April 19, 1939; Hand-written Note, Main prosecutor, May 4, 1939.

15. HHStA Wiesbaden, Abt. 461/7925, fol. 19: Gestapo note, May 12, 1939.

16. HHStA Wiesbaden, Abt. 461/7925, fol. 22+RS: Gendarmerie Gaggenau, note, June 6, 1939.

17. HHStA Wiesbaden, Abt. 461/7925, fol. 22+RS: Gendarmerie Gaggenau, note, June 6, 1939; handwritten note, main prosecutor, June 12, 1939.

18. HHStA Wiesbaden, Abt. 461/7925, fol. 2–4 and 23: Main prosecutor Frankfurt to Reich Ministry of Justice, with handwritten notes, June 13, 1939; Reich Ministry of Justice to main prosecutor Frankfurt, July 14, 1939.

19. HHStA Wiesbaden, Abt. 461/7925, fol. 25–26: Indictment, July 31, 1939.
20. HHStA Wiesbaden, Abt. 461/7925, fols. 39–44RS: Handwritten protocol, August 11, 1939; Judgment (stamp August 18, 1939).
21. HHStA Wiesbaden, Abt. 461/7925, fol. 1–2: Letter, August 14, 1939; HHStA Wiesbaden, Abt. 409/6, no. 73, no fols.: Main Prosecutor, Frankfurt, to prison Frankfurt, August 30, 1939; Summon form for Henriette Schäfer, Main Prosecutor, Frankfurt, August 30, 1939; Archiv Regierungspräsidium Darmstadt, Dezernat II 25 Entschädigung: BEG-Akte des Landes Hessen, Az.: W-03731, fol. 16: Court Bill, September 26, 1939.
22. HHStA Wiesbaden, Abt. 409/6, no. 73, no fols.: Form, Prison Frankfurt-Höchst, September 13, 1939, note on the back, September 14, 1939; HHStA Wiesbaden, Abt. 461, no. 7925, fol. 4: Visitor slips prison Frankfurt-Höchst, September 30, November 4, 1939, and February 3, 1940.
23. HHStA Wiesbaden, Abt. 409/6, no. 73, no fols.: Handwritten note, prison Frankfurt-Höchst, December 14, 1939; HHStA Wiesbaden, Abt. 461, no. 7925, fol. 4RS; HHStA Wiesbaden, Abt. 409/6, no. 73, no fols.: Main prosecutor, Special Court, Frankfurt to Wilhelm Schäfer, December 23, 1939; Note from March 13, 1940 on form, Prison Frankfurt-Höchst, September 13, 1939.
24. Archiv Regierungspräsidium Darmstadt, Dezernat II 25 Entschädigung: BEG-Akte des Landes Hessen, Az.: W-03731, no fols.: handwritten note, Siegfried Meyer, April 2, 1957. Volker Eichler, "Das 'Judenreferat' der Frankfurter Gestapo," in *"Nach der Kristallnacht": Jüdisches Leben und antijüdische Politik, 1938–1945, in Frankfurt am Main*, ed. Monika Kingreen (Frankfurt a.M.: Campus, 1999), 237–258, here 250. See also Monika Kingreen, "Gewaltsam verschleppt aus Frankfurt: Die Deportationen in den Jahren, 1941–1945," in *"Nach der Kristallnacht,"* ed. Kingreen, 357–402, here 383.
25. Gruner, *Widerstand in der Rosenstrasse*; Kingreen, "Gewaltsam verschleppt," 388.
26. YVA Jerusalem, ITS Arolsen, 5086449_0_1, Henriette Schäfer; www.ushmm.org /online/hsv/person_view.php?PersonId=1498269 (accessed June 26, 2020); Alfred Gottwaldt and Diana Schulle, *Die "Judendeportationen" aus dem Deutschen Reich, 1941–1945: Eine kommentierte Chronologie* (Wiesbaden: Marizverlag, 2005), 467; Kingreen, "Gewaltsam verschleppt," 389. YVA Jerusalem, ITS Arolsen, 20170628_161356, Henriette Schäfer. For the situation in the ghetto, see Anna Hájková, *The Last Ghetto: An Everyday History of Theresienstadt* (New York: Oxford University Press, 2020).
27. Cilly Kugelmann, "Befreiung—und dann?: Zur Situation der Juden in Frankfurt am Main im Jahr 1945," in *"Nach der Kristallnacht,"* ed. Kingreen, 435–456, here 440–441. YVA Jerusalem, ITS Arolsen, 70372607_0_1, Henriette Schäfer; Archiv Regierungspräsidium Darmstadt, Dezernat II 25 Entschädigung: BEG-Akte des Landes Hessen, Az.: W-03731, no fols. Letter to Regierungspräsident Entschädigungsbehörde, November 29, 1956.

28. On such problems, see Maximilian Strnad, "A Question of Gender!: Spaces of Violence and Reactions to Kristallnacht in Jewish-Gentil families," in *New Perspectives on Kristallnacht*, ed. Gruner and Ross, 51–68.

29. HHStA Wiesbaden, Abt. 461/7925, fol. 52: Handwritten note, December 6, 1949; Archiv Regierungspräsidium Darmstadt, Dezernat II 25 Entschädigung: BEG-Akte des Landes Hessen, Az.: W-03731, fol. 1–2: Application, February 17, 1950; HHStA Wiesbaden, Abt. 461/7925, no fol.: Main prosecutor Frankfurt to State Court, December 17, 1949; Handwritten notes, no date.

30. HHStA Wiesbaden, Abt. 461/7925, no fol.: Main prosecutor Frankfurt, certificate, December 24, 1949; Main prosecutor Frankfurt to Henriette Schäfer, December 24, 1949; Archiv Regierungspräsidium Darmstadt, Dezernat II 25 Entschädigung: BEG-Akte des Landes Hessen, Az.: W-03731, no fols.: Application, February 17, 1950; Letter to Regierungspräsident Entschädigungsbehörde, November 29, 1956; Certificate of inheritance, April 15, 1957.

31. HHStA Wiesbaden, Abt. 461/7273 Erich Löwenstein, fols. 1–6 and 26–30: Lawyer Wilhelm Jelkmann to clemency office at the State Court Frankfurt, July 20, 1933; Judgment, Special Court Frankfurt, April 1, 1933. On March 31, 1933, the merchant Isaak Leser (b. 1902) had talked in public about the horrific news that thousands of Jews had been hospitalized in Frankfurt. On trial after being denounced, he did not show any regrets. For displaying a hostile attitude toward the state, the Special Court punished him with one year in prison. Since Leser was of Polish origin, the police president in Frankfurt initiated his expulsion after he served the sentence; HHStA Wiesbaden, Abt. 461/7277. At a newspaper stand, the Jewish sales clerk Rahel Lorsch (b. 1914 in Frankfurt) condemned the fact that thirty-five Jewish men had been arrested and beaten. After being interrogated by the Gestapo, she left her home and was nowhere to be found; HHStA Wiesbaden, Abt. 461/7282, Rahel Lorsch, fol. 5–6 and 26: Indictment, Main Prosecutor for Special Court, April 21, 1933; Prosecutor to police President, November 6, 1933. For other cases see: HHStA Wiesbaden, Abt. 461, no. 7273 Erich Löwenstein; no. 7351 Hermann Rosenthal; no. 7306 Bertram Stern.

32. In a barbershop, the store employee Bernhard Mannsbach (b. 1899) complained that the causes of deaths in concentration camps would not be investigated. An SS member denounced him in June 1933 and recommended bringing him to the concentration camp Osthofen so that he could learn in person about the treatment in such camps. Although the Special Court acquitted Mannsbach because the witness was not found trustworthy, he did not receive compensation for the two months he spent in protective custody; HHStA Wiesbaden, Abt. 461/7294 Bernhard Mannsbach.

33. HHStA Wiesbaden, Abt. 461/7281 Hans Oster.

34. Julius Stern (b. 1865 in Nieder-Ingelheim) was sentenced to eight months in prison for his critical words. In August 1933, he claimed that the German radio would

make people dumb, Goebbels would look like an idiot, and corruption was everywhere, as everybody could see with the politician Gauleiter Sprenger in Frankfurt, who had been a simple postman before the Nazis came to power. Although Stern was almost seventy years old and had lost his wine shop after forty years in business, he had to serve the full sentence, despite his wife's plea for clemency; HHStA Wiesbaden, Abt. 461/7317 Julius Stern. In November 1934, Walther Levi (b. 1914) ran into an acquaintance in Munich, who was both a Nazi party and SA member. Levi told him that the misery was getting bigger and bigger under Hitler. Referring to the so-called Röhm putsch, the violent purge of Hitler's perceived opponents, he said, in June 1934 they shot at least 2,000 people. For these comments, the Special Court in Munich sentenced Levi to six weeks in prison; YVA Jerusalem, M55/JM 27135 Staatsarchiv München, Staatsanwaltschaften, no. 8978. Simon Altbaum (b. 1878), a Polish Jew in Mönchengladbach, talked negatively about the Nazis in public. Since the Gestapo expressed suspicions that he had ties to Communists, a trial for treason was prepared, but later canceled. However, Altbaum was expelled to Poland; USHMM Washington, RG 14.001 M Reel 1 Gestapo Düsseldorf, Akte Simon Altbaum, fol. 39.

35. HHStA Wiesbaden, Abt. 461/7306 Bertram Stern; StA Munich, Staatsanwaltschaften, no. 8834.

36. HHStA Wiesbaden, Abt. 461/7436 Max Sternberg.

37. HHStA Wiesbaden, abt. 461/7416, Raimund Ullmann, fols. 19+RS, 17, 183–186: Interrogation Hugo Tormin, n.d. (approximately July 19 or 20, 1935); Handwritten letter, Ullmann, July 22, 1935; Judgment, Special Court, April 17, 1936. During a business visit at a private firm, a divorced sales agent Ernst Meyer (b. 1873 in Diez /Lahn) criticized the buzz around Hitler as well as a recent speech by Gauleiter Sprenger. He also responded to the anti-Semitic newspaper *Der Stürmer*, which depicted a Jew as a murderer, by stating that Jews are not murdering humans. The Special Court in Frankfurt sentenced Meyer to six months in prison for his critical comments; HHStA Wiesbaden, Abt. 461/7435 Ernst Meyer, fol. 39–41RS: Judgment, Special Court Frankfurt/Main, November 13, 1935; see also HHStA Wiesbaden, Abt. 409/4 Haftanstalten, no. 4798.

38. StA Hamburg, 213-11, no. 51188; Wolf Gruner, "Indifference?: Participation and Protest as Individual Responses to the Persecution of the Jews as Revealed in Berlin Police Logs and Trial Records, 1933–1945," in *The Germans and the Holocaust: Popular Responses to the Persecution and Murder of the Jews*, ed. Alan Steinweis and Susanna Schrafstetter (New York: Berghahn, 2016), 59–83, here 64.

39. Based on a public talk, see the article: Joachim Prinz, "Living Without Neighbours," *Jüdische Rundschau*, April 1935, printed in *Persecution and Murder of the European Jews*, vol. 1, ed. Gruner, doc. no. 161, 451–454. See Joachim Prinz, *Rebellious Rabbi: An Autobiography—The German and Early American Years*, edited and introduced by Michael A. Meyer (Bloomington: Indiana University Press, 2008),

102–104; Joachim Prinz, "A Rabbi Under the Hitler Regime," in *Gegenwart im Rückblick: Festgabe für die Jüdische Gemeinde zu Berlin 25 Jahre nach dem Neubeginn*, ed. Herbert A. Strauss and Kurt G. Grossmann (Heidelberg: Lothar Stiehm Verlag, 1970), 231–238; Max Nussbaum, "Ministry Under Stress: A Rabbi's Recollection of Nazi Berlin," in *Gegenwart im Rückblick*, ed. Strauss and Grossmann, 239–247, here 242–246; Speech by Rabbi Dr. Joseph Carlebach in Hamburg, August 19, 1939, in *Jüdischer Alltag als humaner Widerstand: Dokumente des Oberrabbiners Dr. Joseph Carlebach aus den Jahren, 1939–1941*, ed. Miriam Gillis-Carlebach (Hamburg: Verein für Hamburgische Geschichte, 1990), 71. For more examples, see Kwiet and Eschwege, *Selbstbehauptung*, 234–235.

40. LA Berlin, A Pr.Br.Rep. 030, Tit. 95, no. 21617, Bd. 2, Fol. 241. See also Gruner, *Persecution of the Jews in Berlin*, 23; and with a slightly different version: Kreutzmüller, *Ausverkauf*, 294–295.

41. YVA Jerusalem, M55/JM 27134 Staatsarchiv München, Staatsanwaltschaften, no. 8043; LA Berlin, A Rep. 355, no. 4873, no fol.: Copy, General Prosecutor to Special Court, indictment, December 23, 1936, 1–3. One of the notorious Nuremberg Laws of September 15, 1935, prohibited the employment of "Aryan" maids under the age of forty-five in Jewish homes; RGBl., 1935 I, 1146.

42. LA Berlin, A Rep. 355, no. 4502 Klopfer, Paula, no fols.: Copy, General Prosecutor to Special Court (approximately beginning of 1937), indictment, 1–3; Gruner, "The Germans," 35.

43. LA Berlin, A Rep. 355, no. 4897, no fol.: Copy, General Prosecutor at the State Court to Special Court at the State Court, indictment, January 5, 1937. Gertrud Arndt (b. 1878) received six months in prison for insulting Hitler. In Munich, three Jews had told each other jokes about Göring's wife. In a public session, the local Special Court sentenced them all to two months in prison. In July 1937, the Frankfurt Special Court sentenced Rosalie Kowalski (b. 1887) to six months in prison for repeatedly using the debasing term "Hitler pack" and saying that Goebbels lied; LA Berlin, A Rep. 355, no. 4765 Arndt, Gertrud (7.4.1878), fol. 1+RS: Arthur Prinz to local court Berlin-Tiergarten, October 27, 1958; Note, archive of the prosecution, November 3, 1958; YVA Jerusalem, M55/JM 27135 Staatsarchiv München, Staatsanwaltschaften, fol. 1–146; HHStA Wiesbaden, Abt. 461/7722 Rosalie Kowalski, fol. 109–116+RS: Main prosecutor to police headquarters, August 24, 1937. See also, for another case, USC SF/VHA, Inge Stutzel, tape 1, min. 22.

44. HHStA Wiesbaden, Abt. 461/7753 Kurt Ascher, no fol.: Main Prosecutor to Special Court, Frankfurt/Main, indictment, September 28, 1937.

45. YVA Jerusalem, M55/2160, fols. 1–102; YVA Jerusalem, M55/2158, fols. 1–5.

46. YVA Jerusalem, M55/2166, fols. 1–10. On early Jewish forced labor for welfare departments, see Wolf Gruner, *Jewish Forced Labor Under the Nazis: Economic Needs and Racial Aims, 1938–1944* (New York: Cambridge University Press, 2006), 4.

47. LA Berlin, A. Pr.Br.Rep. 030, Tit. 95, no. 21619, Fol. 143–144RS. Later, Adler managed to immigrate to Shanghai; BA Berlin, Residenzenliste, Auskunft Dr. Simone Walther, September 10, 2010. For more details and literature on the summer 1938 attacks, see Gruner, *Persecution of the Jews in Berlin*, 29–31, 106–113.

48. After the November pogrom, he was interned at Buchenwald until January 1939; LA Berlin, A Pr.Br.Rep. 030, Tit. 95, no. 21619, vol. 4, fol. 321+RS: Note, September 26, 1938; YVA Jerusalem, ITS Arolsen, 20170626_163523, Kurt Rosenberg. His business had been totally destroyed. Rosenberg tried to make money by working with a man who secured passages and visas to Bolivia, but operated without authorization and occasionally did not pay the shipping company in Hamburg. In August 1939, Herbert Stein and Rosenberg were arrested. For several months, Rosenberg was in Hamburg-Fuhlsbüttel prison until he was transferred to Berlin. Yet Berlin dropped the case. After fall of 1941, as he claims in his résumé after the war, he had been jailed two times for not wearing the yellow star, once for four weeks and once for six weeks. From November 1941 until the end of the war, he was imprisoned and registered as sick in the police prison in Berlin; LA Berlin, A Rep. 358-02, no. 7670 (microfilm 2224), no fols.: Indictment, Main Prosecutor at the State Court Berlin, March 1, 1940, 1–4; Memo, office of the court Berlin to the prosecutor office Berlin, June 6, 1940; LA Berlin, C Rep 118-01, no. 31531, fol. 1–2: Résumé, 1946; YVA Jerusalem, ITS Arolsen, 20170626_163542, Kurt Rosenberg; ibid., 20170626_163356, Kurt Rosenberg. See also Gruner, *Persecution of the Jews in Berlin*, 30, and Kreutzmüller, *Ausverkauf*, 295. For the Decree of August 23, 1938, see Gruner, *Persecution of the Jews in Berlin*, 114–115.

49. YVA Jerusalem, M55/JM 27136 Staatsarchiv München, Staatsanwaltschaften, no. 9375.

50. YVA Jerusalem, M55/JM 27136 Staatsarchiv München, Staatsanwaltschaften, no. 9357, fol. 1, 18–19: Gestapo Augsburg to main prosecutor Augsburg, January 10, 1939; and Judgment, Special Court Munich, August 17, 1939. Klopfer, upset, exclaimed, "These dirty Bastards, they would squeeze the last penny out of us, if possible." Since Klopfer had frequently criticized the Nazis, the Special Court sentenced her to six months in prison; YVA Jerusalem, M55/JM 27135 Staatsarchiv München, Staatsanwaltschaften, no. 9261, fol. 1 and 17–18: Gendarmerie Krumbach to Bezirksamt Krumbach, November 23, 1938, and Judgment Special Court München, March 15, 1939.

51. Heinrich Mugdan, diary entry, November 20, 1938, in *Jewish Responses to Persecution*, ed. Matthäus and Roseman, vol. 1, 370; cited by Gruner, "The Germans Should Expel the Foreigner Hitler," 38. In Berlin, the 141st police precinct reported the arrest of Erna Oppler (b. 1899) for a political incident on December 29, 1938, after she had argued against the persecution of her fellow Jews in front of four other people in an apartment; LA Berlin, A Pr.Br.Rep. 030, no. 21620, fol. 175: 141. Police precinct, report about a political incident to Stapo, Spandau, December 29, 1938.

Else Cohn said, "Den Führer koennte ich in die Fotzen speien, dass er das Gesetz aufgebracht hat, dass die Juden wegmüssen"; YVA Jerusalem, M55/JM 27135 Staats-archiv München, Staatsanwaltschaften, no. 9295. Nachmann's own wife, who had cheated on him, informed the police; HHStA Wiesbaden, Abt. 461/7878 Ernst Nachmann, fol. 3: Gestapo note, December 8, 1938; HHStA Wiesbaden, Abt. 409/6 Haftanstalten, no. 59.

52. He also said that he had to report twice a week to the authorities. He was registered to emigrate, but lacked the means to do so; HHStA Wiesbaden, Abt. 461/8153, fol. 7–9 and 68–69: Summons, March 13, 1940, and Special Court, judgment, July 24, 1940.

53. WSuLA Vienna, Sondergericht, SHv Strafakten, no. 5067 Dr. Arthur Singer, fol. 1b, 11, 14RS, 65–66RS: Letter housing office to Gestapo, August 21, 1938; Interrogation of the accused, State Court Vienna, September 8, 1939; Interrogation of the accused, State Court Vienna, September 19, 1939; Trial protocol, June 18, 1940; Property dec-laration Arthur Singer. In June 1942, Singer was deported to Maly Trostinez. He lost his remaining property, consisting of 30 Reichsmarks in cash, 5.72 Reichsmarks in savings, bedroom furniture, and other belongings under the decree of November 25, 1941. This decree automatically expropriated all Jews, if they crossed German borders due to emigration or deportation; YVA Jerusalem, ITS Arolsen, Singer, Arthur Transport; www.ushmm.org/online/hsv/person_view.php?PersonId=5221764 (accessed July 2, 2020). Regarding anti-Jewish housing policies in general and in Vienna, see Gruner, "Local Initiatives, Central Coordination," 269–294; Wolf Gruner, *Zwangsarbeit und Verfolgung: Österreichische Juden im NS-Staat, 1938–1945* (Innsbruck et al: Studien-Verlag 2000).

54. YVA Jerusalem, M55/JM 27133 Staatsarchiv für Oberbayern, Special Court Mu-nich-Prosecutor Munich, no. 5463, fol. 3–5, 6–6RS, 9: Gestapo Munich, interroga-tion form, September 12, 1939; Gestapo note, September 13, 1939; Head prosecution office Munich, draft October 1939, to Special Court Munich; see also *Verfolgung und Ermordung der europäischen Juden*, vol. 3, ed. Löw, doc. no. 10, 102–103: Protocol Gestapo, Gestapo Munich (B. Nr. II. B), signed *Kriminal-Oberassistent* Schipferling, September 13, 1939. Her case is mentioned in Schraf-stetter, *Flucht und Versteck*, 39. The retired Arthur Schlesinger (b. 1872) exclaimed in a restaurant in Dresden that the bloodhound Hitler would soon cooperate with the bloodhound Stalin. The Gestapo found out that Schlesinger had earlier criti-cized the persecution of the Jews in some conversations. He had also complained about his exclusion from cinema and theater visits, despite having converted to Protestantism; YVA Jerusalem, M55/2171, fols. 1–24. In November 1939, in an um-brella store in Baden, Margarete Hirsch said that Göring was a bloodthirsty man. Luckily, her charges were dropped under the Hitler war amnesty; WSuLA Vienna, Sondergericht, SHv Strafakten, no. 120 Margarete Hirsch. The day before Germany invaded Poland, the former sales representative Alfred Lauffer (b. 1872) com-

mented to a neighbor in Dresden: "First they expelled the Jews, now this will haunt them" (Erst hat man die Juden rausgeschmissen, das rächt sich jetzt aber alles). After the denunciation by the neighbor in a letter to the local Nazi party group he was arrested. Two months later, the Special Court in Freiberg punished Lauffer with five months in jail under the Treacherous Attacks Law; YVA Jerusalem, M55/2181, fols. 1–82. See also LA Berlin, A Rep. 355, no. 4742 Heinrich, Hugo, no fols.: Abschrift Anklage Generalstaatsanwalt an Sondergericht, August 30, 1940, S. 1–3.

55. StA Munich, Staatsanwaltschaften, no. 9821 Franz Kohn; no. 11287 Julie Wagner; www.bundesarchiv.de/gedenkbuch/en984528 (accessed July 2, 2018).

56. LA Berlin, A Rep. 355, no. 4993, no fol.: Copy, Main Prosecutor to Special Court, follow up indictment, April 15, 1940, 1–2.

57. During his time in prison, his wife did not receive any financial support for her and their child. After the sentence, the police were instructed to hand him over to the Gestapo; StA Chemnitz, 39074, no fols.: indictment, November 1940; copy from *NS-Tageszeitung*, November 22, 1940; copy from *Zwickauer Tageblatt*, November 22, 1940; StA Chemnitz, 30071 Zuchthaus Zwickau/7562, fol. 54 and 56: Letter Martha Korn, January 14, 1941; fol. 56: Gestapo Plauen to Prison in Zwickau, January 22, 1941.

58. LA Berlin, A Rep. 355, no. 5408, no fol.: copy, Main Prosecutor at the State Court, head of the prosecutor office for the Special Court, to the Special Court at the State Court Berlin, arrest issue, June 11, 1940, 1–6; copy judgment, Special Court I, August 23, 1940, 1–2.

59. WSuLA Vienna, Sondergericht, SHv Strafakten, 5149 David Gutwurzel, fol. 1–2, 32–33: Gestapo to Main Prosecutor Vienna, March 18, 1940; Note about criminal charge, 150th Police precinct, Vienna, February 19, 1940; Judgment, State Court Vienna as Special Court, June 10, 1940; DÖW Vienna, Geheime Gestapo-leitstelle Wien, daily report, no. 3, October 5–7, 1940, 4; WSuLA Vienna, Sondergericht, SHv Strafakten, no. 5170, Mirl Rachel Wiener, fol. 1–2, 7, and 33: Gestapo to Main Prosecutor Vienna, May 9, 1940; Note about criminal charge, 54th Police precinct, Vienna, May 2, 1940; Interrogation note, Hildegard Greisinger, May 8, 1940; Judgment, State Court Vienna as Special Court, August 21, 1940.

60. Avraham Barkai, "Im Schatten von Verfolgung und Vernichtung, Leo Baeck in den Jahren des NS-Regimes," in *Leo Baeck, 1873–1956: Aus dem Stamme von Rabbinern*, edited by Georg Heuberger and Fritz Backhaus (Frankfurt am Main: Jüdischer Verlag im Suhrkamp Verlag, 2001), 77–102, here 91.

61. StA Hamburg, 213-11, no. 61296, fol. 1–12. BA Berlin, Residentenliste, KrohnMela-nieBBB11198322_0_1, accessed via USHMM. www.bundesarchiv.de/gedenkbuch /directory.html.en?result#frmResults (accessed January 29, 2018); BA Berlin, Resi-dentenliste, KrohnMelanieBB11198309_0_1, accessed via USHMM. On the deporta-tion and the fate of these Jews: Gottwaldt and Schulle, "*Judendeportationen*," 89–95.

62. A Jewish woman who had spread anti-Hitler rumors and hid a leaflet was arrested, and the Gestapo transferred her to the Vienna Special Court for prosecution; YVA Jerusalem, M38/120 (DÖW), fol. 3. The former tailor Jakob Winter (b. 1880), a veteran of the First World War, was detained in June of 1941. He declared that Germany would lose the war and the Jews would get back all the stolen belongings. The Special Court Vienna sentenced Winter harshly under the Treacherous Attacks Law with two years in prison, because he as a Jew had supposedly denigrated the Nazi movement and the race policy of the Reich in a malicious way; YVA Jerusalem, M38/354, no fols. Olga Goldfeld had been denounced for saying that she still had relationships with Aryans who supported her. She also talked about the deportation of the desperate Jews. According to the report, she blamed the Nazis for handing out oranges to the deportees at the train stations so that the victims could be photographed with friendly faces; WSuLA Vienna, Sondergericht, SHv Strafakten, no. 324 Olga Goldfeld. Widower Friedrich Beer (b. 1892 Vienna) criticized the treatment of the Jews, particularly that only one grocery store was assigned to them in each Vienna district, which meant long walks only to encounter miserable leftovers. He also mentioned the treatment of the very sick and the removal of patients from mental institutions (*Heil- und Pflegeanstalten*). Finally, he called the war a result of Hitler's goal to rule the world. For his words, the Special Court sentenced Beer to fifteen months in prison in March 1942; WSuLA Vienna, Sondergericht, SHv Strafakten, no. 5384 Friedrich Beer, fol. 8 and 62–65: Anne Zidek to local Nazi Party group, Vienna, August 26, 1941; Judgment, Special Court at State Court Vienna, March 13, 1942. Verdict (Leo B.), Special Court Berlin, February 26, 1942, printed in Schimmler, *Recht ohne Gerechtigkeit*, 69–71.

63. LA Berlin, A Rep. 355, no. 5697, no fol.: copy indictment, Main Prosecutor at the State Court, head of the prosecutor office for the Special Court, to the Special Court at the State Court Berlin, June 7, 1941, 1–4. See also CJA Berlin, 2 A 1, Austrittskartei Hertha Reis. About the fate of her, her mother, and her son: Memorial Book entry, www.bundesarchiv.de/gedenkbuch/directory.html.en?result#frmResults (accessed June 22, 2020); YVA Jerusalem, ITS Arolsen, Hertha Reis; CJA, 2 A 1, Austrittskartei Rudolf Alexander Reis; Information from Barbara Welker, CJA Berlin, email, June 22, 2020; Memorial Book entry, www.bundesarchiv.de/gedenkbuch/directory.html.en?result#frmResults (accessed June 22, 2020). For the development of Berlin's policy to expel Jewish tenants, see Susanne Willems, *Der entsiedelte Jude: Albert Speers Wohnungsmarktpolitik für den Berliner Hauptstadtbau* (Berlin: Edition Hentrich, 2002). See more cases mentioned in Gruner, "Defiance and Protest."

64. "*Das ist Hitlerwirtschaft!*," WSuLA Vienna, Sondergericht, SHv Strafakten, no. 5413 Karoline Rist, fol. 2–3: Indictment, Vienna, February 28, 1942. See also no. 6131 Gabriele Reich.

65. "Goebbels, der Scheisser, entfesselt mit seinen Reden Pogrome; nach dieser Zeit kommt eine andere und dann für jeden Juden der gelitten hat, 1000 andere und

noch mehr"; LA Berlin, A Rep. 355, no. 4114 Karpowitz, Otto (b. December 21, 1886), no fols.: Archive of the Prosecution, note, May 8, 1967; Recompensation department to Main Prosecutor, April 27, 1957, 1–3; copy indictment, Main Prosecutor to Special Court Berlin, January 9, 1943; Memorial Book entries, www.bundesarchiv.de/gedenkbuch (accessed October 29, 2020).

Chapter 3. Defying Anti-Jewish Laws

1. The story of Hans Oppenheimer is mainly based on various files from Hesse Main State Archive in Wiesbaden: Abt. 409/4, no. 5439; Abt. 409/3; and Federal archive, Memorial Book. Entry in: Residentenliste, accessed at the USHMM, December 15, 2017.

2. HHStA Wiesbaden, Abt. 409/4, no. 5439, résumé. On the Philanthropin: André Griemert, *Bürgerliche Bildung für Frankfurter Juden?: Das frühe Philanthropin in der Kontroverse um die jüdische Emanzipation* (Marburg: Tectum, 2010); Inge Schlotzhauer, *Das Philanthropin, 1804–1942: Die Schule der Israelitischen Gemeinde in Frankfurt am Main* (Frankfurt: W. Kramer, 1990).

3. Gruner, "NS-Judenverfolgung," 96–97; Kingreen, ed., *"Nach der Kristallnacht."*

4. Wolfgang Wippermann, *Das Leben in Frankfurt zur NS-Zeit*, vol. 1, *Die national-sozialistische Judenverfolgung* (Frankfurt am Main: Kramer, 1986), 86–87; www .frankfurt1933-1945.de/home/ (accessed January 8, 2021).

5. HHStA Wiesbaden, Abt. 409/4, no. 5439, handwritten CV; Wippermann, *Leben in Frankfurt*, vol. 1, 86.

6. HHStA Wiesbaden, Abt. 409/4, no. 5439: CV.

7. See in extensive detail, Gruner, *Jewish Forced Labor*. For Frankfurt: Wolf Gruner, "Der Geschlossene Arbeitseinsatz und die Juden in Frankfurt am Main, 1938–1942," in *"Nach der Kristallnacht,"* ed. Kingreen, 259–288.

8. HHStA Wiesbaden, Abt. 409/5439, CV.

9. For this and the following, StadtA Kelkheim, file "Arbeitseinsatz einer jüdischen Arbeitskolonne (April–Oktober 1939)," no fols. See also Wolf Gruner, "Terra Inkognita?: Die Lager für den 'jüdischen Arbeitseinsatz,' 1938–1943, und die deutsche Bevölkerung," in *Die Deutschen und die Judenverfolgung im Dritten Reich*, ed. Ursula Büttner (Hamburg: Christians, 1992), 131–159.

10. BA Berlin, R 22/3499, fol. 2–3.

11. *VO über die öffentliche Fürsorge für Juden*; RGBl., 1938 I, S. 1649; for details see Wolf Gruner, *Öffentliche Wohlfahrt und Judenverfolgung: Wechselwirkungen lokaler und zentraler Politik im NS-Staat, 1933–1942* (Munich: Oldenbourg Verlag, 2002), 157–211. HHStA Wiesbaden, 519/3.

12. HHStA Wiesbaden, Abt. 409/4, no. 5439; HHStA Wiesbaden, Abt. 461/8896; BA Berlin, R 22, and 3499, fol. 2–3.

13. HHStA Wiesbaden, Abt. 461/8896, indictment, résumé, and letter to his parents.

14. HHStA Wiesbaden, Abt. 409/4, no. 5439: various docs; ibid. Abt. 409/3, card index; 5. *Verordnung zum Reichsbürgergesetz, 27 September 1938*; RGBl., 1938 I, S. 1403.

15. *Verordnung gegen Volksschädlinge*, September 5, 1939; RGBl., 1939 I, 1679. See also Christine Schoenmakers, *"Die Belange der Volksgemeinschaft erfordern . . ." Rechtspraxis und Selbstverständnis von Bremer Juristen im "Dritten Reich"* (Paderborn: Schöningh, 2015), 88–92.

16. While the first draft of Hans's indictment contained a charge for general mischief in nine cases, this specific charge had been erased in the final version; BA Berlin, R 22/3499, fol. 2–3. HHStA Wiesbaden, Abt. 461/8896.

17. BA Berlin, R 22/3499, fol. 1–3.

18. BA Berlin, R 22/3499, fol. 4; HHStA Wiesbaden, Abt. 461/8896.

19. BA Berlin, R 22/3499, fol. 7.

20. HHStA Wiesbaden, Abt. 409/4, no. 5439 and card. For details on Diez prison, see "Justizvollzugs- und Sicherungsverwahranstalt Diez," Wikipedia, de.wikipedia.org /wiki/Justizvollzugs-_und_Sicherungsverwahranstalt_Diez (accessed January 8, 2022).

21. HHStA Wiesbaden, Abt. 409/4, no. 5439.

22. HHStA Wiesbaden, Abt. 409/4, no. 5439.

23. HHStA Wiesbaden, Abt. 409/4, no. 5439.

24. HHStA Wiesbaden, Abt. 409/4, no. 5439, letter, September 1941, letter, March 1942; YVA, ITS Arolsen, card Hans Oppenheimer; HHStA Wiesbaden, 519/3, no. 29972. *Gesetz über Mietverhältnisse mit Juden*; RGBl., 1939 I, 864. For such actions of city governments, see Gruner, "Local Initiatives," 269–294. For Frankfurt: Ute Daub, "Die Stadt Frankfurt macht sich 'judenfrei': Zur Konzentration, Verbannung und Ghettoisierung der jüdischen Bevölkerung zwischen 1938 und 1945," in *"Nach der Kristallnacht,"* ed. Kingreen, 319–356.

25. HHStA Wiesbaden, Abt. 409/4, 5439, letter August 9, 1941. Aminophenazone (or aminopyrine, amidopyrine, Piramidon) is a pyrazolone with analgesic, anti-inflammatory, and antipyretic properties. Aminophenazon, invented by the German chemical firm Hoechst, was taken off the market in the Western world in the 1970s because of its carcinogenic effects; en.wikipedia.org/wiki/Aminophenazone (accessed November 18, 2017).

26. HHStA Wiesbaden, Abt. 409/4, no. 5439, letter August 9, 1941. On anti-Jewish policy in Frankfurt, see Wippermann, *Das Leben in Frankfurt*, vol. 1.

27. HHStA Wiesbaden, Abt. 409/4, no. 5439, fol. 11.

28. HHStA Wiesbaden, Abt. 409/4, no. 5439, fol. 35.

29. HHStA Wiesbaden, Abt. 409/4, no. 5439.

30. HHStA Wiesbaden, Abt. 409/4, no. 5439, letters from January 1942.

31. HHStA Wiesbaden, Abt. 409/4, no. 5439, Letter, March 30, 1942; ibid., note, March 31, 1942.

32. HHStA Wiesbaden, Abt. 409/4, no. 5439: Letter, April 16, 1942; filled-out form about letters to and from Hans and visits, starting on June 7, 1941.

33. HHStA Wiesbaden, Abt. 409/4, no. 5439, fol. 24.

34. HHStA Wiesbaden, Abt. 409/4, no. 5439.

35. HHStA Wiesbaden, Abt. 409/4, no. 5439.

36. "Oppenheimer, Rudolf Rudi," *Memorial Book: Victims of the Persecution of Jews Under the National Socialist Tyranny in Germany, 1933–1945*, Das Bundesarchiv, www.bundesarchiv.de/gedenkbuch/en940921 (accessed March 21, 2022).

37. Entry Anna Oppenheimer, in Residentenliste, doc. no. 44746038_0_1 and doc. no. 44746765_0_1, in ITS Arolsen, all accessed at the USHMM, December 15, 2017; www.bundesarchiv.de/gedenkbuch/en940921 (accessed December 27, 2017); Danuta Czech, *Kalendarium der Ereignisse im Konzentrationslager Auschwitz-Birkenau, 1939–1945* (Reinbek bei Hamburg, 1989), 391.

38. HHStA Wiesbaden, 409/4, no. 5439. On "extermination through work": IMT, vol. 26, doc. no. PS-654, 200–203: Protocol RJM about meeting with RFSS on September 18, 1942; see Adler, *Der verwaltete Mensch*, 251–252; Longerich, *Holocaust*, 324. Decree Müller, October 5, 1942 (PS-1063); cited by Adler, *Der verwaltete Mensch*, 253.

39. HHStA Wiesbaden, Abt. 409/4, no. 5439.

40. HHStA Wiesbaden, Abt. 409/4, no. 4127 Hans Oppenheimer Akte eig. Lippman Israel Lewin, 21.7.1899; HHStA Wiesbaden, Abt. 403; YVA Jerusalem, ITS Arolsen cards, February 5, 1943.

41. *Verordnung gegen den Waffenbesitz der Juden*, RGBl., 1938 I, 1573. StA Hamburg, 213-11, no. 58500 Feldmann, Manfred.

42. To hand over precious metals and jewels: 3. *Durchführungsverordnung zur Verordnung über die Ausschaltung der Juden aus dem deutschen Wirtschaftsleben*, February 21, 1939; RGBl., 1939 I, 282. For cases, see HHStA Wiesbaden, Abt. 461, no. 17287 Moses Rosenbaum; no. 9293 Gustav Beiersdorf; StA Hamburg, 213-11, no. 61336 Hinrichsen, Carl Marcus David; YVA Jerusalem, M38/120 (DÖW), fol. 8RS-9 and fol. 16RS: Norbert Mendrochowicz (b. 1884) arrested on October 3, 1941, Henriette Hoffmann (b. 1862) arrested on October 28, 1941, both in Vienna. USC SF/VHA, Walter Blumenthal, tape 2, min. 18; Kaplan, *Between Dignity and Despair*, 135.

   To deposit liquid assets and money: *Verordnung über Einsatz des jüdischen Vermögens, 3 December 1938*; RGBl., 1938 I, 1709. For cases see: SStA Leipzig, 20114 Landgericht Leipzig, no. 5627, Käthe Kanstein; SStA Leipzig, 20031 Polizeipräsidium, PP-S 1839173 Kanstein, Käthe and PP-S 1839168 Kanstein, Salomon; HHStA Wiesbaden, Abt. 461/8148 Wilhelm Sander and no. 9293 Gustav Beiersdorf. See also a trial against a Jewish couple in Vienna in 1940: Wolfgang Form, and Oliver Uthe, eds., *NS-Justiz in Österreich. Lage- und Reiseberichte, 1938–1945* (Vienna: Litverlag, 2004), 382.

   To leave valuables behind in Germany: *Runderlass Mitnahme von Umzugsgut durch Auswanderer*, April 17, 1939; JNBL, April 25, 1939, 1; USC SF/VHA, Irene

Hofstein, tape 3, min. 1:31–2:58. See some cases in Kaplan, *Between Dignity and Despair*, 134–135; Kulka and Jäckel, eds., *Die Juden*, doc. no. 3009: Regierungspräsident Niederbayern and Oberpfalz, Report for October 1939, Regensburg November 8, 1939.

43. USC SF/VHA, Hilde Watermann, tape 1; Irene Hofstein, tape 3; StA Hamburg, 213-11, no. 60192, Goldschmidt, Aron; StA Munich, Staatsanwaltschaften, no. 9612 (Rosa and Gustav Plaschke); Kaplan, *Between Dignity and Despair*, 135.

44. HHStA Wiesbaden, Abt. 461/8148, no fols.: Judgment Special Court, July 10, 1940, 4; HHStA Wiesbaden, Abt. 461/9293, fol. 2–9RS, 42–44RS: Gestapo to Devisenstelle, September 26, 1940; October 17, 1940 form, October 17, 1940; Judgment, Special Court Frankfurt, January 13, 1941.

45. StA Hamburg, 213-11, no. 67101 Martha Frank, fol. 1–25, 55; YVA Jerusalem, ITS Arolsen, Martha Frank TD; Memorial Book entry Martha Frank, in www .bundesarchiv.de/gedenkbuch/en1012568 (accessed April 24, 2018).

46. As mentioned in many memoirs of Jewish survivors. See Miron, "Lately," 127. For some other examples: WSuLA Vienna, Sondergericht, SHv Strafakten 6276 Edith Weiss; USC SF/VHA, Anita Siegel, 45, tape 2, min. 45; USC SF/VHA, Renata Adler, tape 2, Seg. 56 bis 58. For the curfew decree see: StA Freiburg i. Br., Landratsamt Mühlheim, no. 365, no. 243, no fols.: RFSS decree, September 6, 1939, in circular decree Stapoleitstelle Karlsruhe, September 10, 1939.

47. WSuLA Vienna, Sondergericht, SHv Strafakten, 5216 Laura Rechnitz, fol. 2 and 23: Note, Police, February 3, 1941; Judgment, Special Court Vienna, April 25, 1941. Multiple examples from Vienna can be found at: DÖW Wien, Gestapo-Leitstelle Wien, Tagesrapporte October–December 1940, no fols.: Gestapo Vienna daily report, no. 9, December 18–19, 1940, 2; DÖW Wien, Gestapo-Leitstelle Wien, Tagesrapporte January–March 1941, no fols.: Gestapo Vienna daily report, no. 4, February 7–9, 1941, 4; Gestapo Vienna daily report, no. 5, February 10–11, 1941, 4.

48. Facsimile of the decree ordering Jews to hand over radios in September 1939, in Irmgard Harmann-Schütz and Franz Blome-Drees, *Die Geschichte der Juden in Sundern* (Sundern: Stadt Sundern, 1988), 156; *Verordnung über ausserordentliche Rundfunkmassnahmen*, September 1, 1939; RGBl., I/1939, 1683. See also Michael P. Hensle, *Rundfunkverbrechen: Das Hören von "Feindsendern" im Nationalsozialismus* (Berlin: Metropol, 2003). In Frankfurt, dentist Walter Mosbach (b. 1899 in Schwerte-Ruhr) first denied but then admitted to listening to British radio stations together with a non-Jewish female physician. He had also visited half a dozen forbidden movies at night and, therefore, broken the curfew. In addition, he was indicted for distribution of illegal texts but acquitted on these counts. The court sentenced him to two years in prison in January 1942. Before finishing his sentence, the Gestapo deported him to Auschwitz on December 8, 1942; HHStA Wiesbaden, Abt. 461/8299, Erna Oeser, fol. 13, 59, 167: Interrogation in prison, June 13, 1941; Judgment, Special Court, January 26, 1942; Zentralspruchkammer Hessen/Süd an

Staatsanwaltschaft Frankfurt, January 5, 1950. For other cases see WSuLA Vienna, Sondergericht, SHv Strafakten, 5612 Irma Plehn; 5770 Rudolf Konitzer; 5950 Stella Kubs; DÖW Wien, Gestapo-Leitstelle Wien, Tagesrapporte January–March 1941, no fols.: Gestapo daily report, no. 6, February 12–13, 1941, 3 (Rudolf Kornitzer, b. 1900, Vienna); StA Hamburg, 213-11, no. 59780, Gustav Wagner.

49. USC SF/VHA, Ruth Epstein, tape 2, min. 23:40–24:15. See also: USC SF/VHA, Hannelore Noe, tape 3, min. 62.

50. StA Hamburg, 213-11, no. 61799, Max Grossmann; YVA Jerusalem, M1 DN/188 Frankfurt; DÖW Vienna, Geheime Gestapo-leitstelle Wien, Gestapo daily report, no. 9, January 22–23, 1941, 3–4.

51. Kulka and Jäckel, eds., *The Jews*, doc. no. 3009: *Regierungspräsident* Niederbayern and Oberpfalz, Report for October 1939, Regensburg, November 8, 1939. The police also incarcerated Jakob Kolb (b. 1896 in Michelndorf) for ten days in the fall of 1940, since he was engaged in illegal trade with foodstuffs; DÖW Vienna, Geheime Gestapo-leitstelle Wien, Gestapo daily report, no. 2, September 17 and 18, 1940; Gruner, *Holocaust in Bohemia and Moravia*, 279.

52. The family had moved from Magdeburg to Berlin-Neukölln in July 1937, and was arrested in August 1940. The wife's sister lived in Pittsburgh. In October 1939, her brother-in-law Nathan Kann dispatched affidavits for the family to the U.S. Consulate in Berlin. In February 1941, the Zadeks obtained third-class passage bound for New York. However, they did not receive the U.S. visas. They were deported to the Warsaw ghetto on April 2, 1942; LA Berlin, B Rep. 020, Acc. 1201, no. 6948, fol. 134–135: Neukölln 211th Police precinct, logbook entry, August 25, 1941 (no. 359); and August 28, 1941 (no. 362); www.bundesarchiv.de/gedenkbuch (last accessed on January 11, 2022) and BLHA Potsdam, Rep. 36 A, Kartei; Michael E. Abrahams-Sprod, *Life Under Siege: The Jews of Magdeburg Under Nazi Rule* (Dissertation, University of Sydney, 2006), 307–308 (ses.library.usyd.edu.au/bitstream/2123/1627/19/09Ch.7. pdf, last accessed January 11, 2022). For the Berlin decree on limited shopping hours of July 4, 1940, see Gruner, *Persecution of the Jews in Berlin*, 137. The Zadek family had already been denounced by the same woman in June, because at their home several Jews would get together, jeering and playing loud music using a gramophone. These gatherings had supposedly started since the invasion of the Soviet Union. The female denunciator told the police, the Nazi party, and the Gestapo that the Jews would expect the defeat of Germany and express their happiness with their annoying noise; LA Berlin, Rep. 020, Acc. 1201, no. 6948 Neukölln 211th Police precinct, fol. 105: Entry, June 23, 1941.

53. Robert Prochnik (b. 1915 in Vienna), his father Leon (b. 1886, Vienna) and partner Karoline Hause (b. 1896, Vienna). Prochnik was sent a few days later on a train to the Theresienstadt ghetto; YVA Jerusalem, M69/3500 (Öst. Staatsarchiv Wien), fol. 10.

54. LA Berlin, A Pr.Br.Rep. 030-02-05, no. 382, no fol.: Judgment, court Berlin, Oktober 23, 1941, 1; form, women's jail Berlin-Barnimstrasse, January 23, 1942;

www.bundesarchiv.de/gedenkbuch (accessed on June 20, 2018); Gottwaldt and Schulle, "*Judendeportationen,*" 240–242. For more cases, see Gruner, *Arbeitseinsatz,* 190. See various cases in 145. Police precinct logbook alone; LA Berlin, B Rep. 20, no. 6939, fol. 84, 90, 126. In October 1940, a private employer denounced twenty-nine-year-old Bernhard Bottstein at the Gestapo in Berlin-Charlottenburg for resisting his forced labor orders; LA Berlin, B Rep. 20, no. 6934, no fol.: Entry no. 248, October 25, 1940. In 1942, he was deported first to Theresienstadt and from there to Auschwitz; www.bundesarchiv.de/gedenkbuch (last accessed on January 11, 2022).

55. For more details, see Gruner, *Arbeitseinsatz,* 142–143.

56. Linde Apel, *Jüdische Frauen im Konzentrationslager Ravensbrück, 1939–1945* (Berlin: Metropol, 2003), 69–72. In September 1941, twenty-year-old Helga Basch resisted her forced labor duties at the Siemens plant in Berlin. The firm's own security personnel accompanied her to a police station, from where officers handed her over to the Gestapo. Helga Basch was murdered at a former euthanasia facility in Bernburg (Saale) in March 1942; LA Berlin, B Rep. 20, no. 6939, fol. 73: Log book 145. Police precinct, entry no. 207, September 5, 1941; www.bundesarchiv.de /gedenkbuch (last accessed on January 11, 2022).

57. *Dritte Bekanntmachung über den Kennkartenzwang;* RGBl., 1938 I, 922; 2. *Verordnung zur Durchführung des Gesetzes über die Änderung von Familien- und Vornamen;* RGBl., 1938 I, 1044. Fortunately, Antlers was able to emigrate in June 1939, probably to San Francisco; LA Berlin, A Pr.Br.Rep. 030, Tit. 95, no. 21620, Bd. 5, fols. 204–205RS: Note, February 7, 1939; *Berliner Adressbuch für das Jahr 1939* (Berlin: Verlag August Scherl Nachfolger, 1939), 41; BA Berlin, Residenzenliste, Auskunft Dr. Simone Walther, September 10, 2010; BLHA Potsdam, Rep. 36 A (II), no. 802, no fol.: February 8, 1943.

58. Note, November 29, 1938, printed in *Jewish Responses to Persecution,* ed. Matthäus and Roseman, vol. 1, 369.

59. SStA Leipzig, 20031 PP-S 4173 Schneider, Ida; PP-S 2857 Johanna Quaas; PP-S 4172 Schütze, Frieda. The forty-seven-year-old Johanna Staub received four months in jail for not adopting the discriminatory name; SStA Leipzig, 20031 PP-S 4928 Staub, Johanna. In October 1939, police detected that Ernestine Moschkiewitz (b. 1896 in Raschkow), who worked as a forced laborer at the time, had not applied for the name "Sara" and the new identification card. She argued that she had no information about it. A court sentenced her to pay 16 Reichsmarks or spend four days in prison; SStA Leipzig, 20031 PP-S 2317/31 Moschkewietz, Ernestine. The widow Henriette Bach (b. 1876 in Bremen) was a music conductor and lived as a Catholic in Munich. She never applied for the middle name "Sara" or the special identification card for Jews. She was denounced in November 1942. The local court in Munich sentenced her to a penalty of 120 Reichsmarks or thirty days in prison for two offenses in January 1943; StA Munich, Polizeidirektion München, no. 11510, no fols.; Apel, *Jüdische Frauen,* 65–69.

60. StA Hamburg, 213-11_0282_41, fol. 28–36: Judgment, local court Hamburg, November 12, 1940; Luise Solmitz diary, entry March 18, 1941, in *Verfolgung und Ermordung der europäischen Juden*, vol. 3, ed. Löw, doc. no. 165, 425–426; StA Hamburg, 213-11, no. 64786 Kaste, Dreisa; SStA Leipzig, 20031 PP-S 8264 Stelzer, Frieda. See also: DÖW Wien, Gestapo-Leitstelle Wien, Tagesrapporte January–March 1941, no fols.: Gestapo daily reports, no. 4, February 7–9, 1941, 4.

61. YVA Jerusalem, M55/JM 20757/StA Würzburg, Gestapo Würzburg, no. 10707, no fols.: Note Gestapo Würzburg, March 10, 1941; StA Hamburg, 213-11, no. 62691 Katzenstein, Adolf David. The court sentenced Betty Rosenthal (b. 1880) to three Reichsmarks or one day in prison for not mentioning her status as a Jew in applications in the summer of 1939; SStA Leipzig, 20031 PP-S 3400/80 Rosenthal, Betty. See also the case of Gertrude Lehment (b. 1888 in Hamburg), who pretended to be "Aryan" when she applied for a passport in 1937; she received a fine of 300 Reichsmarks or fifteen days in prison; StA Hamburg, 213-11, no. 53525, Gertrude Lehment. In the beginning of 1940, the widow Caroline Falck (b. 1879) received a sentence of 20 Reichsmarks or two days in jail for not revealing her Jewish identity in a complaint letter to a Hamburg moving company; StA Hamburg, 213-11, no. 62743, Falck, Caroline. With a similar attitude, Adolf Hermann (b. 1871) continued to sign his ration cards for food without the name "Israel," although he had been previously fined 20 Reichsmarks for not using the discriminatory middle name. Moreover, Hermann defied the orders of the Hamburg labor office for segregated labor deployment by working on his own for a private employer, for which he received a sentence of five months in prison; StA Hamburg, 213-11, no. 65182 Adler, Hermann. In letters to the Frankfurt chamber of commerce, Ludwig Sindheimer (b. 1880 in Hardheim/Baden) did not identify as a Jew and refused to close down his leather product business. The city denounced him at the prosecutor's office in November 1940; YVA Jerusalem, M1 DN/188 Frankfurt, fol. 24–26.

62. SStA Leipzig, 20114 Landgericht Leipzig, no. 6075. List with names (CD), in Judith Buber-Agassi, *Die jüdischen Frauen im Konzentrationslager Ravensbrück: Wer waren sie?* (Berlin: Lit-Verlag, 2010). (I thank Linde Apel, Hamburg, for this document); www.bundesarchiv.de/gedenkbuch/en859114 (accessed November 21, 2017). For the "13f14" program in Ravensbrück, see Apel, *Jüdische Frauen*, 296–316; Wachsmann, *KL: A History*, 243–255.

63. WSuLA Vienna, Rassepolitisches Amt der Stadt Wien, Gauleitung, Diverses, A-Z no. 1, 1938–1944, no fols.: Newspaper clipping, *Völkischer Beobachter*, January 18, 1940; letter to Gauleitung Vienna, January 9, 1941; StA Hamburg, 213-11, no. 60935; WSuLA Vienna, Sondergericht, SHv Strafakten, 6276 Edith Weiss. In 1941, a Nazi party group denounced Berta Bocher (b. 1877) for pretending to be "Aryan" in Vienna. She had declared she did not possess any personal documents. The Nazi party group proposed to remove her from the area and deport her immediately; WSuLA Vienna, Rassepolitisches Amt der Stadt Wien, Gauleitung, Diverses, A-Z

no. 1, 1938–1944, no fols.: Ortsgruppe Klagbaum to Rassenpolitisches Amt Vienna, January 9, 1941. See also YVA Jerusalem, M38/122 (DÖW), fol. 11. Gorta Grünberg (b. 1874) and Dr. Georg Grünberg (b. 1897) were both arrested in August 1942 since they hid their Jewish identity and defied anti-Jewish laws. After the investigation, the Vienna Gestapo did not bother to send them to court, instead transferring them directly to the assembly point for deportation; YVA Jerusalem, M69/3492 (Öst. Staatsarchiv Wien), fol. 4.

64. *Jüdisches Nachrichtenblatt* (Berlin edition), no. 67, October 24, 1941, 1; YVA Jerusalem, M58/JM 11808, fol. 318 and 356: Note, Jewish community Olmütz, September 29, 1941, 2; Note, Jewish community Olmütz, October 23, 1941, 2; YVA Jerusalem, M58/JM 11809, fol. 195: Note, Jewish Community Prague/Olmütz branch, April 21, 1942, 2; *Der Neue Tag*, October 18, 1941, 5. YVA Jerusalem, M38/120 (DÖW 65732), fol. 3.

65. Samuel Huneke, "The Duplicity of Tolerance: Lesbian Experiences in Nazi Berlin," *Journal of Contemporary History* 54 (2019), no. 1, 30–59, here 43–44.

66. Schrafstetter, *Flucht und Versteck*, 37–38, 106; Detjen, "Zum Staatsfeind ernannt," 262; SStA Leipzig, 20031 PP-S 6957 Zimmermann, Fanny. Since Bader denied the accusation and no other witnesses surfaced, the case was closed; USHMM, RG 14.001 M Reel 1 (Akten der Gestapo Düsseldorf), Akte Moritz Bader, fol. 3: Franz Damm to Gestapo, March 24, 1942; YVA Jerusalem, M38/122 (DÖW), fol. 26.

67. BA Berlin, R 30/4d, Bl. 121 and 139–140: OLR administrative report (classified), November 1941, Moravska Ostrava, November 22, 1941, Annex 1, report about the political situation, 4; OLR administrative report (classified), for December 1941, Moravska Ostrava, December 20, 1941, Annex 1, report about the political situation, 3–4. See Gruner, *The Holocaust in Bohemia*, 280–281; YVA Jerusalem, M38/122 (DÖW), fol. 9–11.

68. LA Berlin, A Rep. 408, no. 4 Logbook Criminal police 17th precinct, entry no. 21, January 7, 1943; entry no. 73, January 21, 1943; entry no. 91, January 23, 1943; entry no. 246, March 5, 1943; entry no. 258, March 8, 1943; entry no. 385, April 8, 1943; entry no. 415, April 19, 1943; Addendum for no. 415, May 5, 1943; entry no. 593, July 5, 1943; entry no. 837, September 20, 1943. See also judgment, Special Court Berlin, February 5, 1943, in Schimmler, *Recht ohne Gerechtigkeit*, 106–108. For details about hiding: Lutjens, *Submerged*, 198; Kaplan, *Between Dignity and Despair*, 207.

Chapter 4. Protest in Writing Against Nazi Persecution

1. BA Berlin, R 3018/2999, vol. 1, fol. 2–3RS and 56: Arrest form, Gestapo Munich, March 24, 1942; Judgment, no date; StadtA Munich, Gedenkbuch Datenbankauszug, Neuburger, Benno. (I thank Maximilian Strnad, Munich, for the documents from the Munich City Archive.)

2. Anna was born on April 15, 1877; StadtA Munich, PMB N 22 Benno Neuburger; www.bundesarchiv.de/gedenkbuch/directory.html.en?result#frmResults (accessed

November 15, 2017). Another son, Ernst, passed away only six days after his birth in September 1914; BA Berlin, R 3018/2999, vol. 1, fol. 3: Arrest form, Gestapo Munich, March 24, 1942; StadtA Munich, EMA-NS Benno Neuburger; StadtA Munich, PMB N 22 Benno Neuburger; StadtA Munich, Gedenkbuch Datenbankauszug, Neuburger, Benno; LA Berlin, A Rep. 369 HR Haftkarte Neuburger; LA Berlin, A Rep 366 1560_1942 Haftkarte Neuburger; Hanny's Story, Interview conducted in Long Beach, California, December 13, 1983; Private Archive Neuburger-Stoll family.

3. Letter from Anna and Benno Neuburger to Johanna and Fritz Neuburger, August 4, 1938; Private Archive Neuburger-Stoll family. StadtA Munich, Gedenkbuch Datenbankauszug, Neuburger, Benno; BA Berlin, R 3018/2999, vol. 1, fol. 3–4, 56: Arrest form, Gestapo Munich, March 24, 1942; Judgment, no date. Hanny's Story, Interview conducted in Long Beach, December 13, 1983, and Fred's story, Interview conducted in San Francisco, September, 1983; Private Archive Neuburger-Stoll family.

4. Letters from Benno and Anna Neuburger, Munich, to Johanna and Fritz Neuburger, September 24, 1938, and several letters (undated, approximately October 1938); Private Archive Neuburger-Stoll family.

5. Letter from Anna Neuburger, Munich, to Johanna and Fritz Neuburger, November 12, 1938; Private Archive Neuburger-Stoll family. www.bundesarchiv.de /gedenkbuch/en935538 (accessed January 15, 2022). On the pogrom in Munich: Andreas Heusler and Tobias Weger, *"Kristallnacht": Gewalt gegen die Münchner Juden im November 1938* (Munich: Buchendorfer, 1998), 37, 75, 78, 115–116, 144.

6. Heusler and Weger, *"Kristallnacht,"* 123–133; StadtA Munich, Gedenkbuch Datenbankauszug, Neuburger, Benno.

7. Letter from Anna Neuburger and Hedi Holzer, Munich, to Johanna and Fritz Neuburger, November 12, 1938, Private Archive Neuburger-Stoll family. www.ale mannia-judaica.de/traunstein_juedgeschichte.htm (accessed September 20, 2021); "Die Vertreibung der jüdischen Familie Holzer: 'Reichskristallnacht' in Traunstein vor 70 Jahren," in *Traunsteiner Tageblatt,* 45/2008, no. 45: www.traunsteiner-tagblatt.de/das-traunsteiner-tagblatt/chiemgau-blaetter/chiemgau-blaetter-2021_ ausgabe,-die-vertreibung-der-juedischen-familie-holzer-_chid,752.html (accessed April 23, 2022, thanks to Bruce Neuburger). On the destruction of homes: Gruner, "Worse Than Vandals," 25–49.

8. Letter from Anna Neuburger, Munich, to Johanna and Fritz Neuburger, November 25, 1938; Private Archive Neuburger-Stoll family.

9. Letter from Anna and Benno Neuburger, Munich, to Johanna and Fritz Neuburger, December 15, 1938; Private Archive Neuburger-Stoll family.

10. Letters from Anna and Benno Neuburger, Munich, to Johanna and Fritz Neuburger, 8, 9, 22, January 26, March 31, April 30, and May 8, 1939; Private Archive Neuburger-Stoll family.

11. Letters from Anna and Benno Neuburger, Munich, to Johanna and Fritz Neuburger, September 9 and 14, 1939; Private Archive Neuburger-Stoll family. Gruner, Local Initiatives, 275–283.

12. Letter from Benno Neuburger, Munich, to Johanna and Fritz Neuburger, early November 1939 (no date); Private Archive Neuburger-Stoll family. Munich had 9,000 Jewish inhabitants in 1933, 4,500 in 1939, and 3,400 in 1941; Heusler and Weger, "Kristallnacht," 16.

13. Letters from Anna and Benno Neuburger to Johanna and Fritz Neuburger, December 26, 1939, February 1940, September 26, and December 14, 1940, February 20 and 24, March 6, March 14, 1941; Private Archive Neuburger-Stoll family.

14. Letters from Benno Neuburger to Johanna and Fritz Neuburger (no date, before March 15, 1941), March 15 and 29, April 3 and 9, 1941; Private Archive Neuburger-Stoll family. For the United States and its immigration policy toward the Jews from Europe, Barry Trachtenberg, The United States and the Nazi Holocaust: Race, Refuge, and Remembrance (New York: Bloomsbury, 2018).

15. Letter from Benno and Anna Neuburger, Munich, to Johanna and Fritz Neuburger, April (?), August 1, and September 20, 1941; Private Archive Neuburger-Stoll family. For the closing of the consulates see en.wikipedia.org/wiki/June_1941 (accessed June 27, 2018).

16. In German: "Der ewige Massenmörder Hitler Pfui!"; BA Berlin, R 3018/2999, vol. 1, fol. 5: Arrest form, Gestapo Munich, March 24, 1942; BA Berlin, R 3017/5257, no fols.: Indictment, 1–2; StadtA Munich, Gedenkbuch Datenbankauszug, Neuburger, Benno.

17. Domarus, ed., Hitler: Reden und Proklamationen, vol. 2, Halbband 2, 1772–1773; Willy Cohn, Kein Recht—nirgends: Breslauer Tagebücher, 1933–1941, ed. Norbert Conrads (Bonn: Bundeszentrale für Politische Bildung, 2009), 324.

18. Heusler and Weger, "Kristallnacht," 188–190; Memorial Book entries: www.bundes archiv.de/gedenkbuch/en939730; www.bundesarchiv.de/gedenkbuch/en939735 (accessed January 15, 2022). For the transport, see Gottwaldt and Schulle, "Judende-portationen," 101–106.

19. Forty-six Jews took their own lives in 1941; Heusler and Weger, "Kristallnacht," 140.

20. Benno's writing in German: "Der Herrgott ist im Himmel, der 4rer ist ein Greuel-mensch, der Herrgott bestimmt für alle alle[s] und duldet andere Götter nicht— Heil ist er ja selbst ein Gott." Other comments were: "Was ist Recht?," "So ein Idiot war noch nie da so lange die Welt ist, so ein Gemeiner," "Terrorregierung," "Mörder von 5 000 000" or "Bestie Mörder Strolch"; BA Berlin, R 3017/5257, no fols.: Indictment, 2–4; BA Berlin, R 3018/2999, vol. 1, fol. 4–5: Arrest form, Gestapo Munich, March 24, 1942. BA Berlin, R 3017/5257, no fols.: Indictment, 1–2; StadtA Munich, Gedenkbuch Datenbankauszug, Neuburger, Benno.

21. N. H. Baynes, ed., The Speeches of Adolf Hitler, 1922–1939 (London: Oxford University Press, 1942), 737–741. Reprinted by www.yadvashem.org/odot_pdf/Micro

soft%20Word%20-%201988.pdf (accessed November 15, 2017). Original speech in German, January 30, 1939, in *Hitler: Reden und Proklamationen,* ed. Domarus, vol. 2, Halbband 1, 1939–1940, 1047–1067; vol. 2, Halbband 2, 1829. See the argument about Hitler's speech used by Benno cited in the indictment: BA Berlin, R 3017/5257, no fols.: Indictment, 4;

22. BA Berlin, R 3017/5257, no fols.: Indictment, 1; BA Berlin, R 3018/2999, vol. 1, fol. 4: Arrest form, Gestapo Munich, March 24, 1942; StadtA Munich, Gedenkbuch Datenbankauszug, Neuburger, Benno; StadtA Munich, EMA-NS Benno Neuburger. On the establishment of such camps in 1941: Gruner, *Jewish Forced Labor,* 61–74.

23. Maximilian Strnad, *Zwischenstation "Judensiedlung": Verfolgung und Deportation der jüdischen Münchner, 1941–1945* (Munich: Oldenbourg, 2011), 30–65, 83–90; Wolf Gruner, "Die Arbeitslager für den Zwangseinsatz deutscher und nichtdeutscher Juden im Dritten Reich. Kapitel: Zu den Arbeits- und Wohnlagern für deutsche Juden im Altreich (1941–1943/44)," *Gedenkstättenrundbrief* 80 (1997), 27–37.

24. Strnad, *Zwischenstation "Judensiedlung,"* 83–90; BA Berlin, R 3018/2999, vol. 1, fol. 57: Judgment (n.d.), 4.

25. BA Berlin, R 3018/2999, vol. 1, fol. 5RS: Arrest form, Gestapo Munich, March 24, 1942, 5; LA Berlin, A Rep. 369 HR arrest card Neuburger; LA Berlin, A Rep 366/1560, 1942 arrest card Neuburger; BA Berlin, R 3018/2999, vol. 1, no fols.: Criminal record, May 12, 1942; StadtA Munich, Gedenkbuch Datenbankauszug, Neuburger, Benno; StadtA Munich, EMA-NS Benno Neuburger; BA Berlin, R 3017/5257, no fols.: Indictment, 1–4; BA Berlin, R 3018/2999, vol. 1, fol. 57: Judgment, no date, 4; BA Berlin, R 3018/2999, vol. 1, fol. 6 and vol. 3, fol. 5: Final report, Gestapo Munich, March 31, 1942, 1 and Envelope with 3 photos with measurement written on the backside.

26. BA Berlin, R 3018/2999, vol. 1, fol. 5–7: Arrest form, Gestapo Munich, March 24, 1942, 4–5; Final report, Gestapo Munich, 1–2 and Note to investigating judge, March 31, 1942; See also BA Berlin, R 3017/5257, no fols.: Indictment, 1–4; LA Berlin, A Rep. 369 HR Haftkarte Neuburger; LA Berlin, A Rep 366 1560_1942 Haftkarte Neuburger; BA Berlin, R 3018/2999, vol. 1, no fols.: Criminal record, May 12, 1942; StadtA Munich, Gedenkbuch Datenbankauszug, Neuburger, Benno; StadtA Munich, EMA-NS Benno Neuburger.

27. BA Berlin, R 3018/2999, vol. 1, and 2: note, Gestapo Munich, March 31, 1942 and stamp on note, April 4, 1942; Court Munich, hearing protocol, April 4, 1942; Court Munich, arrest warrant, April 4, 1942; arrest note, April 4, 1942. See also BA Berlin, R 3017/5257, no fols.: Indictment, 1. 9:

28. BA Berlin, R 3018/2999, vol. 1, fol. 9: Main Prosecutor Court Munich to Reich Main prosecutor, April 11, 1942; BA Berlin, R 3017/5257, no fols.: Reich Main Prosecutor Berlin, Indictment, May 6, 1942, 1–4; see also BA Berlin, R 3018/2999, vol. 1, fol. 14–16; ibid, vol. 2, fol. 4–10. On the People's Court: Jürgen Zarusky, "Widerstand

als 'Hochverrat,' 1933–1945." Eine Mikrofiche-Edition des Instituts für Zeitgeschichte, *Vierteljahrshefte für Zeitgeschichte* 42 (1994), no. 4, 671–678.

29. BA Berlin, R 3018/2999, vol. 1, fol. 23–24: Letter from Benno to Anna Neuburger,
    May 19, 1942.

30. BA Berlin, R 3018/2999, vol. 1, fol. 25 and 41: note, court prison Munich, May 21,
    1942; Letter, Koenigsberger to Munich judge, June 30, 1942.

31. BA Berlin, R 3018/2999, vol. 1, fol. 18, 22, 28, 30, 38, 50: note, Second Senate, May
    28, 1942; note, Second Senate, May 27, 1942 and handwritten note of May 28; Letter
    Dr. Bergmann, June 17, 1942; Note, Reich Main Prosecutor Berlin, June 27, 1942;
    Prison Munich Stadelheim card, July 4, 1942; Trial protocol, July 20, 1942; LA
    Berlin, A Rep. 369 HR Haftkarte Neuburger; ibid., A Rep 366 1560_1942 Haftkarte
    Neuburger. On Engert and the People's Court see: Karl Engert, "Die Stellung und
    Aufgaben des Volksgerichtshofes," *Deutsches Recht*, 1939, vol. 1, 485–486; transl.
    and cit. by Wayne Geerling and Gary Magee, *Quantifying Resistance: Political
    Crime and the People's Court in Nazi Germany* (Singapore: Springer, 2017), 156;
    de.wikipedia.org/wiki/Karl_Engert" (last accessed June 8, 2021).

32. BA Berlin, R 3018/2999, vol. 2, fol. 20, 50–52RS, 54, 57: form, no date; Trial proto-
    col, July 20, 1942; Draft judgment, no date; Judgment draft, no date, 4. When his
    lawyer Bergmann dropped Benno's case for another trial, the People's Court ap-
    pointed Dr. Friedrich Wübken as defense counsel instead; BA Berlin, R 3018/2999,
    vol. 1, fol. 44–46: letter from Dr. Bergmann to the People's Court, July 13, 1942; note
    to People's Court, July 16, 1942, and letter to Dr. Bergmann, July 17, 1942.

33. BA Berlin, R 3018/2999, vol. 1, fol. 57RS-58RS: Judgment draft, no date, 5–7.

34. LA Berlin, A Rep. 369 HR Haftkarte Neuburger; LA Berlin, A Rep 366 1560_1942
    Haftkarte Neuburger; BA Berlin, R 3018/2999, vol. 2, fol. 26+RS: Handwritten note,
    August 2, 1942, 1–2. See also BA Berlin, R 3018/2999, vol. 1, fol. 59–61RS: Judgment,
    July 31, 1942, 1–7; BA Berlin, R 3018/2999, vol. 4, fol. 9: Reich Ministry of Justice to
    Reich Main Prosecutor, September 3, 1942, 1; BA Berlin, R 3018/2999, vol. 3, fol. 7:
    Head of the prison Munich-Stadelheim to Reich Main Prosecutor, July 30, 1942, 1;
    quote: fol. 6+RS: Head of the detention prison Alt-Moabit to Reich Main Prosecutor,
    July 29, 1942, 1–2.

35. BA Berlin, R 3018/2999, vol. 4, fol. 7 (envelope): Copy, decree Reich Minister of
    Justice, September 3, 1942, 1; fol. 11–16: Order Reich Main Prosecutor, September
    11, 1942, 1–7; Order President People's Court, September 14, 1942, 1.

36. BA Berlin, R 3018/2999, vol. 4, fol. 18: Note Reich Main Prosecutor, September 17,
    1942, 1.

37. BA Berlin, R 3018/2999, vol. 1, fol. 64: Letter, September 17, 1942, 1–2.

38. BA Berlin, R 3018/2999, vol. 4, fol. 19+RS: Note Reich Main Prosecutor, Septem-
    ber 18, 1942, 1–2. See the list of names in *Der Tod von Plötzensee: Erinnerungen,
    Ereignisse, Dokumente, 1942–1944*, ed. Victor von Gostomski and Walter Loch
    (Frankfurt am Main: Bloch, 1993), 307.

39. BA Berlin, R 3018/2999, vol. 1, fol. 67–67RS: Receipt, November 4, 1942, 1–2. See also vol. 2, fol. 30–31. At the end of September, the Munich branch of the Dresdner Bank informed the Reich Main Prosecutor that in his account there were still 7,700 Reichsmarks; BA Berlin, R 3018/2999, vol. 2, fol. 32–34: Letter Dresdner Bank, September 29, 1942; Main Prosecutor Munich to Reich Main Prosecutor, September 1942; vol. 4, fol. 8: Draft of press release, after September 18, 1942.

40. Text in convolute of translated letters; Private Archive Neuburger-Stoll family.

41. Letter to Anna Neuburger, July 23, 1942, from Camp Munich-Milbertshofen; Private Archive Neuburger-Stoll family. The Gedenkbuch notes the July 22, 1942; www.bundesarchiv.de/gedenkbuch/en935671 (accessed January 16, 2022); the civil registry card says: July 23, 1942; StadtAM, EMA-NS Benno Neuburger. For both transports see Gottwaldt and Schulle, *"Judendeportationen,"* 121, 226–229. See also her last letter to Ilse from July 23, 1942; Private Archive Neuburger-Stoll family.

42. See for scope and detail, Pegelow-Kaplan and Gruner, *Resisting Persecution.*

43. Kwiet and Eschwege, *Selbstbehauptung,* 218. Julius Fromm to the Berlin police president, January 4, 1934, printed in *Persecution and Murder of the European Jews,* vol. 1, ed. Gruner, doc. no. 95, 303–307. On Fromm, see Götz Aly and Michael Sontheimer, *Fromms: How Julius Fromm's Condom Empire Fell to the Nazis* (New York: Other Press, 2009); Paula Tobias letter, May 14, 1935, in *Persecution and Murder of the European Jews,* vol. 1, ed. Gruner, doc. no. 167, 465. See also Gruner, *Persecution of the Jews in Berlin,* 19. For a more detailed discussion of written petitions authored by Jewish organizations and individuals in Greater Germany, see Wolf Gruner, " 'To not live as a Pariah . . .' Jewish Petitions as Individual and Collective Protest Against Nazi Persecution in the Greater German Reich," in Pegelow-Kaplan and Gruner, *Resisting Persecution,* 28–50.

44. RGVA Moscow 721-1-3161, fol. 38–44: Letter from Max Loewy to the Police President, July 29, 1935 (Thanks to Christoph Kreutzmüller, Berlin, for this document). See Kreutzmüller, *Ausverkauf,* 316–319. For the police chief order, see Gruner, *Persecution of the Jews in Berlin,* 84. For details about the weeklong organized riots, based on different sources, see Hannah Ahlheim, *"Deutsche, kauft nicht bei Juden!": Antisemitismus und politischer Boykott in Deutschland 1924 bis 1935* (Göttingen: Wallstein Verlag, 2011), 379–390; Gruner, *The Persecution of the Jews in Berlin,* 79–84; Kreutzmüller, *Ausverkauf,* 145–150.

45. StA Munich, Gestapo-Leitstelle München, no. 54, fols. 320 and 328: Daily reports, Munich, January 1940; Daily reports, Munich, October 1939. For the number of inhabitants, see Heusler and Weger, *"Kristallnacht,"* 16. For dozens of petitions from 1939 to 1941, see WSuLA Vienna, Rassepolitisches Amt der Stadt Wien, Gauleitung, Diverses, A-Z no. 1, 1938–1945; Gruner, "To not live as a Pariah . . .," 39; DÖW Vienna, Geheime Gestapo-leitstelle Wien, daily report, no. 2, September 17–18, 1940, 1–2.

46. YVA Jerusalem, M55/JM 27134 Staatsarchiv München, Staatsanwaltschaften, no. 7686; YVA Jerusalem, M55/JM 27135 Staatsarchiv München, Staatsanwaltschaften, no. 9062.

47. Letters from April 17 and November 10, 1937, in *Persecution and Murder of the European Jews*, vol. 1, ed. Gruner, doc. no. 273 and 3–7, 682–683 and 768–769.

48. StA Munich, Staatsanwaltschaften, no. 9278.

49. YVA Jerusalem, M55/2173 (Special Court Freiberg/Saxony), fol. 1–33.

50. The letter was intercepted by the mail inspection service of the German army; LA Berlin, A Rep. 358-02, no. 2544, Cohn, Paul. The Gestapo deported him from Berlin to the Riga ghetto on January 19, 1942; www.bundesarchiv.de/gedenkbuch /en1026408 (accessed on June 22, 2018).

51. LA Berlin, A Rep. 355, no. 4217 Friedmann, Walter Joseph; YVA Jerusalem, M38/347, no fols.

52. Document printed in *Jewish Responses to Persecution*, ed. Matthäus and Roseman, vol. 1, 18. For another example after the annexation of Austria, see *Jewish Responses to Persecution*, ed. Matthäus and Roseman, vol. 1, 283.

53. LA Berlin, A. Pr.Br.Rep. 030, no. 21640, fol. 599: Police, report, July 19, 1935.

54. For example, see Kulka and Jäckel, eds., *Die Juden*, CD-no. 1078 and 1190: Gendarmerie Steinach/Saale, report for July 1935, Steinach/Saale, July 22, 1935; Landrat Schlüchtern, report for August 1935, Schlüchtern, August 30, 1935; Kwiet and Eschwege, *Selbstbehauptung*, 240–241. For a petition, see Luise Solmitz, diary entry, November 15, 1935, in *Jewish Responses to Persecution*, ed. Matthäus and Roseman, vol. 1, 196–197.

55. Kulka and Jäckel, eds., *The Jews*, doc. no. 1593: Gestapo Regierungsbezirk Arnsberg, report for January 1936, Dortmund, no date [January 1936]; LA Berlin, A Rep. 408, no. 8, Fol. 169 and RS: Log book Criminal police, 63th Police precinct, entry 394, December 14, 1936; Alfred M. was later sentenced to six years in prison and deported in 1942; Kwiet and Eschwege, *Selbstbehauptung*, 241–243.

56. Original pamphlets in StA Munich, Staatsanwaltschaften no. 8544, no fols.; YVA Jerusalem, M55/JM 29284-1 (StA München, Polizeidirektion München 13909), no fols.; Detjen, *Staatsfeind*, 257. For context, see Thomas Weber, *Hitler's First War: Adolf Hitler, the Men of the List Regiment, and the First World War* (Oxford: Oxford University Press, 2011), 177, 276, 298. Tim Grady, *The German-Jewish Soldiers of the First World War in History and Memory* (Liverpool: Liverpool University Press, 2011), 134. In March 1943, he was deported to Auschwitz; www.bundesarchiv .de/gedenkbuch/en863228 (accessed on April 17, 2018); YVA Jerusalem, ITS Arolsen, 24302904_0_1, Siegfried Heumann.

57. LA Berlin, A Pr.Br.Rep. 030, Tit. 95, no. 21620, Bd. 5, fol. 87–89; LA Berlin, B Rep. 020 Acc 1201, no. 6949, fol. 441: Police Journal, Berlin-Schöneberg, entry no. 331. In the same way, Edith Wolff also protested against the 1933 boycott, the introduction of the Yellow Star in 1941, and the execution of Jewish representatives at the end of

1942; Kroh, *David kämpft,* 104–105; Kwiet and Eschwege, *Selbstbehauptung,*
243–245; Gruner, "The Germans Should Expel the Foreigner Hitler," 38–39.

58. "Süsse holde Gestapo. Dir klopfen wir noch den Po. Bis die deutsche Köterrasse
kommt in unsere Ghettogasse, Hosiannah unser Grünschpan, Heldenjüngel von
Paris. Wo entfesselt nun der Mordwahn ist, kommt ihr auch bald ins Geschiss.
Nieder knallt den Hund, den Hitler!"; DÖW Vienna, Gestapo-leitstelle Wien,
daily report, no. 11, November 24–25, 1938, fol. 39789. See Gruner, "Worse than
Vandals," 36.

59. Note, November 29, 1938, printed in *Jewish Responses to Persecution,* ed. Matthäus
and Roseman, 369. For the German original, see *Verfolgung und Ermordung der
europäischen Juden,* vol. 2, ed. Heim, doc. no. 181, 512.

60. Goeschel, *Suicide,* 111–112; Kaplan, *Between Dignity and Despair,* 183; DÖW
Vienna, Gestapo-Leitstelle Wien, Tagesrapporte January–March 1941, fol. 39788:
Gestapo Vienna, daily report, no. 2, February 3–4, 1941, 4. For more, see DÖW
Vienna, Gestapo-Leitstelle Wien, Tagesrapporte January–March 1941.

61. WSuLA Vienna, Sondergericht, SHv Strafakten, 6002 Emil Israel Deutsch, fol.
1190–1380.

62. LA Berlin, A Rep. 355, no. 5860, no fol.: copy judgment, Special Court II at the
State Court Berlin, November 25, 1939, 1–4; LA Berlin, Pr.Br.Rep. 30 Berlin C, tit.
198A, no. 152; LA Berlin, A Rep. 370, arrest card, Lewithan, Image_00011414; LA
Berlin, A Rep. 355, no. 5495, no fol.: General Prosecutor to Special Court, indictment, December 2, 1940; LA Berlin, A Pr.Br.Rep. 030-02-02, no. 41, MF-no. 001, no
fols.; LA Berlin, A Pr Br. 030-02-01, no. 152, no fols. By contrast, the memory book
entry states that he was deported to Sobibor in June 1942; www.bundesarchiv.de
/gedenkbuch (accessed on January 13, 2022).

Chapter 5. Acting in Physical Self-Defense

1. Doc., petition for naturalization, May 10, 1947, in BA Berlin, Residentenliste
(Thanks to Christoph Kreutzmüller, Berlin, for the copy). For images of Daisy
Gronowski, see the slideshow: vhaonline.usc.edu/viewingPage?testimonyID=228&r
eturnIndex=0.

2. USC SF/VHA, Interview Diane Jacobs (Daisy Gronowski), Code 1032, Interviewer
Merle Goldberg, January 25, 1995, tape 3, min. 5:40–6:05 and 8:18–9:50.

3. On the original file the wrong year for the interview, 1994, appears, while a stamp
bears the correct year, 1995, USC Shoah Foundation, Pre-Interview Questionnaire,
Diane Jacobs, January 25, 1995, 3; Gedenkbuch Bundesarchiv, entry Bruno
Gronowski (last accessed January 20, 2022); USC SF/VHA, Interview Diane Jacobs,
tape 1, min. 7:03–7:05, 9:56, 10:38–11:45, 13:27–13:44; USC Shoah Foundation, Pre-
Interview Questionnaire, Diane Jacobs, January 25, 1995, 5 and 17. According to the
Diane Jacobs story, Daisy remembered that he owned two cinema theaters and

other businesses; *Escape from Berlin: The Diane Jacobs Story*, a biography by Frank J. Zanca (Orlando, Fla.: Destiny Horizons, 2008), 4.

4. USC SF/VHA Interview, Diane Jacobs, tape 1, min. 9:40–10:00, 12:00–13:00, 14:27–15:00, tape 2, min. 23:45–26:10, tape 6, min. 0:17–0:30; USC Shoah Foundation, Pre-Interview Questionnaire, Diane Jacobs, January 25, 1995, 17; *Escape from Berlin*, 5.

5. YVA Jerusalem, ITS Arolsen, Reichsvereinigung, School enrollment card, Daisy Gronowski, October 1933. On the school, see *Schulführer für Charlottenburg-Wilmersdorf (Öffentliche Grund-, Ober- und Sonderschulen)* (Berlin: Projektagentur, 2008), 36; René Ejury, *Regionale Schulentwicklung in Berlin und Brandenburg, 1920–1995, Sozialgeschichtliche Analyse der Wechselbeziehungen zwischen Schulreform und regionalen Ungleichheiten der Bildungsbeteiligung* (Dissertation, Freie Universität Berlin, 2004), 92.

6. She remembered attending a private school, not a public school; USC Shoah Foundation, Pre-Interview Questionnaire, Diane Jacobs, January 25, 1995, 7; USC SF/VHA, Interview Diane Jacobs, tape 1, min. 10:14, 16:50–17:05; YVA Jerusalem, ITS Arolsen, Reichsvereinigung, card Daisy Gronowski, October 1933. For the hostile environment at this school, see Frank Mecklenburg, "Nächstes Jahr in Worms: Deutschjudentum und Antizionismus vor 1933," in *Was war deutsches Judentum?, 1870–1933*, ed. Christina von Braun (Munich: De Gruyter Oldenbourg, 2015), 39–49, here 39.

7. Gruner, *The Persecution of the Jews in Berlin*, 19–20, 35, 69, and 175. See also Gruner, "Reichshauptstadt," 257; René Ejury, *Regionale Schulentwicklung*, 101.

8. Her apartment was in Berlin-Charlottenburg, Kantstrasse 116; YVA Jerusalem, ITS Arolsen, Reichsvereinigung, card Daisy Gronowski, October 1933. In 1939, Jewish students had to leave the "Fürstin-Bismarck-Schule," as was true for all schools. The former principal left the city and emigrated to the United States; de.wikipedia.org/wiki/Sophie-Charlotte-Oberschule (accessed December 26, 2017); www.tagesspiegel.de/berlin/stadtleben/berliner-lebensadern-6-sybelstrasse-die-welt-im-westen/1893292.html (accessed October 11, 2017).

9. USC SF/VHA, Interview Diane Jacobs, tape 1, min. 20:00–20:15.

10. USC SF/VHA, Interview Diane Jacobs, tape 3, min. 6:05.

11. Prinz, *Rebellious Rabbi*, 72–80, 101–104; Joachim Prinz, "A Rabbi Under the Hitler Regime," 231–238. For the talk and article see "Das Leben ohne Nachbarn: Versuch einer ersten Analyse, Ghetto 1935," by Joachim Prinz, *Jüdische Rundschau*, vol. 40, no. 31/32, April 17, 1935, 3. Cited following the translation in *Persecution and Murder of the European Jews*, vol. 1, ed. Gruner, doc. no. 161, 451–454.

12. For the quote: Prinz, *Rebellious Rabbi*, 114. For more details: Prinz, *Rebellious Rabbi*, 88–256. For the order of remarks during the March on Washington, see www.ourdocuments.gov/doc_large_image.php?flash=false&doc=96 (accessed July 6, 2020).

13. USC SF/VHA, Interview Diane Jacobs, tape 3, min. 3:15–4:20, 6:28–7:53, 15:10–15:30. On Hashomer Hatzair, the group banned 1938 by the Nazis, see Cox, *Circles of Resistance*, 18–21 and 87.

14. USC SF/VHA, Interview, Diane Jacobs, tape 3, min. 13:15–16:15. See also USC Shoah Foundation, Pre-Interview Questionnaire, Diane Jacobs, January 25, 1995, 10. On the camouflage tactics, Marten Düring, *Verdeckte soziale Netzwerke im Nationalsozialismus: Die Entstehung und Arbeitsweise von Berliner Hilfsnetzwerken für verfolgte Juden* (Berlin: De Gruyter Oldenbourg, 2015), 167.

15. Stefanie Schüler-Springorum, "Die jüdische Jugendgruppe 'Schwarzer Haufen,'" *Tel Aviver Jahrbuch für deutsche Geschichte* 28 (1999), 159–200; Cox, *Circles of Resistance*; Kim Wünschmann, *Before Auschwitz: Jewish Prisoners in the Prewar Concentration Camps* (Cambridge: Harvard University Press, 2015), 100–101; Altgeld and Kissener, "Judenverfolgung und Widerstand," 31–32.

16. USC SF/VHA, Interview Diane Jacobs, tape 1, min. 20:45–22:00, min. 27:45–28:00, tape 2, min. 27:00–29:00, tape 3, min. 16:25–16:42.

17. BA Berlin, R58 (former ZwA Dahlwitz-Hoppegarten), ZB1/637, fol. 23: Note, SD Berlin, August 1, 1935. Later, the SS leadership decided that in case of a war all 29 existing German retraining camps would be turned into forced labor camps supervised and guarded by the SS; Gruner, *Arbeitseinsatz*, 229–231; Gruner, *Jewish Forced Labor*, 44. On emigration, see David Jünger, *Jahre der Ungewissheit: Emigrationspläne deutscher Juden, 1933–1938* (Göttingen: Vandenhoeck & Ruprecht, 2016).

18. USC SF/VHA, Interview Diane Jacobs, tape 2, min. 27:00–29:00, tape 3, min. 1:50–3:00; and tape 4, min. 0:10–00:34. For the camp capacity, see also Wolf Gruner, "Die Arbeitslager für den Zwangseinsatz deutscher und nichtdeutscher Juden im Dritten Reich. Kapitel 2: Zu den Lagern der Reichsvereinigung (ab 1941 Arbeitslager) im Altreich," in *Gedenkstättenrundbrief* 79 (1997), 3–17, here 13.

19. USC SF/VHA Interview Diane Jacobs, tape 3, min. 5:40–6:05 and 9:35–10:10.

20. USC SF/VHA, Interview Diane Jacobs, tape 3, min. 10:10–11:05.

21. USC SF/VHA, Interview Diane Jacobs, tape 3, min. 11:05–11.42.

22. Memorandum Joint, November 30, 1938, in *Persecution and Murder of the European Jews*, vol. 2, ed. Heim, doc. no. 185, 524–525. For the establishment of the non-Zionist retraining camp Gross-Breesen by the Central Association of Jews in Germany in 1936 and its existence until 1938, see Johann Nicolai, *"Seid mutig und aufrecht!": Das Ende des Centralvereins deutscher Staatsbürger jüdischen Glaubens, 1933–1938* (Berlin: be.bra Verlag, 2016), 202–217. Quote in Gruner, *Jewish Forced Labor*, 45.

23. Memorandum Joint, November 30, 1938, in *Persecution and Murder of the European Jews*, vol. 2, ed. Heim, doc. no. 185, 524; Gruner, *Jewish Forced Labor*, 45–47; Gruner, "Die Arbeitslager: Kapitel 2," 13.

24. USC SF/VHA Interview, Diane Jacobs, tape 3, min. 11:42–12:15 and 17.40–19.08.

25. USC SF/VHA Interview, Diane Jacobs, tape 3, min. 19:10–22:14; USC SF, Pre-Interview Questionnaire, Diane Jacobs, January 25, 1995, 11.

26. USC SF/VHA Interview, Diane Jacobs, tape 3, min. 23:15–29:09.

27. USC SF/VHA Interview, Diane Jacobs, tape 4, min. 0:42–03:10.

28. USC SF/VHA, Interview Diane Jacobs, tape 4, min. 3:10–6:10.

29. Franz Rudolf von Weiss worked at the consulate in Cologne since 1920. In 1937, he was appointed Consul, and in 1943, Consul General; de.wikipedia.org/wiki/Franz-Rudolf_von_Weiss; dodis.ch/P1061; dodis.ch/46705. Quote in report, November 13, 1938 (all accessed April 18, 2022). On Frölicher, see de.wikipedia.org/wiki/Hans_Fr%C3%B6licher (accessed April 18, 2022).

30. USC SF/VHA Interview, Diane Jacobs, tape 4, min. 6:10–7:20.

31. USC SF/VHA Interview, Diane Jacobs, tape 4, min. 9:20–10:34, 10:50–18:50; USC Shoah Foundation, Pre-Interview Questionnaire, Diane Jacobs, January 25, 1995, 11. On the children transport: Judith Baumel-Schwartz, *Never Look Back: The Jewish Refugee Children in Great Britain, 1938–1945* (West Lafayette, Iowa: Purdue University Press, 2012); Jennifer Craig-Norton, *The Kindertransport: Contesting Memory* (Bloomington: Indiana University Press, 2019).

32. USC SF/VHA Interview, Diane Jacobs, tape 4, min. 18:50–20:20; doc. no. 0006_89725188_1, in ITS Arolsen, accessed at USHMM, December 15, 2017; Gedenkbuch Bundesarchiv, entry Bruno Gronowski; www.bundesarchiv.de /gedenkbuch/directory.html.en?result#frmResults (accessed October 13, 2017); doc. no. 11266888_0_1, in ITS Arolsen, accessed at the USHMM, December 15, 2017. Similarly, only days before, all Jews in three transports from Berlin, Munich, and Frankfurt had been shot in Kowno; Gottwaldt and Schulle, *"Judendeportationen,"* 104–112, 121; Andrej Angrick and Peter Klein, *Die "Endlösung" in Riga: Ausbeutung und Vernichtung, 1941–1944* (Darmstadt: Wissenschaftliche Buchgesellschaft, 2006), 160–161. For the discussion among historians, see Christian Gerlach, "The Wannsee Conference, the Fate of German Jews, and Hitler's Decision in Principle to Exterminate all European Jews," in *The Journal of Modern History* 70 (1998), no. 4, 759–812.

33. According to the VHA interview, her mother was taken to Twarnici in 1942. Some postwar documents had confused this town with the actual destination, Trawniki, a small place located 50 kilometers southeast of Lublin. Diane also claimed in her interview that her sister Inez went together with her mother. Inez's registration in the German Memorial Book shows, however, that the Gestapo deported her on March 28, 1942, from Berlin to Piaski. There was no entry under Ellen Phillip or Ellen Gronowski. A search at the International Tracing Service resolved the issue of her mother's name. An Ellen Eppenstein, thus, appears in the Memorial Book on the same transport to Piaski as Inez; USC SF/VHA Interview, Diane Jacobs, tape 5, min. 1:30–1:44; USC SF, Pre-Interview Questionnaire, Diane Jacobs, January 25, 1995, 5; Memorial Book, Bundesarchiv, entries Ines Gronowski and Ella

(Ellen) Eppenstein; www.bundesarchiv.de/gedenkbuch/en1068535; www.bundes archiv.de/gedenkbuch/en1036965 (last accessed January 22, 2022); Various documents (EppensteinEllaA89725195_0_1, EppensteinEllaB89725197_0_1, EppensteinEllaBB11191669_0_1) from ITS Arolsen, accessed at the USHMM, December 2017 (My thanks go to Betsy Anthony). For more details about the deportation: Jani Pietsch, *"Ich besass einen Garten in Schöneiche bei Berlin": Das verwaltete Verschwinden jüdischer Nachbarn und ihre schwierige Rückkehr* (Frankfurt: Campus Verlag, 2006), 219, fn. 12; Gottwaldt and Schulle, *"Judendeportationen,"* 137 and 188; Gruner, *The Persecution of the Jews in Berlin*, 178.

34. Gottwaldt and Schulle, *"Judendeportationen,"* 137 and 187.

35. USC SF/VHA, Interview Diane Jacobs, tape 4, min. 21:40–24:35, and tape 5, min. 0:47–1:20, 2:00–6:45.

36. I use her given name, Daisy Gronowski, for the time before the name change. USC SF/VHA, Interview Diane Jacobs, tape 5, min. 6:45–8:44, 8:44–10:48; USC SF, Pre-Interview Questionnaire, Diane Jacobs, January 25, 1995, 11; doc., petition for naturalization, May 10, 1947, and doc., U.S. District Court, Los Angeles, July 25, 1952, in Residentenliste, accessed at the USHMM, December 15, 2017; doc., U.S. District Court, Los Angeles, July 25, 1952, in Residentenliste, BA Berlin (Thanks to Christoph Kreutzmüller, Berlin, for the copy); "Republican Group Appoints Officers," *Los Angeles Times*, February 5, 1987.

37. USC SF/VHA, Interview Diane Jacobs, tape 5, min. 10:48–11:00, and tape 6 (statement Dr. Alfred Jacobs), min. 5:15–5:20; USC SF, Pre-Interview Questionnaire, Diane Jacobs, January 25, 1995, 3 and 7; doc. no. 0005_89725172_1, doc. no. 0001_84993283_1, doc. no. 0002_99475720_1, doc. no. 0009_89725191_1, 0005_89725199_1, doc. no. 0001_99475722_1, doc. no. 0010_84993292_1, 0003_84993296_2, doc. no. 0001_84993294_1 (Diane Jacobs to ITS, June 17, 1996) and doc. no. 0009_84993310_1, in ITS Arolsen, accessed at the USHMM, December 15, 2017.

38. USC SF/VHA, Fanny Lust, tape 1, min. 11. Other instances happened in Giessen, Falkenstein (Vogtland), Berlin, Breslau, Frankfurt am Main, Braunschweig, Königsberg: USC SF/VHA, interviews of Joan Winter; Eva Wertheimer; Alexander Stockdale; Margot Segall-Blank; Henry Schatz; Herman Schaalman; Eli Rosner; George Rosenberg; Alice Ressegui; Walter Reece; Gunter Perry; Bernhard Penner; Herbert Nathan; Gerry Maass; Fanny Lust; Abraham Lowy; Egon Koenig; Rudy Kennedy; Freddy Kahn; Bernard Joseph; Helmut Gruenfeld; Werner Greenbaum; Peter Glucksmann; Herbert Freudenberger; Peter Forstenzer; Adrian Factor, Ruth Ehrmann; Erwin Deutsch; Ellen Kerry Davis; Kenneth Blumenstein; Ariane Abdalah; Ruth Epstein.

39. USC SF/VHA, Bert Wallace, tape 2, min. 24; Haviva Salomon, tape 1, min. 15; Helmut Gruenewald, tape 4, min. 25; and Joan Winter, tape 2, min. 56; Audio testimony in *Three Sisters from Breitenbach* (documentary, no director, no date),

min. 38:54–40:15; www.youtube.com/watch?v=F9hh3X0nYXI (last accessed September 20, 2021).

40. Kulka and Jäckel, eds., *The Jews*, doc. no. 831 and 972: Landrat Schlüchtern, Report March–April 1935, April 23, 1935; Regierungspräsident Wiesbaden, report, July 1, 1935.

41. HHStA Wiesbaden, Abt. 461/16778 Oskar Junghans, fols. 4–12, 52–63, 87–88.

42. HHStA Wiesbaden, Abt. 461/16946 Max Cohn.

43. *Persecution and Murder of the European Jews*, vol. 2, ed. Heim, doc. no. 131, 381; for his biographical information see 331.

44. Paul Szustak was tried for this crime in 1950; Solomon Perel, *Europa, Europa* (New York: John Wiley, 1997), 69–70; pogrome1938-niedersachsen.de/peine; www.myheimat.de/peine/kultur/kristallnacht-als-im-reich-die-synagogen-brannten-d2723453.html (both accessed January 19, 2019); "Der Mord in der Peiner Kristallnacht," *Hannoversche Presse*, July 6, 1950. (Thanks to Monica Simpson, San Diego, a relative of Hans Marburger, for bringing this case to my attention.)

45. According to Ruth's recollection, mother and grandmother dragged the corpse out of the house and hid it in a large pile of manure; USC SF/VHA, Interview Ruth Winick, tape 1, min. 2:00–4:53, 18:16–22:00.

46. USC SF VHA, Hardy Kupferberg, tape 2, min. 19:50–25:34. The interviewee mentioned the Synagogue Levetzowstrasse, but this synagogue was not arsoned during the November pogrom. The Nazis destroyed the interior. Probably, she meant the synagogue Fasanenstrasse, which was burned to the ground.

47. USC SF/VHA, Interview Frank Theyleg, tape 2, min. 13–18.

48. Despite increased Nazi repression during the war, the teenager Helmut Gruenfeld (b. 1928 in Darmstadt) ended up in a brawl with uniformed Hitler Youth in 1942; USC SF/VHA, Helmut Gruenfeld, tape 3, Segment 80–81; Kosmala and Schoppmann, *Überleben im Untergrund*; Wolfgang Benz, ed., *Überleben im Dritten Reich: Juden im Untergrund und ihre Helfer* (Munich: Beck, 2003); Claudia Schoppmann, "Die 'Fabrikaktion' in Berlin: Hilfe für untergetauchte Juden als Form humanitären Widerstandes," *Zeitschrift für Geschichtswissenschaft* 53 (2005), no. 2, 138–148. On the difficulties of life in hiding, see Kaplan, *Between Dignity and Despair*, 209–212; and Lutjens, *Submerged*. For more details on the factory raid, see Gruner, *Widerstand in der Rosenstrasse*, 77–84. For details on the spies in Berlin, see Doris Tausendfreund, *Erzwungener Verrat: Jüdische "Greifer" im Dienst der Gestapo, 1943–1945* (Berlin: Metropol, 2006), 69–210.

49. LA Berlin, A Rep. 408, no. 4, no fol.: Log book, Criminal Police precinct 17, Weinbergsweg 12, entry no. 495, May 26, 1943. For his work as a plumber at the firm Otto Walter, Berlin, Zehdenicker Str. 4–5, see BLHA, Rep. 36 A (II), no. 10515, fol. 11. In Auschwitz, he managed to survive. In January 1945, the SS transferred him with one of the evacuation marches first to Buchenwald and then to Theresienstadt, where he died in July, two months after the liberation; www.bundesarchiv.de

/gedenkbuch/en1009580 (last accessed on January 22, 2022), and BLHA, Rep. 36 A (II), no. 10516.

50. LA Berlin, A Rep. 408, no. 4, no fol.: Log book Criminal Police precinct, Weinbergsweg 12, entry no. 785, August 30, 1943, and post scriptum to 785/43. (I am grateful to Richard Lutjens for pointing out this document to me.) For more details on Jacobson, see BLHA Potsdam, Rep. 36 A, Kartei. For Jacobson's profession, see *Berliner Adressbuch 1941:* Einwohner, Band 1 (Berlin: Verlag August Scherl Nachfolger, 1941), 958.

51. As a *Geltungsjude,* he somehow survived the war in Berlin; BA Berlin, Residenzenliste, Auskunft Dr. Simone Walther, September 10, 2010.

52. USC SF/VHA, Interview Diane Jacobs, tape 5, min. 12:44–13:01, 24:00–25:10.

Conclusion

1. LA Berlin, A Rep. 358-02, no. 7657, fol. 2–6.

2. Philip Zimbardo, "Comment: Pathology of Imprisonment," *Society* 9 (1972), no. 6, 4–8, here 6.

3. *Verfolgung und Ermordung der europäischen Juden,* vol. 3, ed. Löw, doc. no. 70 and 311, 206 and 734; YVA Jerusalem, M58/JM 11808, fol. 209 and 235: Note, Jewish community Olmütz about summons at the Gestapo, December 5, 1941; Note, Jewish community Olmütz about summons at the Gestapo, December 17, 1941. For defiant Jewish behavior in the Protectorate, see Gruner, *Holocaust in Bohemia and Moravia.*

4. Gruner, *Persecution of the Jews in Berlin,* 137–150.

5. For these older notions of German indifference, see Ian Kershaw, *Popular Opinion and Political Dissent in the Third Reich: Bavaria, 1933–1945* (Oxford: Oxford University Press, 1983). For some examples of non-Jewish protest and solidarity, see, early on, Gellately, *The Gestapo and German Society,* 159–184; more recently, Gruner, "Indifference?," 59–83; Schimmler, *Recht ohne Gerechtigkeit,* 106–108; Simon, *Untergetaucht,* 59–60, 173–175; *Protest in Hitler's "National Community": Popular Unrest and the Nazi Response,* ed. Nathan Stoltzfus and Birgit Maier-Katkin (New York: Berghahn, 2016); Geheran, *Comrades Betrayed,* 66 and 108–110; Roseman, *Lives Reclaimed.*

6. BA Berlin, R 58/152, fol. 128: Report no. 105 (*Meldungen aus dem Reich*), July 15, 1940.

7. On the Gestapo in Vienna, see Elisabeth Boeckl-Klamper, Thomas Mang, and Wolfgang Neugebauer, eds., *The Vienna Gestapo, 1938–1945: Crimes, Perpetrators, Victims,* translated by John Nicholson and Nick Somers (New York: Berghahn, 2022), 174–208.

8. LA Berlin, A Rep. 355, no. 4854 Wilzig, Nachmann, 1: copy, Judgment Special Court, 1–7.

9. Letter from Kurt Tucholsky to Arnold Zweig, December 15, 1935, in Kurt Tucholsky, *Briefe: Auswahl, 1931–1935*, 2nd ed. (Berlin: Verlag Volk und Welt, 1983), 570–577, here 571. See also Wolf Gruner, "Verweigerung, Opposition und Protest: Vergessene jüdische Reaktionen auf die NS-Verfolgung in Deutschland," in *Shoah: Ereignis und Erinnerung*, ed. Alina Bothe and Stefanie Schüler-Springorum, Jahrbuch Selma Stern Zentrum für Jüdische StudienBerlin-Brandenburg (Berlin: Hentrich, 2019), 11–30.

10. See *Berliner Zeitung* (July to November 1945), *Neue Zeit* (August to November 1945), *Tagesspiegel* (October 1945 to April 1946), and *Das Volk* (July to October 1945). On the public discussion about the extermination of the European Jews, see the chapter "Myth of Silence" in Jockusch, *Collect and Record!* For the situation of Jews in Germany after the end of the war, see Michael Brenner, *Nach dem Holocaust: Juden in Deutschland, 1945–1950* (Munich: Beck, 1995); Atina Grossmann, *Jews, Germans, and Allies: Close Encounters in Occupied Germany* (Princeton: Princeton University Press, 2007).

11. CJA Berlin, 5 A 1, no. 3, fol. 1: Situation report for April 1946, Jewish Community Berlin. Cf. protocols of meetings: CJA Berlin, 5 A 1, no. 5, fol. 1–30: meeting minutes, November 1945–November 1947; CJA Berlin, 5 A 1, no. 3, fol. 22: "Die Lage der Jüdischen Gemeinde zu Berlin und ihrer Mitglieder," 17; CJA Berlin, 5 A 1, fol. 4: Letter to the meeting of representatives, December 14, 1945; CJA Berlin, 5 A 1, no. 8, fol. 23: Minutes of meeting of representatives, June 24, 1947; Wilhelm Meier, "Unsere Sorgen," *Der Weg: Zeitschrift für Fragen des Judentums* 1/12, May 17, 1946, 1–2. Cf. *Der Weg* 1–46 (March to December 1946). Exceptions were an article about the rebellion of the Sonderkommando in Auschwitz in 1944 as well as the mentioning of resistance groups and the attack on the Berlin propaganda exhibition "Das Sowjetparadies" in a speech commemorating the pogrom in 1938; Wilhelm Meier, "Die Toten kehren nicht zurück . . .," *Der Weg* 30, September 20, 1946, 1–2; radio speech, "Julius Meyer spricht zum 9. November," *Der Weg* 38, November 15, 1946, 2.

12. "Die Kristallnacht," *Der Weg* 1/37, November 8, 1946, 1. Cf. with a critique regarding this position: Hans-Erich Fabian, "Verkehrte Fronten," *Der Weg* 44, December 27, 1946, 2.

13. Leo Winter, "Der Gelbe Stern," *Tagesspiegel*, October 9, 1945, 2.

14. For questions of relations and networks, see Düring, *Verdeckte soziale Netzwerke*; Beer, *Die Banalität des Guten*. For a 1936 case of an informal Jewish group raising money to support fellow Jews in Bad Kissingen, see Gruner, *Öffentliche Wohlfahrt*, 79. Still during the horrible time of deportations, young Jewish Berliners met regularly for dancing at a private home; Kaplan, *Between Dignity and Despair*, 167.

15. On the case of the Berlin textile merchants, see Kreutzmüller, *Ausverkauf*, 296–297. See also Zahn, " 'Nicht mitgehen, sondern weggehen!'," 165–173; Kwiet and Eschwege, *Selbstbehauptung*, 243–245; Cioma Schönhaus, *The Forger*. For the

Chug Chaluzi group, see also Aviram, *Mit dem Mut der Verzweiflung*, 52–142; Johannes Tuchel, ed., *Silent Heroes Memorial Center: Resistance to Persecution of the Jews, 1933–1945* (Berlin: Silent Heroes Memorial Center, 2010), 105; Schüler-Springorum, "Die jüdische Jugendgruppe," 159–200; Cox, *Circles of Resistance*; Gruner, "The Germans," 16.

16. Nicolai, *"Seid mutig und aufrecht!"*; Arnold Paucker, *Deutsche Juden im Kampf um Recht und Freiheit: Studien zu Abwehr, Selbstbehauptung und Widerstand der deutschen Juden seit dem Ende des 19. Jahrhunderts* (Berlin: Hentrich, 2003); Avraham Barkai, *"Wehr Dich!": Der Centralverein deutscher Staatsbürger jüdischen Glaubens, 1893–1938* (München: Beck, 2002); Avraham Barkai, "Jewish Self-Help in Nazi Germany, 1933–1938: The Dilemmas of Cooperation," in *Jewish Life in Nazi Germany*, ed. Nicosia and Scrase, 71–88; Karol Jonca, "Jewish Resistance to Nazi Racial Legislation in Silesia, 1933–1937," in *Germans Against Nazism: Nonconformity, Opposition, and Resistance in the Third Reich: Essays in Honour of Peter Hoffmann*, ed. Francis R. Nicosia and Lawrence D. Stokes (New York: Berghahn, 2015), 77–86, here 80–83.

17. For examples, see Wolf Gruner, "Poverty and Persecution: The Reichsvereinigung, the Jewish Population, and the Anti-Jewish Policy in the Nazi-State, 1939–1945," *Yad Vashem Studies* 27 (1999), 23–60; Gruner, *Öffentliche Wohlfahrt*; and *Persecution and Murder of the European Jews*, vol. 2, ed. Heim, doc. no. 119, 356–353. For a different view on the collaboration and/or defiance, see Meyer, "Gratwanderung," 291–337. For Vienna, see Doron Rabinovici, *Instanzen der Ohnmacht: Wien, 1938–1945: Der Weg zum Judenrat* (Frankfurt: Jüdischer Verlag, 2000).

18. Thanks to Marion Kaplan who emphasized this aspect.

19. Nussbaum, "Ministry Under Stress," 239.

INDEX

Page numbers in italics refer to figures